A Banarasi On Varanasi

A Banarasi On Varanasi

Kunal Sinha

BLUEJAY BOOKS

An imprint of Srishti Publishers & Distributors
New Delhi & Kolkata

BLUEJAY BOOKS
An imprint of SRISHTI PUBLISHERS & DISTRIBUTORS
64-A, Adhchini
Sri Aurobindo Marg
New Delhi 110 017
srishtipublishers@yahoo.com

First published by *BLUEJAY BOOKS* 2004

ISBN 81-88575-24-0
Rs. 495

Photographs and book design by the author

Typeset in Goudy Old Style 11 at
Creative Concept

Book cover design by
Creative Concept, New Delhi

ACKNOWLEDGMENTS

There are just so many people who made this book possible, that I may not be able to thank all of them. But I must begin with my parents. My father, who moved to Varanasi in 1962 and loved the city so much that he decided to settle here, would probably not have dreamt that I would eventually write a book about the holy city. Though he passed away many years ago, I could feel Baba's presence, as if guiding me along my journey of self-discovery. My mother, on the other hand, was a constant advisory board for me, asking if I had covered certain aspects of the city, correcting impressions that had been formed when I was very young and filling me up on history. My elder brother contributed with suggestions and encouragement. My wife Sumona, whose first visit to Varanasi was only a day after our wedding, was the active listener – and a gauge of whether certain anecdotes made for interesting reading or not.

Several long-time residents of Varanasi were of immense help during the one year that I took to compile material for the book. Naba da (N.K. Sarkar) helped me find sources from the Banaras Hindu University. My old friend, Mukul Shah, who is well connected in the city, thanks to his flourishing accounting practice, put me in touch with a few people who could provide me an insider's perspective on the culture of the city. Among them were Alok and Deepak Shahpuri, owners of Deepak Cinema and trustees of the Jagannath Temple Trust, Mayank

Agrawal and Chand Bhai, who spent time explaining the intricacies of the Banarasi saree.

The numerous auto-rickshaw drivers, *rickshaw-wallahs* and *mallahs* (boatmen) who transported me across the city earn my gratitude, as does my young neighbour Rohit Bhattacharya for lending me his 5-speed bicycle for my explorations.

From the past, my teachers – both at St. John's School and the Banaras Hindu University – must be thanked for kindling my curiosity. For most of my life in Varanasi, I was indeed a student. Gopal Das, my guitar teacher, made me appreciate the nuances of Hindustani Classical music. And finally, to my publisher for asking me to write this book. Thanks to him, I embarked on this voyage to discover my own city, and came away enlightened as never before!

This book is dedicated
to my mother,
a Banarasi by enculturation
on account of her love for paan,
fluency in Bhojpuri, and
devotion to Baba Vishwanath.

CONTENTS

PROLOGUE

Hairat Hairat Hey Sakhi, Hairat Gaya Hiray
Boond Samani Samand Mein, So Kit Hairat Jai

Seeking and searching all the time,
I lost my own track,
When the drop of water falls in the ocean,
How can one get it back?

Kabir

ଓ

Long before Pankaj Mishra wandered through its lanes in search of locales and characters for his first novel 'The Romantics', long before Deepa Mehta attempted to shoot her film 'Water' in the face of protests from the Vishwa Hindu Parishad and the Bajrang Dal, long before Abhishek Bachchan and Renoo Nathan pranced on its ghats, and on the sandbanks on the other side of the Ganga, Varanasi was drawing pilgrims, writers, singers, monks and mendicants – all in search of eternal salvation, and sometimes inspiration. How long ago that was, no one knows. About the antiquity of the holy city, Mark Twain wrote, "Banaras is older than history, older than tradition, older than even legend, and looks twice as old as all of them put together."

Somewhere in between, more than three decades ago, the city was preparing for one of its countless festivals. The rich and the poor were buying lamps and oil to light up their homes at dusk. The *halwais* were putting out the mountains of *mithai* – juicy *gulabjamuns, chumchums, kheerkadams, pedas* and *laddoos*, which they had toiled to prepare all of the previous night, for eager residents to buy. Housewives were collecting fragrant blossoms from their backyard, or buying them from the flower sellers near the neighbourhood temple, and scrubbing clean with *imli* their brass images of Lakshmi and Ganesh, in preparation for the evening Puja. Traders were bringing out their brand new ledgers – the *bahi khatas* – which they would place in front of the Goddess of Wealth.

While the city was abuzz with this frenetic activity, in a ward of Sir Sundarlal Hospital, in the leafy Banaras Hindu University, my mother went into labour. The family prayed that her child be born before dusk – as legend had it that one born on Diwali night would surely grow up to be a dacoit, or at least a ruffian. I did not disappoint my family. I made my appearance at 9:20 in the morning, kicking, crying, with all ten toes intact.

Another Banarasi had made his appearance to swell the ranks of its teeming lakhs.

ॐ

Was it a momentous occasion? Possibly not. The Census of India 2001 puts the population of Banaras precisely at 1,211,749. In reality, at any given point of its centuries old history, the city plays host to nearly as many pilgrims and seekers, mendicants and migrants. I was but a tiny addition in the Registrar General's Statistics, nothing more. Sant Kabir stood vindicated.

On the other hand, if Death in Banaras was what I was talking of, that would be something. Every pious Hindu aspires to die somewhere in that teeming, medieval agglomeration of temples, homes, shops and lanes bound by the rivers Varuna and Assi; to be liberated from the endless cycle of birth, death and re-birth. Search as I did for any magical or spiritual qualities that could possibly be bestowed on me on account of my birth in the city, I could not find anything in the Texts. I would have to, like any ordinary mortal, create my own *karma*.

ॐ

Older than Antiquity

THE HISTORY OF VARANASI

Paat bharanta dekhi ke hansath kupaliya,
Hum chali tum chalihey, dhauri baapuliya!

At the falling dry leaf,
the tender leaf does sneer,
Says the falling leaf, "Today my turn, tomorrow yours.
Have patience, dear."

Kabir

ଓ

It has been impossible for any historian, however meticulous or learned, to put a date as to when the city of Banaras was established. The Reverend M. A. Sherring postulated that 'it may even date from the time when the Aryan race first spread itself over Northern India'. Quite possible, though there are few texts to ratify this. When the Aryans moved into the Gangetic plain from their earlier settlements in Northwest India around 2000 B.C., this was the outpost of a tribe called the Kashis. There are indeed references to the Kashi kingdom, dating to the early part of the first millenium B.C. in the Puranas, leading scholars to speculate that this was the capital of the kingdom. By the time Gautama Buddha travelled from Gaya, where he attained enlightenment, to Sarnath, a suburb of Banaras, to preach his first sermon in the sixth century B.C., it was a bustling city.

It is from this time onwards, as the Buddhist texts, as well as the Mahabharat and the Puranas were written, that the history of north India, and Banaras, becomes somewhat clearer. The Jataka tales, which are the fables of the earlier lives of the Buddha, describe 'Baranasi' as the capital of the kingdom of Kashi, a magnificent city encircled by walls twelve leagues around – the 'chief city in all of India, coveted by kings all round.'

In that age, North India was divided into sixteen great kingdoms, called the *janpadas.* The prosperous kingdom of Kashi caught the fancy of its powerful neighbours – Magadh in the east, and Koshala in the north. There were several reasons for this. The city was already famous for its cotton and silk cloth. The *Mahajanpadas,* written at the time, mention *malmala* cloth being exported to Europe. After the body of Buddha was draped in the softest *Kasikuttama,* the fame of the material spread to wherever his devotees went – China, Cambodia, Java, Sumatra and Korea. Being at the crossroads of two of the greatest trading routes, the Ganga, and the Northern Road, Kashi was an important commercial centre.

In the seventh century B.C., the Koshala king conquered Kashi. In the Jataka tales, he is referred to as the Conqueror of Banaras : 'Baranasiggaho'. In the sixth century B.C., the Magadh king challenged his dominion. Eager to appease his neighbour, the Koshala king offered his daughter's hand to the Magadh king, Bimbisara, giving away Kashi as dowry, so long as the revenues from the city went to the queen for her adornment. By the time Bimbisara's son Ajatashatru ascended the throne, Magadh had become the predominant kingdom of North India, and Pataliputra its capital. Kashi was ruled by Sishunag, of the Naga dynasty in the third century B.C., and by the Nandas when Alexander invaded India in 326 B.C.

In the latter part of the third century B.C., the Mauryas came to power in north India. Chandragupta Maurya continued to rule from Magadh from 231 to 297 B.C. Emperor Ashoka, the other famous Mauryan king built the great stupa at Sarnath after renouncing his kingdom. The commander of the Mauryan army, Pushyamitra Sunga, killed his king and assumed power in 184 BC. The Sungas ruled till 72 B.C; the only significance as far as Kashi was concerned was that the mother of the Sunga king Bhagabhadra belonged to the city. Towards the end of the Sunga period, and into the Kushana period (72 B.C. to 300 A.D.), Kashi developed into an important trading centre.

Between 305 and 1090 A.D., the Guptas rose to prominence. Seals from Rajghat suggest their presence, as Shaivite and Vaishnavite traditions of Hinduism took root. Jainism and Buddhism flourished; and the Chinese traveller Hiuen Tsang visited Kashi during the reign of Harshavardhana in 620 A.D. His description is of a city inhabited by wealthy, cultured people who were polished in their manners and given to study. He writes of a luxuriant city with a hundred temples, forest groves and streams; something that is borne out by a similar description of the Forest of Bliss in the Puranas. Nothing of that remains today, though I would like to think that the grove that abutted our colony near Durga Kund, when we moved into our home in 1977, was a remnant of the same Forest of Bliss. Sadly, even that is gone now.

After the Gupta period, Banaras remained under the control of various Hindu kingdoms, till the beginning of the thirteenth century, when the Delhi Sultanate was established. It was during this period that the city became a stronghold of Brahminical Hinduism.

The next phase of Banaras's history is representative of the predominant movement of the time – Tantra. Eighth century Banaras is best described in the writings of a pilgrim named Pantha, as a place where the netherworld, heavens and earth had met. He writes of establishing a fearsome image of the Goddess Chandi; of a city where people came from afar to die and obtain salvation. Even today, the Tantric tradition lives on in the ashrams of the Aghoris, as can one find evidence of the horrific goddesses they worshipped among the paintings of Molaram at the Bharat Kala Bhavan, and on the walls of the Durga Saptasati temple in the southern suburb of Nagwa.

By the eleventh century, the Gahadavala kingdom rose to prominence in the Gangetic plains, making Kashi their capital.

They were devout Hindus, even though their beliefs were eclectic : while some kings called themselves worshippers of Shiva, others were followers of Vishnu. The centre of the capital lay north, in the area of what is now the Rajghat Plateau, and here was established the temple of Adi Keshava 'The Original Vishnu'. The most famous king among the Gahadavalas was Govindachandra, who was believed to be the incarnation of Vishnu. His two queens, however, were staunch Buddhists. Under his patronage, the erudite Brahmin Lakshmidhara compiled one of the most comprehensive 'literature reviews' of the era : the fourteen volume *Krityakalpataru*, 'The Magical Wishing Tree of Duties'. The volume contains quotations from the Puranas, the Dharmashastras and the epics, arranged by topics that range from religion to duty to philanthropy to ritual. The last Gahadavala king, Jayachandra also got himself initiated as a Vaishnava and gifted thirty-two villages to five hundred Brahmins.

In his quest for domination over North India, Jayachandra became a fierce rival of King Prithviraj of Kannauj. Their squabbles weakened both, as a consequence of which they became easy targets for the advancing Muslim army of Muhammad Ghauri. In 1194, Ghauri's forces, commanded by General Qutubuddin Aibak, roundly defeated Jayachandra, beheaded him, and entered Banaras. They sacked and looted the city, carrying away the plunder on the backs of 1400 camels. More than a thousand temples were razed to the ground, and mosques raised on the foundations. Nearly a thousand years later, the Vishwa Hindu Parishad now wants to avenge the 'humiliation'.

The Gangetic plain remained under Muslim domination for over five hundred years. The religious way of Banaras was disrupted repeatedly, with its temples being destroyed at least five more times : by Firoz Shah Tughlaq, then by the Sharqi kings of

Jaunpur, who were followed by Sikandar Lodhi, and finally by the Mughals Shah Jahan (so what if he built the Taj Mahal!) and Aurangzeb. Aurangzeb even tried to rename the city as 'Muhammadabad', (just as he renamed Vrindavan as Muminabad), but the spirit of the Banarasis prevailed. The only respite was during the reign of the Mughal emperor Akbar, whose Rajput allies built the *ghats* on the waterfront – which have become the trademark of the city now, the observatory at Mansingh Ghat, and many temples.

In this turbulent period, the people of Banaras took their religious and intellectual spirit underground. The most reliable source of the city's history, the *Kashi Khaṇda*, was written in the mid-fourteenth century. Part of the *Skanda Purana*, it is hundred chapters long, and contains geographical information, myths, *mahatmyas* – hymns of praise, and ritual prescriptions. So were written the *Kashi Rahasya*, 'The Secret Lore of Kashi', which provides a mystical view of the city, and the *Kashi Kedara Mahatmya*, in praise of the Kedara shrine in the southern party of the city. The late medieval period is known by the arrival of several Vaishnava saints from different parts of the country. Among them were Ramanand, Chaitanya, Nanak and Vallabha. They gave birth to the *Bhakti* movement – wherein traditional Sanskrit prose made way for a lyrical, poetic literature expressed in the language of the people. The *Bhakti* movement found its proponents in Kabir, in the fifteenth century, and Tulsidas, in the sixteenth.

When the Mughal empire crumbled, the city of Banaras returned to Hindu dominion, and the same dynasty has continued to preside over the city since. In the early eighteenth century, Mansaram and his successor Balwant Singh ruled the city. They were followed by Maharaja Chet Singh, who took on the British Governor General Warren Hastings by not paying taxes, escaping even after being imprisoned, and rallying his people to drive away Hastings in 1781. Eventually, by 1794, Banaras came under British dominion, and the role of its rulers shifted from a political to a religious and cultural one. From Maharaja Ishwari Prasad Narain Singh in the nineteenth century, to Maharaja Vibhuti Narain Singh who passed away in 2000, and his son Anant Narayan Singh. The *Kashi Naresh* is the chief patron of the arts and music in the city, and seen by the residents as the incarnation of Lord Shiva on earth.

The city assumed much of its current form in the eighteenth century. After providing shelter to the great Maratha, Shivaji, it received the patronage and the energy of the Marathas. According to one historian, A.S Altekar, "Modern Banaras is largely the creation of the Marathas". They reconstructed a large number of temples, and several *ghats*. The British followed by building the main roads – from the Cantonment to the river, at Dasashwamedh, the Chowk road through the business district – and a Sanskrit College in 1853, in a completely incongruous Gothic style.

Today, the city looks and feels as antiquated as it actually is. While new 'colonies' have sprung up over lush green farmlands, they can scarcely detract from its medieval underpinnings. Every few years comes along a zealous ruler – the District Magistrate – who launches ambitious drives to push through a wider road or to 'beautify' the city by constructing parks and fountains, but moves on to another posting before he is able to uproot any of the fixtures that have remained in Varanasi for many centuries. Chaos rules supreme, and the city lurches on.

ꕥ

The Varanasi of my childhood, in complete contrast, was an orderly, fragrant, idyllic spot in heaven. It was as if I had attained *moksha* upon birth. Our family had a prestigious address – A/6/i Principal's Colony, Banaras Hindu University, thanks to my father being one of the senior-most professors in the university. We lived in a sprawling bungalow, with trimmed hedges of periwinkle and hibiscus surrounding our garden. As an infant, my mother would vigorously massage me with mustard oil, and leave me on a charpoy in the *aangan* (courtyard) to soak in the winter sun. I was spoiled for *maalish*, for life.

My father had planted a mango tree in the middle of the courtyard. It was fully grown by the time of my birth and bore at least five hundred succulent *langdas* in summer. We would easily eat five or six every day. A vine that bore sweet green grapes in summer curled up on one side, and two papaya trees, laden with those symbols of fertility, rose high beyond my reach in a corner. Outside, the lawn was surrounded by flower beds, while bougainvillea and jasmine crept up our windows. A *gulmohar* tree, its trunk hidden by the giant leaves of a money-plant creeper, showered petals on the garden in summer; while the *harsinghar* and the *rangbadal* bloomed just in time for Durga Puja. The guavas that grew in our garden had red cores; while the smell alone of the *mahua* outside our gate was intoxicating. A gravel path led to our garage, wherein my father's black 1936 Austin would be parked, as would Bihari's cycle-rickshaw. Every morning, Bihari would take his rickshaw out, clean it, and set off to make his living. Never did he refuse me a free ride. There were large fields in front of our house, all the way till the students' hostels. In the day, peacocks pranced in the fields. At night, foxes would howl and emerge from their hide-outs in the tall *arhar,* and make a beeline for the corn that grew in the kitchen-gardens of some of the professors' homes. As little children, our parents warned us about them.

As I grew, my world expanded beyond Principal's Colony. At the age of four, my mother took me to a nursery school, Malaviya Shishu Vihar, and I happily entered a world of friends. Every morning, we would ride in a covered rickshaw to a school where teachers behaved like fussing aunts. A year and a half in this school, and I suddenly felt grown up as I started going to St. John's, the same school where my seven-year older brother went. In a bus ! Some seven kilometres away, in another part of the city – the Diesel Locomotive Works campus. Till then, my trips to the town had been with my parents, sometimes standing with my head popping up from the sunroof of our Austin. Then, I learned to ride the Hillman bicycle that was handed down from my brother, could visit friends in other colonies and took my first tentative steps towards independence.

Three months after my ninth birthday, we moved into the house that my father built, in the city. Suddenly, the bustle of Varanasi was upon me. Even though we moved to a colony where there were not more than a dozen homes, the proximity to the 'real action' excited me. Our new home was close to three very revered temples : the Durga Temple, Sankat Mochan, and Tulsi Manas Mandir, and it immediately gave me the chance to mingle with those who were part of the city's history – not just a cosmopolitan collection of transplanted academicians. I was ready to undergo my initiation rites.

☙

What's in a Name?

ETYMOLOGY & ORIENTATION

Kaaba phir Kasi Kasi bhaya, Ram bhaya Rahim
Mot choon maida bhaya, baithi Kabira jeem.

In essence, Kaaba is the same as Kasi,
Ram and Rahim are the same;
Same is the powder of all the grains,
Man eats all of them.

Kabir

ঙ

About a year ago, I received a call from one of my friends who had just visited my home in Banaras. "Tell me quick, I have just had a bet with someone. Did I go to Kashi when I was in Varanasi? I said that I had, but this guy tells me that Kashi is a small place on the outskirts of Varanasi." Her dilemma is not uncommon. The three terms Banaras, Varanasi and Kashi have been used interchangeably for so long that one must clarify things right at the outset.

Kashi is the oldest name of the city. It is mentioned in the most ancient of the available texts, and there are three suggestions to its etymology, each quite different. The common one takes from the Sanskrit '*kasha*', which means 'to shine, to look brilliant or beautiful'. It is written in the Kashi Khanda : "Because that light, which is the unspeakable Shiva, shines (*kashate*) here, let its other name be Kashi." One version suggests that the name came from an ancient king, Kasha; while it has sometimes also been suggested that it is named *kasha*, the tall silver flowering grass that grows aplenty along the banks of the Ganga.

Name aside, Kashi is geographically defined by the Kashi Darpana as the area that is bound by the Panchakoshi Road and the Ganga : a sacred area that extends far into the countryside. Literally, this is an area in a radius of five *koshas* (the kosha equalling about two miles) with Madhyameshwara at its centre. Devotees circumambulate the city in what is called the

Panchakoshi Yatra, which takes five days to complete on foot. During this journey, they must stop and pray at 108 sacred spots – temples and shrines to Shiva, Devi and their protectors : Ganeshas and Bhairavas. To make the journey easier, there are many *dharamshalas* en route.

The name Banaras appears in texts much later. Kabir (15th century) uses the name, referring to a mythical magnate Raja Banar. Later, the British archaeologist James Prinsep also states that Banaras was governed by a certain Raja Banar, who was defeated by one of Mahmud's generals in 1017 A.D. But we know that was not the case, and conclude that the name 'Banaras' was simply a corrupted form of the name 'Varanasi', which finds mention in the more ancient Mahabharat and the Jataka Tales.

As any citizen will tell you, Varanasi refers to the area that lies between the Varuna in the north, Assi in the south, Dehli Vinayaka in the west, and the Ganga in the east (see map). Even though the Assi can hardly be called a river – it is at best an apology of a drain – its importance as a boundary was underscored in the Puranas. The Padma Purana states : "The Varuna and the Assi are two rivers, set there by the Gods. Between them is a holy land *(khsetra)*, and there is none more excellent on earth." The Kurma Purana puts it succintly: "Varanasi is the city between the Varuna and the Assi." In the final analysis, this is the sacred area where every pious Hindu must come to die; should they be desirous of liberation. Doctors at the Sir Sundarlal Hospital, which is a mere two hundred metres south of the Assi (and hence outside the sacred area), will tell you many a tale of relatives of dying men and women pleading that they be allowed to take their loved ones to Varanasi to breathe their last. To avoid any confusion, dear reader, any further, I shall hereafter use this current name, Varanasi, in the remainder of this book to refer to the city.

Within a radius of two hundred bow-lengths from the holy temple of Vishwanath, the area called Avimukta 'Never Forsaken' is the holiest part of the city. This part of Varanasi has no equal in the Universe, for it is guarded by Attahaseshwara in the east, Bhutadeshwara in the south, Gokarneshwara in the west, and Ghantakareshwara in the north. The name emphasizes an emotional and devotional attachment to the place, and the most devout follow this injunction by taking the *khsetra sannyas* – a vow never to leave the place. This is where the *linga* of Shiva was first established, and worshipped. The Puranas say that even in times of *pralay* (universal destruction), Shiva protects this part of the city, holding it above the waters on his *trishul* (trident).

The fact is, real Kashi and Varanasi are superphysical and spiritual rather than material or physical. The Skanda Purana says :

"Briefly, the body of man is the temple of God; herein are all the Tirthas, the holy places in living form. Spirit and Matter meet and combine in this living tabernacle and herein again, in a way the Finite and the Infinite touch each other more closely at special centres than elsewhere. Kashi, the Illuminator lies between the *Ida* nerve symbolized by Assi and the *Pingala* nerve symbolized by Varuna."

☙

Some accounts in the Puranas describe Varanasi as a city that rests on the three points of Shiva's trident. The city is thus divided from north to south into the three *khandas* of Omkara, Vishweswara and Kedara, which were seen at one time as the peaks of three hills. A millenium ago, Omkara was the preeminent Shiva *linga* in Varanasi. The Omkara Temple was an imposing structure, occupying the entire hilltop. Today,

Omkareswara has all but disappeared behind a maze of lanes and homes that is the Muslim dominated area of Machhodari (Matsyodari, in Sanskrit). The Vishweswara Khand, better known as Vishwanath, and geographically synonymous with Avimukta, assumed its pre-eminence later. I shall deal with it later, as will I describe in detail the temple at the centre of the Kedara Khand, situated in the south of the city. In Varanasi, Kedara 'the field where grows the crop of liberation' is the worldly representative of the other Kedareswara, high up in Uttarakhand in the Himalaya. It sits on the banks of the Ganga, just as Kedareswara sits on the banks of the Mandakini.

Having described how religious leaders, regents, scholars and its residents have mapped the city by belief, I cannot but resist writing about the divisions that have been created more recently, for administrative purposes. Modern day Varanasi is divided into territories that are governed by eight *thanas,* or police stations, each of which is presided by the S.O. (Station Officer). If you are travelling to Varanasi, and (Lord Shiva forbid) should you need to contact the police, this piece of information might just prove to be more useful to you than all those historical and religious territorial markings. The aforementioned *thanas* are : Lanka, Chowk, Bhelupur, Manduadih, Nadesar, Dasashwamedh, Adampura (more familiar to residents and rickshaw-wallahs as Pilikothi), and Lahurabir.

ଓ

Making Sense out of the Maze

GEOGRAPHY

Kabira bhanbar mein baithkey, bhauchak mana na joye,
Dooban ke bhay chhadiye, Karta kare so hoye.

In the midst of perilous whirl,
lose not courage or common sense,
Give up all fear of drowning,
It is God alone who dispenses.

Kabir

ଓ

The first time visitor may enter Varaṇasi from any direction, by any mode of transport. Faced with the immense disorderliness that characterizes the city, Kabir's words might just put you in the right frame of mind.

If you have flown in, then you will certainly enter the city from the north, where Babatpur Airport is situated. Since there are flights that come in from Kathmandu, it enjoys the lofty status of an International Airport, complete with immigration, customs, and I imagine, Duty Free Shopping. At the other extreme, I have known of a former colleague who made the trip by boat from Allahabad, after attending the Mahakumbh Mela. It took him three days and two nights, and he was *charas*-induced ecstatic about it. Yet another intrepid traveller – then a student at Allahabad University - had made the same journey on road, but by cycle rickshaw. Once again, this was done in a similarly elevated state, with he and his friend taking turns cycling the rickshaw, along with its grateful owner. It took them only a day to cover the 120 kilometres. Lesser mortals usually trundle in by train or bus, from the east or the west. When one enters the city from the east, the first view of the city, from the Malviya Bridge at Rajghat, can indeed be a rewarding one – as one sees the entire city strung out along the river.

☙

Varanasi Mapped

Very crudely, Varanasi can be thought of as a triangle, with the Rajghat plateau, the Banaras Hindu University and the Cantonment railway station at its three corners. A thousand narrow lanes and streets crisscross the ancient territory contained within, and there is no one who can provide a reliable, detailed map of the city. Even old time residents are, at best, familiar with only the part of the city they live in, and the notable places outside that domain.

The main railway station sits right astride that ancient north Indian trading route – the Grand Trunk Road. Varanasi was put firmly on the Indian Railways map by one of its zealous residents, Pandit Kamlapati Tripathi, who, as Railway Minister in Indira Gandhi's cabinet, ensured that the city was connected to every part of the country. He also re-built the station façade in the style of a sprawling Hindu temple. As if to proclaim that the Ashok Chakra had its origins in neighbouring Sarnath, a giant wheel sits on top of the central *shikhara.* For many years, when I was young, I would see a scale model of the new station displayed near the entrance, and wonder if it would ever be ready. It is chaotic outside the station. Crowds from the adjoining bus station mingle with the melee that the trains disgorge. Pilgrims and returning residents fight with rickshaw pullers and auto-rickshaw drivers over the best fares. Whenever I return, I lapse into the local dialect Bhojpuri to declare my origins. The milestone outside the station simply declares, Varanasi 0, Delhi 710, Calcutta 680. They have evidently forgotten that the eastern city has reverted to its Bengali name.

I will attempt to orient you, dear reader, with the city, by taking you on a journey from the railway station in the north to the university in the south, and then back again up – somewhat parallel to the Ganga. The first *mohalla*, or part of the city, that one passes through, on the way to the heart of Varanasi, is Sigra. On the left, one of its three universities, Kashi Vidyapeeth, can be recognized by its muddy yellow buildings, and slogans in blue exhorting students to vote for various candidates to the last Student Union elections painted on their walls. Next to Kashi Vidyapeeth is the unusual Bharat Mata Temple. Built in 1936 during the freedom struggle, it contains a relief map of India, in marble, in place of the conventional deity. Just fifty metres further, along the road, a wholesale vegetable market, the *satti,* is in full swing every morning at Chandua, making it difficult for any vehicle to pass through. Farmers from the villages bring in their fresh vegetables on every possible mode of transport, and vendors from the city drive a hard bargain at the top of their voices, before their competitors can snap up the best greens. Both look out for cows and goats, milling about among humans, lest they take off with the best bits, for free. Just as you cross this market, an incongruous traffic island springs up in the middle of a road junction, with an obelisk that announces the Four Truths as espoused by the Rotary Club. The next stretch is somewhat out of place with the character of the city: a wide road with large shops and the *Saajan* cinema hall, new apartment and office buildings and an ornate new temple, the *Kaiwalya Gyan Mandir*, a patch of green behind which are the Sampurnanand Stadium, and the headquarters of the horribly inefficient and corrupt Varanasi Municipality, and St. Paul's Church. Another minor crossing, at which a left turn will take you to an area called Sidhhgiri Bagh. The only time I had ever been there was when we had installed a security service at our home : the office and residence of Colonel Bannerjee, a genial old army fellow who ran the agency, were in this part of town.

Back on the main road bound south. Rathyatra *Chowhmani* comes next. Its importance as a crossroad can be gauged from the presence of the only traffic signal to function in the entire city. Next to the road has been constructed Varanasi's first shopping mall. For at least two years after it was built, I saw only two occupants in this building – Raymond Suitings and Titan Watches. In the ancient city, the idea of a mall seems quite irrelevant – especially since the significance of Rathyatra lies in the annual chariot procession that is taken out in the honour of the eastern deity Jagannath, once a year in autumn. Should you turn right, you will go to Mahmoorganj, a residential area, better known for the offices of All India Radio, and a couple of well known private hospitals. I have had the misfortune of undergoing a CT scan in one of them. The road going left takes you to Godowlia, and further to the river at Dasashwamedh Ghat, but we shall visit those later in our explorations.

Just after crossing Rathyatra, on the left, you will find an unobtrusive entrance to one of Varanasi's old schools : The Besant Theosophical Society School. The road curves along a wall plastered with cinema posters, and is lined with little shops, till one takes a right turn at the temple of Shri Shayri Mata – which you would hit if you kept going straight. This is Kamachchha, home to an outpost of the Banaras Hindu University : its Faculty of Education, and the Central Hindu Schools are located in a campus here. Another vegetable market, less obtrusive and disruptive to traffic than the one at Chandua, prospers in a large courtyard, on the left. My father's department had a laboratory assistant called Kishun Ram, who sold vegetables early in the mornings and late in the evenings in this marketplace. As the road curves, you can see the remnants of the old Power House, once the object of much curiosity on my part on account of its multiple 'fountains' (actually part of the plant's cooling system). That is immediately followed by the red and white building of the Chintamani Anglo-Bengali School, and its grounds.

Then follows the Bengali dominated area of Bhelupur. Significant here are the Parsvanath Digamber Jain temple, and the palace of the erstwhile Maharaja of Vizianagaram – who came from the south of the country. The former is believed to be the birthplace of the twenty-third Jain Tirthankara, and contains a century-old stone image of Rishabnatha, seated on a lion throne with a seven-hooded snake canopy. Vizzy's statue, in full cricketing gear, graces the traffic junction at Bhelupur. The outer walls of his palace grounds, however, sport posters of all the Hindi films that run in Varanasi's theatres. As long as I can remember, this wall has served as the window to the saucy world of Bollywood for the residents. Suddenly, for about half a kilometre, it seems that the city has changed character. The road widens to include a green traffic island, among the very few in the city, with two statues: one of the last Mughal emperor Bahadurshah Zafar, the other of the Bengali poet and Nobel laureate Rabindranath Tagore. It then branches on the left towards Ravindrapuri, the residential colony for some of the wealthiest of Varanasi's traders.

The road goes straight towards Durga Kund, where lie the temple of the goddess Durga (well known to foreigners as the Monkey Temple) and the tank that abuts it. Before that you will pass by the small shrine of Murkatta Baba 'The Headless Holy-Man', the relatively new ISKCON Temple and the Tantric Temple of Rani Barahi to the left of the traffic junction of Gurudham. On the eastern bank of Durga Kund is a lovely garden, at the centre of which is a marble memorial to Swami Bhaskarananda, built by his devotee, the Raja of Amethi. In the morning, local residents gather here to sing hymns. At one of the two eastern corners of the Kund is a small shrine of Gangadhar Mahadev, at the other lies the temple of Durg Vinayak, while a narrow lane next to the garden leads to the Bankati Hanuman temple. Just before Durgakund, a narrow lane right heads towards Nawabganj, where the Nawab of Avadh Wajid Ali Shah spent his latter years, and the grain market and potters' quarter of Khojwan. The Western tourists that one might espy heading down this lane are interested in neither, rather they make a beeline for one of the city's best (and newest) bookshops – Pilgrim.

Diagonally opposite the Durga temple, looking completely nondescript behind a row of auto-rickshaws is a small white-washed *mazaar* that comes to life only when a *taazia* is placed there for the Muharram procession. It is the remnant of a larger palace complex of unknown antiquity. My home lies barely five hundred metres from the temple, making it within earshot of every *aarti* that is performed in the temple, but vulnerable to periodic invasions by the monkeys that reside on the temple's precincts. When we moved to Durgakund in 1977, the crumbling palace and its bush and creeper covered grounds were a favourite spot for me and my friends to play hide-and-seek, unafraid of the ghosts that might have dwelt within. But it was within a year that all but the little *mazaar* was razed to make way for apartment blocks.

The relatively new Tulsi Manas Mandir, resplendent in marble, and bright lights in the month of *Saawan* (July – August), comes next, before the road narrows to a mere five metres. Just a hundred metres down, the road crosses the Assi *Nala,* and one has left the boundaries of the holy city. Purists may shudder at the term that I use here to describe the Assi – it is a river, according to the sacred texts. But locals like me prefer reality: that narrow, black, smelly strip of water is a *nala*, a drain, nothing more!

This part of the city is called Sankat Mochan, after the eponymous temple which attracts most Banarasis in search of boons that Hanuman, the Monkey God, the *Ramsewak* might grant them. While the temple itself is in a complex away from the road, close by are two interesting structures on the left. One is a marble temple dedicated to Ram and Sita, empty most of the time, and an Indo-Saracenic building that is actually a hostel 'Mahendravi Lodge' for the students of the Banaras Hindu University's Faculty of Social Sciences.

The kilometre-long stretch that follows, before the imposing BHU gates is named after the land that Ram conquered – Lanka. Apart from its name, there is nothing here that suggests mythology. It is quite simply the marketplace where the students and staff of the university shop. Many years ago, the students coined a term for hanging out here in the evening, 'Lanketing'. The presence of two large hospitals nearby has ensured the proliferation of support services – pathology and X-Ray labs, and a profusion of chemists.

At the southern end of Lanka is the statue of Pandit Madan Mohan Malaviya, the man who built the huge, immensely pretty university, simply by going around the country asking kings and businessmen to be charitable. The university deserves a much more detailed description, and I have saved that for later. The road going left from Malviyaji's statue takes you to the factories of the Diesel Locomotive Works, the one on the right goes on to Ramnagar. One must cross a pontoon bridge in the dry season, or take a ferry in the monsoons, in order to reach the fort of the Maharaja of Banaras located on the opposite riverbank. A new bridge has been built somewhat upstream, but involves a much longer journey. For now, we shall turn back – as we have two more sides of that triangle that Varanasi falls within, to explore.

Turning back, another road from Lanka leads to Assi, one of the parts of the city where westerners tend to congregate. Those here have long shed their blue jeans and trekking pants, their Berghaus and Lowe Alpine knapsacks. Clad in thin cotton tees and pajamas or *lungis* with bright Hindu iconography screen printed on them, they are here to study Indian classical music, the Hindu religion, and / or smoke pot. Keeping in touch with their civilizations through the numerous cybercafes and eateries like Haifa (opened by enterprising locals who have undoubtedly been trained by some homesick tourist), offering everything from pasta to humus they remain as long as their visas allow them to. On this road is the Raghav Mandir, set in a spacious compound. The temple houses images of Ram, Sita, Hanuman, Lakshmi, Narayan, and Ramanandacharya. Headed by Shri Ramdheen Dasjee Maharaj, it is a retreat for *sadhus*, and home to the Guddar Das Ka Chhota Akhara – one of the many sects that you will encounter in the holy city. From the right of Assi Ghat, a road winds its way along the Ganga to Guru Ravi Dass Park. This is purely a symbol of Dalit ('lower-class' Hindu) emancipation constructed by their leader, the abrasive chief minister of Uttar Pradesh - at the time of my writing, I must emphasize, given the fickle nature of Uttar Pradesh politics. Out of sight from the main town, and with a cool breeze blowing even in the peak of summer, it has turned out to be a favourite spot for young lovers, especially from the university.

From Assi onwards, every fifty metres or so, a lane 'gali' on the east side of the main street takes you to a *ghat* on the riverbank. One such lane goes to Lolark Kund, a tank at the bottom of four long flights of stairs, where those in search of offspring and cure for illness take a bath in the month of Bhadra (August-September). The tank was built by the Raja of Cooch Behar, in Bengal, after he was healed of leprosy from the waters of a small pond. A small temple dedicated to Lorarkeshwara is on the southern side of the Kund, under a *peepul* tree. On the walls is an icon depicting the Sun in a chariot, drawn by six white horses. Looming over the northern wall of the Lolark complex is an imposing palace. Unfortunately, it houses the electrical transformers of the local power company, and is off limits for visitors. Further down the Assi Road, Mata Anandamayee ashram and its charitable hospital are followed a short distance later by the new Bread of Life Bakery. Opposite lies the unkempt Ratnekar Park, a favourite spot for rickshaw-wallahs to spend their summer nights sleeping after a round of *ganja.* Sure enough, there's a 'Government Bhaang Shop' just down the road. A relatively wider street to one of the two cremation grounds, Harishchandra Ghat, follows, and then one arrives in the Bengali dominated precinct of Sonarpura.

In a short stretch of hundred metres, you would be faced with a smorgasbord of different establishments here. The famous sweet shop, Ksheer Sagar, and the old saw mills – Gita Saw Mill, Ganga Saw Mill and Kanhaiya Saw Mill - spilling their sweet smell of freshly sawn logs on to the main road. Two really old educational institutions, the Durga Charan Inter College for Girls, and the Bengali Tola School, which compete for attention during the Durga Puja. Two majestic homes, one rundown yet offering immense possibilities for a film set; the other recently restored and inviting the curious to step in. The first, directly opposite the saw mills, was built by the Raja of Cooch Behar as a family retreat. Its gates are shut most of the year, but in October, when the Friends Sporting Club hosts their Durga Puja on the grounds of the villa, its lawns are festooned with coloured lights, and the building receives a fresh coat of lime paint.The second, some fifty metres later, belongs to the Biswas family (no relation to Naipaul's Caribbean character), and we knew them well in the '70s. The men in the family had two passions: vintage cars, and hunting. They possessed a 1910 Sunbeam and a 1930s Studebaker, and were the only ones who could be trusted with keeping our Austin in running condition. Their sprawling living room was strewn with skins of animals – leopard, tiger and deer – that the men had hunted down in the neighbouring jungles of Mirzapur; lanterns, stuffed chaise lounges, and deep pile rugs made by the craftsmen in Bhadohi. Tucked behind the Bengali Tola School (Primary Section) lies the precinct of Devnathpura, where craftsmen fashion idols of Durga, Kartik, Saraswati, Lakshmi and Ganesh feverishly before post-autumn Durga Puja.

From the next *mohalla*, called Pandey Haveli, the evidence of Varanasi's famed silk sarees begins to spill on to the streets. Showroom after showroom – Enaar Sarees, National State Sarees, Hakimco, Modern Silk Stores, Taj Baba, Taj Exotica, Ishrat Sarees, Zubair Sarees, Safia, Jeco Textiles, Anwar Sarees, Madani Seraj and Emco Fabrics are just some of the shops with glistening silks and brocade put on display to tempt the visitor. The average Banarasi carries on as if these were just another set of posters for candidates for the local municipal elections. The Muslim-dominated area of Madanpura shows evidence of recent Gulf money, with marble towers rising from the street; as men in blue-check *lungis* and white skull-caps lounge around in the numerous tea and *pakora* shops. Every now and then, a little boy or girl darts across the road, emerging from a lane on the left, and headed for one on the right, or vice-versa. My father called them shooting stars, to be wary of when driving down this road – in the days when it was possible to do speeds in excess of 10 kmph.

Jangambari, up next, is where Banarasis shop for furniture. The ghat side of this part of the city is where old-timer Tamilians, Kannadigas and Andhra-ites reside, as do visitors from Southern India who head to find a place for 'boarding-lodging' on their pilgrimage to the holy city. The entrance to the brightly coloured Jangambari Math, on the main road, is often teeming with women in nine-yard sarees and men in white *lungi* and *veshti*. Here, the courtyard is teeming with Shivlingas, numbering some sixty-thousand, left behind by devout pilgrims. If the traffic on the road slows to a crawl by now, that's because one is now approaching the city's busiest intersection - Godowlia. Things come to a standstill, routinely at 3:00, 6:00 and 9:00 pm everyday, as the Susheel Cinema disgorges its Hindi-film crazy audience on to the streets. Opposite Susheel are two well stocked bookshops – Universal, and Indica. The first keeps all the bestsellers. As you enter the latter, a wind chime above the door announces your entry into a world of books on religion, philosophy, tantra, travel and the arts. It is run by a kindly European called Alvarro Enterria. Next to Susheel lies the City Book Shop.

Godowlia Crossing is quite simply, the most chaotic spot in Varanasi. Rickshaws, scooters, motorcycles, bicycles, the odd horse-pulled *tonga*, determined locals, backpacking foreigners and confused Indian pilgrims on foot mingle and dart about in different directions. Mercifully, auto-rickshaws have been banished to the nearby Girjaghar Crossing fifty metres away. I think that the traffic here flows something like fish swim in a river or the sea, two shoals flowing in opposite directions. Each vehicle rider is keenly aware of its neighbour, and reacts to it, moving away to avoid hitting it. The side-view mirrors of the two-wheelers are turned in, to avoid being broken. Perchance one of the 'fish' were to stray into an oncoming shoal, the other 'fish' would make room, but not without much honking and bell-ringing. Eventually, the errant vehicle finds its way back to its own school. Sometimes, a traffic policeman tries to keep order by swinging his *lathi* at a poor rickshaw-wallah, but that is all he can do. Loudspeakers, alternately broadcasting religious songs and political speeches add to the din.

The road carries on to the heart of Varanasi's commercial district – Chowk. It seems to me that the crowds are automatically sorted at this point. Most locals (unless they had specially planned to visit Lord Vishwanath and take a dip in the river, which they usually do in the morning) are Chowk-bound. Most out-of-towners take the right turn (or if they are coming from the Girjaghar side, carry straight on) to Dasashwamedh – the Vishwanath *Gali* and the Dasashwamedh *Ghat*. Chowk sits on top of a hill, which would not be discernible if you were not making this journey on a rickshaw, or observing those on the road. For the poor rickshaw-wallahs must now disembark and pull their vehicles, since the slope is too steep to pedal up with their human burden. Shops selling sarees and salwar-kameezes

(Gopal Vastralaya, Banaras Art Palace, Pitambari Sarees), 'suiting-shirting' (Vimal, Raymonds), electronic goods and cassettes, watches and wall-clocks (Chakravarti & Co., Time Zone, New Time House), photographers' studios (Bright Studio, Photo House, Grace Studio, Camera Şcanner), doctors' clinics (Dr. Faran Durrani, Ram Gopal Tandon – ENT Specialist, Dr. Rajni Kant Dutta), dentists (Dr R N Bannerjee with Baranwal Dental Clinic opposite him), opticians (Das Optical, Sri Hari Opticians, Chashma Ghar) and home appliances stores (Satyanarayan & Co., Girdhardas and Sons, Nalanda and Co.), three cinema halls (Kanhaiya Chitra Mandir, Deepak and Chitra), a library (Carmichael Library), cosmetics and gift shops – all seem to be crammed into such a short distance. My favourite, of course, had been the two sporting equipment stores : Rajput & Co, and Dina & Co. at Bansphatak, which I would frequent to buy badminton and tennis racquets, shuttlecocks and Symonds tennis balls. (Cricket equipment would be bought at the 'auctions' held at BHU – where the top bid for a cricket bat could close at as low as Rs 25). Dina and Co. has since shut down. For those interested in books on culture and religion, there is again much to choose from – Motilal Banarasidass, Chowkhamba Classica and Chowkhamba Vidya Bhavan, Thakur Prasad Booksellers and Bhargava Book Depot. If you ask a local shopowner, he will guide you to the flower market – Phoolmala Bazaar, which comes alive every late afternoon, carrying on till evening by when the fragrant blossoms and garlands made out of marigold, jasmine, hibiscus and periwinkle are sold out. Just before the entrance to the flower market is the shop of Laltaprasad Ramsaranlal Attarwala, seller of perfumed oils and potions; following it is a tall building with filigreed iron railings painted in yellow and green, inside which lies the Satyanarayan Temple.

The Chowk, or Square, of every north Indian city, is its central, indigenous old market. Varanasi's Chowk, a kilometre north of Godowlia, is best known for its *thana*, the police station. Just before the lawkeepers' offices, a lane on the left takes you to Daalmandi. The place is however not a wholesale market (*mandi*) for pulses (*daal*). The folks of Varanasi come here to buy their crockery – tableware for sale in shop after shop. As a young man, one had heard that this was also Varanasi's red-light district, but I am yet to find out the precise location of the brothels.

As you return to the main street, and head north, more shops follow, till you reach another major crossing at Vishweshwarganj. This is also the city's wholesale grain market. Labourers clad in vests and lungis, bent under sacks of wheat and rice, carry out the orders of traders in their spotless white dhoti-kurtas. At the crossing is the Digambar Jain Temple and dharmashala, and two busts – one of the assassinated former prime minister Rajiv Gandhi, the other of Maharaj Agrasen. A right turn will take you to the *mohalla* of Maidagin, which has one of the two important taxi stands in the city: rows of white Ambassador cars, and Maruti Omnis are found parked here. At Maidagin lies the venerable Nagari Pracharani Sabha, the Society for Spread of Nagari – which is an euphemism for Hindi, not in a literary, but in a cultural-political sense. Its red building stands graciously in an independent compound, a rare sight in this crowded part of the city. Opposite it towers impressively Varanasi's Town Hall, today called Gandhi Bhawan. Gandhiji's and Kasturba's statues stand in a small park in front of the town hall – they were a present to the city from Dr. Vijaya of Vizianagaram according to the wishes of his mother Lalita Kumari Devi, Dowager Maharani of Vizianagaram. The Town Hall houses the offices of the Bhartendu Academy, a centre for social, cultural and literary studies, and the Kotwali Police Station. A fork in the road ahead will take you to Macchodari – where the old Shiva temple of Omkareshwar lies hidden behind a cluster of Muslim homes. The road going left from Vishweshwarganj goes to Kabirchaura. The Kabir Temple here is bereft of idols and religious artifacts, keeping in mind Kabir's belief in the formlessness of God. Varanasi's overcrowded, government-run Shiv Prasad Gupta Hospital is also located in Kabirchaura. North of Kabirchaura, are the *mohallas* of Jaitpura and Adampura, which are the real centres for the weaving of Banarasi sarees. Next up is Lohatiya, the part of the city where ironmongers sell their wares; among these shops towers the gateway to the Radhaswami Temple. This road carries on to Lahurabir, yet another busy commercial area, then bisects the Grand Trunk Road, to reach the relatively cleaner, better laid out parts of the city. Nadesar, and the leafy Cantonment, are parts where well-heeled foreigners choose to stay, possibly to recover their sense of sanity after every day they spend in the ancient, holy city.

I must take you back to Godowlia, simply to be able to map out the few in-between parts of the city. Next to Godowlia, as I had mentioned before, is Girijaghar, a crossing marked by the Church of St Thomas. In the south lies one of the weaving areas : Reori Talab. Next to the narrow road can be seen skeins of yarn wrapped around wooden poles, and bobbins being repaired. Varanasi's first English-medium school, Jai Narain Inter College, was established here in 1814, by a nobleman from Bengal called Raja Jai Narain Ghoshal. The old school building was built in stone, and had a red-clay tiled roof. In the late 1970s, a two-seater Piper aircraft, on a training flight from BHU, crashed into the school after its trainee pilot apparently decided to swoop down to wave at his friends in the city. A new, undistinguished building has now taken the place of the old one. West of Girijaghar is the somewhat soapy sounding part of the city called Luxa. First, there are two cinema halls next to each other: Saraswati (I can imagine the Goddess of Learning squirming), and the older Mazda, once owned by the family of one of my brother's classmates. This is where the second of the main taxi stands of the city can be found. Further on is Ramakrishna Mission, and its charitable hospital. The part of the city dominated by the Punjabi community follows –

Gurubagh. Two features make it easy to discern : a Gurudwara, and rows of shops selling salwaar kameezes.

Nai Sarak – New Street, heads north of Girijaghar. This is once again, an area populated by Muslims. A mosque's minaret rises above all else, smells of biryani and kebab waft on to the street in the evening, and Urdu calligraphy adorns the signboards. A hundred metres on is a row of shops selling *namkeen* – salted savouries. Behind it lies Benia Bagh, a park that is often the scene of political rallies and speeches today. Only a hundred years ago, this was an inland lake : the Veni Lake, which was fed by the Ganga river by a stream that ran the length of Godowlia. The British drained it, built the park, and called it Victoria Park. The renaming saga continues. Currently, the park is called Raj Narayan Udyan, after the maverick Janata Party politician whose claim to fame was a massive election victory over Indira Gandhi in the 1977 general elections. His statue adorns the park, while the palms leading up to it offer a shady place for tired rickshaw-wallahs to grab a snooze. Next to Benia Bagh is a busy bus stand, from where commuters catch public transport to the railway junction of Mughal Sarai 16 kms away. Nai Sarak carries on to Chetganj, a part of the city named after one of its 17th century maharajas, Chet Singh, best known for outwitting Warren Hastings, before finally reaching Lahurabir. Statues of noted Hindi litterateur Munshi Premchand, and freedom fighter Chandra Shekhar Azad were erected in the traffic islands here at various points of time, to coincide with some anniversary or the other.

At the northern tip of the city, near the summit of the Varuna river and the Ganga, lies the temple of Adi Keshava. Two thousand years ago, this was the heart of Varanasi. Today, a shady winding road off the highway takes you to a grassy plateau called Rajghat, home to the Krishnamurti Foundation School, the Annie Besant College and the Gandhi Foundation, and a site for ancient excavations. The Malviya Bridge carries all train and road traffic east, and offers a spectacular view of the city as it curves around and rises above the banks of the Ganga.

☙

The Famous Galis of Varanasi

What makes Varanasi so unique, and such a maze to easily get lost in – are its narrow, labyrinthine lanes, better known in local parlance as *galis.* (Not to be confused with *gaalis,* which means abuses. More on that later.) As old as the city itself, they belong to an era well before the discipline on town-planning had spread beyond Mohenjodaro. No visitor to the city can avoid them, as most temples and well-known shops are located inside some *gali.* For the Banarasi, they are an integral part of life, and provide opportunity to flaunt his or her familiarity with the contours of the city.

Barely wide for two persons of ample girth to pass through, twisting, turning and branching out every few metres, enclosing pilgrims in the atmosphere of the city and assaulting them with sights, sounds and odours, the *galis* are Varanasi's nervous system. Buildings three or four floors high, some with brightly painted gateways, others with narrow doors from which steeply rise stone steps, ornate verandahs on the floors above, and crammed, bustling shops on the ground floor, line every *gali.* Only at noon, when the sun is directly above, does a ray hit the stone-flagged pavement. Pilgrims jostle for space with residents, bulls and beggars amble past, the former occasionally stopping to swipe a bunch of succulent spinach from vegetable vendors, or a garland from a flower seller. The odd monkey swings from one balcony to another, and pigeons nest on the window ledges and in cornices. Depending on the time of the day, different sets of people seem to populate the *gali.* In the morning, chattering schoolchildren in uniform head out to the main road to catch their rickshaw or bus to school. Sweepers with brooms and wheelbarrows clear out the detritus of the previous 24 hours. Housewives haggle with vegetable vendors, who sell their fresh stock from baskets atop their heads, or handcarts. The men, still clad in their *lungis,* settle on tea-shop benches with a crisp issue of *Aaj,* or *Dainik Jagaran* and catch up with the national and regional news, exchanging local news with the *chaiwallah* and other customers. Worshippers, some still in their clothes wet from a dip in the Ganga, occasionally ushered or harried by *pandas,* make their way to the temple, to perform Puja on an empty stomach: the *prasad* being the first thing they would consume in the day. Local residents bow before the lesser shrines before they depart for work.

As the day progresses, the shops open their shutters. The *halwai* and *mithai* shops are the first to get into action, to feed the columns of pilgrims that emerge from the temples hungry. Then, the bangle sellers, cloth merchants, souvenir and toy sellers, sellers of charms and God-images lay out their wares and, in the manner of medieval merchants, call out to and invite passersby. Most shopowners are multilingual, even if their vocabulary in each tongue is limited. Bengalis are invited by 'Boudi, dekhe jan', as do Israelis provoke a 'Shalom', as are Spaniards addressed as 'Senor' and 'Senorita'. When there are power outages (and in Uttar Pradesh they are not infrequent), generators raise the decibel level within the narrow confines of the *gali* to unbearable limits, and the acrid smell of kerosene mingles with that of stale urine, cowdung, jasmine and incense.

The total length of Varanasi's *galis* is said to be 480 kms. No one has ever attempted a map of all the city's lanes and bylanes, and I shall desist attempting the impossible. What I will do, however, is to provide the highlights of the city's best known *galis.* The most famous, and hence, most crowded of Varanasi's *galis* is the half-kilometre long Vishwanath Gali. Easily recognizable from the main road that goes from Godowlia to

Dasashwamedh Ghat - owing to the recent, garish stone gate constructed at its entrance, it is the path to the Kashi Vishwanath Temple, as well as the lesser known Annapurna Temple, and the shrines of Sakshi Vinayak, Dandapani, Dhundiraja Ganesh and Shani. As one approaches the temple, the number of shops selling rosaries, *shivlingas, supari* (arecanut), incense sticks, *sindoor* and oil lamps increases. Then comes a fork in the lane, and all visitors who look confused are immediately pointed in the direction (right) of the Vishwanath Temple. Policemen frisk you and ask you to leave behind any bags you might be carrying behind, since this is a 'high-security' area – ever a communal flashpoint after December 6 1992, when the Babri Masjid in Ayodhya was demolished by fanatical Hindus. Sweet-shop owners urge you to take off your shoes, which they would keep safely, while you went inside the temple, and ask you the value of your offering to the Lord. Shoes off, a small packet of *mithai, bel leaf,* a garland and a vessel containing a mixture of water and milk – to pour over Shiva's linga, is thrust into your hand.

Back to the fork in the lane. The left turn carries on to Gyanvapi, the 'Wisdom Well'. More shops, except this time, they sell clothes, and ornaments. For thirty years, my mother patronized one such store – she bought yarn for all the sweaters she'd knit for the family. Kachauri Gali, named after the scrumptious fried *kachauris* on sale every morning, runs parallel to this lane. Here is also located the temple of Kashi Karvat, a manifestation of Bhima Shankar. The *linga* lies twenty feet underground, and is approached through a tunnel. The nearby Khoya Gali is where halwais congregate to pick up *khoya* - that vital ingredient for the best of Banarasi *mithai, chhena* (cottage cheese), ghee (clarified butter) and milk. The air is thick with the aroma of milk products. At festival time, housewives, out to prepare the best home-made sweets for their family and relatives, join the rush of customers and the price of *khoya* shoots up.

Just after Chowk, a lane on the right takes you to Rani Kuan, and Kunj Gali - the wholesale trading centre for Banarasi sarees. Every day, in the many shops owned by prosperous Hindu traders, the Muslim *julehas* (weavers) bring their lustrous creations, fling them out on the spotless white sheets that are laid on the shopfloor and haggle for the best price. Yet another lane in this part of the city, Thatheri Bazaar, serves as the main market for brass and copper utensils for religious ceremonies and daily use. Of the original twenty or so traders, only four remain today, but do brisk business. Devotees also pick up idols of Gods and Goddesses: Krishna, Shiva, Ganesh, Lakshmi, and tiny saris and dhotis in silk and gold brocade to clothe the idols in. It is here that one can see the famous Sherwali Kothi 'The Mansion of the Tiger' – a large house built in 1891, that has two roaring tigers carved in Italian marble on either side of its main door. On the opposite side of the road from Thatheri Bazaar, inside yet another lane, is the legendary Raja Darwaza. It is today a market for jewellery. Tiny shops, elevated from the street by two feet and accessible only by stone steps or a short jump, populated by their dhoti-clad owners, deceive you by not displaying their precious wares, which are kept out of sight. When their shops are not doing brisk business, which may often be the case, the owners sit langourously on the white sheets on the floor, reading the newspaper, chewing *paan*, sipping tea, or just looking at passersby.

Venturing further into the interior, one reaches a grimy, oil-soaked market for machine parts, Kashipura. This is also the home of Varanasi's braziers and coppersmiths. One of the lanes that lead to Maidagin is the fascinating Paan Dariba, the wholesale market for the acclaimed Banarasi *paan*. Every ingredient that could possibly impart and add to the *paan's* flavour and taste can be found here, in bulk. The shopowners put out small mountains of *surti*, that coarse tobacco not to be confused with the more refined *zarda* which is found in tins, and now pouches.

There are mounds of *supari*, betel nuts, some chopped, others whole, and wicker baskets lined with wet straw in which rest wads of shiny, green *paan* leaves, waiting to be snapped up by hundreds of *paanwallahs* – Varanasi's ubiquitous *paan* shop owners.

The lane to Kedar has its beginnings at Sonarpura. Like most other *galis,* it ejects young schoolchildren and welcomes devotees early in the morning. Should you venture here in the evening, you would almost immediately be enticed by the smell of mutton, fish and chicken cutlets, being fried at a tiny shop barely 20 metres into the lane. As you carry on, you might discover that this is more of a residential, and less of a commercial area.

If you enter one of the old, stone faced, balconied homes – like the one where Dr Bishwanath Chakraborti, a doctor at the Ramkrishna Mission Hospital resides - you would suddenly find yourself in a large courtyard. This, open space is surrounded by rooms that rise three or four stories high, and they must be reached by narrow, dark flights of stone steps. Some courtyards have a well, and almost certainly a *tulsi* plant in the centre. Smells of cooking emanate from kitchens on various floors, a maid scrubs clothes in a corner, and a transistor radio, or lately, cassette player plays at top volume in one of the rooms. Once home to large Bengali joint families, they are now populated by several tenants, with the owners possibly keeping only a floor to themselves. A Shiva Temple, nearly 1500 years old – locals couldn't tell me who built it – has lovely figurines carved under the eaves. The *gali* carries on past Kedar, where beggars and flower-sellers line up outside, both hoping to make some money. A wide range of *matths* and *ashrams* follow,' catering to the spiritual and material needs of travellers from the eastern and southern parts of India. Up from Mansarovar Ghat is the Sreeramataraka Andhra Ashram, and later the Akhila Bharatiya Brahmana Kariveem Nityanand Satram, which has its headquarters at Srisailam in Andhra Pradesh. For the Bengali pilgrim, there's Sri Guru Sangha Ashram. Duck into a doorway, and you'll find the Ramadulareshwar Mahadeva Temple, which was established in 1810 A.D. by two brothers from Calcutta, Ashutosh Deb (Chhatu Babu) and Pramatha Nath Deb (Latu Babu) in memory of their father Ram Dulal Deb. The temple is in pretty good condition, thanks to a renovation in 1954 by their descendants.

What follows are several commercial establishments catering to Western and Oriental tourists – cybercafes aplenty, Monalisa Restaurant and Monalisa Peace Cottage, Denns Restaurant, Kumiko Guest House and music schools. The lane suddenly seems to change character, as if it had morphed to serve the needs of low-budget foreign travellers. You see many of them, busy sending messages from the numerous cybercafes, or picking up bottles of mineral water, kept out by shopkeepers. Keep going, and you will eventually emerge at Dasashwamedh. Just before the lane deposits you on the main road, is a small temple of the Goddess Kali. Every time, my family visits the area, we never fail to do *pranam* to the Goddess. As Bengalis, we were also patrons of Chintamani's grocery store – he was the only one in the city to stock authentic ingredients for Bengali cooking.

The lanes of Madanpura are another story: they are a place of work, and home to the weavers. They reverberate with the clackety-clack of the weaver's loom, and silk yarn is laid out on the terraces, in the sun, to dry after being dyed in rich colour. The men weave, and the women draw threads and fill up the bobbins. The aroma of cooking in rich spices permeates the air, and the call of the muezzin pierces the atmosphere five times a day.

Khojwan lies in the southern part of Varanasi, a production centre for wooden craft and stone products. Inside dark workshops, bare chested men can be seen hammering and chiselling away at blocks of stone or wood. You will come across the Arya Kashtha Kala Mandir (Aryan Temple for Wooden Art), and find lifelike wooden idols of Hindu Gods and Goddesses. The stone workers churn out idols, as well as candlestands, boxes, coasters, ashtrays, incense holders and lamp bases. The lane to Khojwan begins at Durga Kund. Winding past Pilgrims Book House, it enters Nawabganj, where a modern 'shopping complex' has sprung up. Small shops selling grain, daily needs and a couple of butchers follow. Fifity metres further is the temple of Santoshi Ma, inevitably broadcasting devotional songs over its loudspeakers. A few metres later is the Sankat Haran Hanuman Temple, with an image of Baba Tarkeshwar Nath in a niche near the doorway. A larger temple dedicated to the seer Pracheen Baba Agyavan is next, and plays host to an *akhara* and gymnasium at its rear. The incongruous Oxford Boys Hostel makes its appearance, and opposite it is a small Sati temple. This one was built as recently as 1978, to honour Sharda Devi, the wife of Gopaldas Sahu. Almost inexplicably after a short distance, the lane widens to a small *chowk* to the right, quite medieval in its appearance. A large stone platform with a *peepul* tree right in the middle reminds you of a village *chaupal*, and the fact that Khojwan was indeed once a village. Around this square are shops that sell grain, spices and condiments.

ᗡ

Spirituality & Religion

THE TEMPLES OF VARANASI

Sabay hamarey ek hai, Jo sumire Hari naam
Bastu lahi pahachan ke, Baason so kya kaam
All who meditate on my Lord,
are equal in my vision
It is the thing contained that matters,
not the pot that did contain.

Kabir

☙

As Hinduism's pre-eminent centre, Varanasi is home to every one of the three hundred and thirty mil lion Hindu Gods and Goddesses. Harvard professor of religion Diana Eck calls it the 'Sacred Circle of All the Gods.' Its divine status was cemented the day Lord Shiva chose to descend from the heavens and make the city his home. Even if the entire world degenerates into a state of sin and ruin, Varanasi remains unscathed and pure. Today, it is believed that there are fourteen hundred temples in Varanasi. In addition, the city is home to over three hundred religious institutions, two thousand religious ascetics in permanent residence at the various monasteries and fifteen hundred Sanskrit scholars.

As if to reflect Kabir's words, most of the abodes of the Gods and Goddesses are simple structures. None of the ostentation that you would associate with the temples of south India; none of the grandeur of Khajuraho will be found here. No deity expects elaborate offerings; all worshippers can come close to and touch Shiva's most revered *linga* at Vishwanath. Shiva is an austere God, and is often content to sit below *peepul* trees on the side of a road. He does not ask much of His devotees : a few *bel* leaves, a little *Gangajal* – preferably mixed with milk, that's all. Ganesh is painted simply on the doors of many homes, standing guard. Images of Ram and Sita, and Hanuman are ubiquitous – little framed pictures with garlands around them. Blue or black images of Kali stare out of shrines on the roadside.

ଓ

SHIVA

To trace the legend, the unkempt, ascetic Shiva married Parvati, daughter of the Himalayas after ending his perpetual meditation. As a householder, he needed a home for himself and his wife. After scanning the earth, it was Kashi that caught his eye – a city of numerous gardens, palaces and temples. He decided to come down from the heavens with Parvati, and his entourage of protectors. In the beginning, Parvati did not like the city, but Shiva refused to go back saying, "I will not leave my home, as my home is Avimukta - Never Forsaken". Out of their familiarity with the Lord, the locals simply refer to Him as 'Baba' – father, and to emphasize his ubiquity, say *"Kankar kankar mein Shankar"* (Shiva lies in every pebble).

Omkareshwar

More than a thousand years have passed since the era when the holiest Shiva-*linga* in Varanasi stood and was worshipped at Omkareshwar. It was enshrined in a grand structure on the banks of the Matsyodari Lake. The *linga* is said to have appeared on its own, as Brahma performed penance at this spot. After Muslim marauders destroyed the temple, and settled down in this part of the city, it never recovered its original glory. The decline was hastened by the draining of the Matsyodari Lake in the 19th century. What we can see today is but a small temple, built in the eighteenth century by the Maratha Queen, Bhavani. She entrusted the priestly duties of the temple to a Brahmin family, which to this date is responsible for the upkeep of the temple. In spite of its apparent nondescriptness, most locals are able to direct you towards the temple. After going past the much grander Swaminarayan Temple, you'll spot a lane next to a police station. You will have to walk for about a kilometre, through Koela Bazaar and Hasanpura till you come into Chittanpura, where everyone seems to be busy spinning yarn for Banarasi sarees, or stretching out the yarn on frames before the actual weaving can begin. A narrow path next to the Garib Nawaz Hotel will take you to Omkareshwar Temple, a structure barely twenty feet high painted in lime and ochre. Two images of trumpeteers are painted on either side of the door, which remains locked for much of the day. There are Muslim graveyards on the mound atop which the temple sits, and the few Hindus who live here are unable to support the upkeep of the temple. It is only during the festival of Shivaratri that the odd pilgrims make their way here, but for much of the year, Omkareshwar is lost, neglected, but possibly not yet forgotten.

Vishwanath

The temple of Vishwanath, standing in the centre of the holiest of the three circles, Avimukteshwara, has been the most important Shiva shrine in Varanasi, for nearly a millenium. The first mention of the temple was made in the text Kritya Kalpataru, written by Lakshmidhar Bhatt around 1110 A.D. Sources thereafter refer to the destruction of the temple during the Muslim invasion of 1194 A.D. and a mosque at the site around 1236 A.D. It is likely that Raja Sawai Jai Singh of Amber constructed the Adi Vishweshara temple at a different site, adjacent to where the current temple stands. Between the 14th and the 17th centuries, the seat of Vishwanath was repeatedly razed by a succession of Muslim invaders, including the Sharqi Sultans (1394-1479) and Sikandar Lodhi (1486-1507) and rebuilt, on one occasion during the reign of Akbar, by Todarmal. Then, in the mid 16th century, Aurangzeb assumed the reins of the Mughal empire. Among the Hindu kings who fought him was the great Maratha, Shivaji. Defeated by Aurangzeb and imprisoned at Agra, Shivaji escaped and chose to take refuge in Varanasi. In 1669, Aurangzeb took his wrath out on the city, ordering the destruction of all temples and *pathshalas* (schools). The Vishwanath Temple was destroyed once again, but not before the priests had managed to spirit away the *linga.* One version of the story has it that the *linga* was hidden in the Gyanvapi Well, before being taken to a *pujari's* house. Aurangzeb ordered the construction of a mosque, which is today identified as the Gyanvapi Mosque. For a hundred years, the most important *Shivalinga* in Hindu religion stayed under wraps.

The temple you see today was built by Rani Ahilyabai Holkar of Indore in 1785. Apart from the sanctum of Vishwanath in the centre, it houses various shrines of Gauri, one of the manifestations of his consort Parvati, Vishnu, Kal Bhairav and Dandapani, the protectors, and Vighneshwara, and Avimukta Vinayak, both forms of his son Ganesh. One enters through a gate, guarded by policemen, with a marble sign forbidding non-Hindus from entering. The spire is plated with 820 kgs of gold, donated by the Sikh ruler Maharaja Ranjit Singh, in 1835. Foreigners refer to Vishwanath as the Golden Temple, since the spire is all they can see from the terrace of a nearby home, or from the window of Udai Silk Shop. The courtyard inside the temple is paved with marble, wet from *ganjajal* that worshippers have sprinkled or spilled. Almost immediately, one feels swept away by the tide of devotion, hearing people of all ages, who have travelled thousands of kilometres, or just a few hundred metres, hail the Lord crying out 'Bol Bam', 'Om Namah Shivay', 'Jai Shambhu', 'Har Har Mahadev' and 'Baba Vishwanath Ki Jai ho'. Bells ring incessantly, and on the main days of worship, including Mondays, Shiva's holy day, the crowds become a seething mass of humanity. The main shrine, built in 1828 by Baijabai Scindia, is to your right. As you enter through a doorway made of carved silver, you spot the shiny black *Shivlinga,* set in a recessed tank full of *bel* leaves, flowers and milky *gangajal.* On a less crowded day, pilgrims can spend a little time with the Lord, say their prayers, drink the *charnamitra* – the life-giving water that touches His feet, and get a *teeka* from the presiding priest. On a crowded day, you just flow with the crush of devotees, who are asked to keep moving by the zealous constables of Uttar Pradesh Police. When I visited Vishwanath with my wife, brother and sister-in-law, just after our wedding, the crowds were so pushy and eager that my wife and sister-in-law ended up with having *gangajal* poured on them !

Being in the Vishwanath Temple during one of the daily *aartis* can be a completely enchanting experience. Every day, there are five *aartis.* The Mangala Aarti is performed at the Brahma *muhurta* of 3:30 am, to wake the Lord up. The blowing of the conch serves as a wakeup alarm, and that is followed by the singing of a hymn in the honour of Lord Ganesh, who must be appeased before any rite. This is as per the boon that was granted by Shiva himself to atone for his cutting off his son's head and replacing it with an elephant's. The Bhog Aarti is performed at 12:00 noon, when the Mukhashuddhi (ritual purification of the mouth) is performed and Vishwanath is fed. A *tulsi* leaf is placed on every dish to ward off the evil eye; thereafter the doors are shut to let Him have His lunch in peace. The Saptarishi Aarti is performed at 7:30 pm, when dusk falls; Shringar Aarti at 11:00 pm when He is adorned, followed immedately by Shayan Aarti, when He is put to bed. The rituals are elaborate. Amid chants, 11 priests go about the task of bathing the *linga* in *gangajal,* anointing it with *chandan* - sandalwood paste, and then with His favourite intoxicants, *ganja* and *bhang*, and bathing Him again with milk. Next, they heap flowers, garlands and *bel* on the *linga* till you can barely see the black stone. The chants cease, to be replaced by the lighting and waving of lamps, the blowing of conches, the ringing of all the bells on the temple's precincts, and the beating of Shiva's drum, the *damaru.* While the older priests seem to be involved in the creating of light, waving the many lamps, the young create the sound. It is an unfailing pattern that has been repeated every day, for centuries.

Kedareshwar

The Skanda Purana contains a section containing thirty-one chapters: the Kashi Kedara Mahatmya. It describes Kedar as the field where the crop of liberation grows. While Kedarnath, the most important of the Himalayan shrines, sits on the banks of the Mandakini, one of the tributaries of the Ganga, its replica rises high on the banks of the Ganga itself, in Varanasi. According to the scriptures, anyone who saw the Himalayan Kedar would be liberated from the cycle of rebirth. Only a few pilgrims could however make it there. The Gods realized that, if the Kedar at Varanasi bestowed visitors with the same boon, everyone could be liberated, and heaven would get too crowded. Shiva agreed to imbue the Kedar temple at Varanasi with a lesser status: only those who died here would go straight to heaven, mere sight was not enough. The presence of a large number of elderly widows around Kedar bears testimony to the resultant belief that death in the vicinity is a sure pathway to eternal salvation.

The original Kedar temple was destroyed by Aurangzeb. It was rebuilt around 1898, partly by Raja Chet Singh of Varanasi, and by the Raja of Vijayanagaram. From the river, Kedareshwar is easily distinguished by its red and white stripes. From the lane inside, it is less easier to locate architecturally – one finds his or her way by spotting a doorway between rows of alms-seeking widows and flower sellers. At the entrance near the lane is a small image of Ganesh. A dark passageway takes you to the inner courtyard, surrounded by *Shivalingas,* with a temple in the centre. The pillars around the *mandap* are styled after those in the Kashi Kamakoti temple at Harishchandra Ghat. The inner sanctum is guarded by Nandi, Shiva's bull, and in a dimly lit chamber, sits an outcrop of misshapen rock with a white line running through it : the Kedar *linga.* Priests will tell you that this *swayambhu* (self-manifest) *linga* changed composition through the ages: from being a gem in Satayuga - the

Age of Perfection, gold in Dwapar, silver in Treta, and finally stone in Kaliyuga - the current Age of Decadence.

The atmosphere in Kedar is charged with quiet piety. Out of the usual pilgrim's radar, it is revered by local Bengalis and South Indians, who first bathe in the river, then walk up the steps to pray to Kedar. While the women carry *gangajal* in small brass pots, the men fill it in enormous pots and mount the steps crying out, 'Har Har Mahadev'.

Other notable Shiva-lingas

One of the oldest *lingas*, that of Mahadeva, can be found in the Trilochana Temple, above Trilochan Ghat. It is a self-manifest *linga,* and some refer to it as the establishing deity of Varanasi. Krittivaseshwara, located in a mosque near Maidagin, and out of bounds for Hindus except on Shivaratri, refers to the 'Lord Who Wears the Elephant Hide'. It takes its name from Shiva's victory over the elephant demon, after which he wore the hide of the elephant as a garment. The original temple was destroyed during the reign of Aurangzeb. In a lane that goes from Chowk to Sankata Ghat can be found another self-manifest *linga,* that of Vireshwara, the 'Hero's Lord'. Legend has it that Shiva appeared out of the *linga* to grant his devotee Vishwanara the boon of a son, who later became the God of Fire, Agni. Today, women ask Vireshwara for the same blessing. Tilbhandeshwara is a simple temple near Madanpura, housing a metre-high *linga* that is said to be growing by the height of a *'til'* (sesame seed) every day. During Shivaratri, it is covered with a five-faced copper mask. Finally, there is Kameshwara, 'Desire's Lord', a short distance away from Omkareshwara, in Machhodari.

DEVI

Shiva came to Kashi with Parvati, but he also sent sixty-four *yoginis,* who represent the whole range of female deities in Hindu mythology. Today, the small, nondescript Chaunsatti (Sixty-Four) Devi Temple, situated in a lane near Bengali Tola in Varanasi, above Chaunsatti Ghat, is the only one anywhere where all sixty four Goddesses can be worshipped together. Parvati herself assumes different forms, from the fiery Kali to the luminous Kamala. These goddesses are referred to as the Mahavidyas. The term sometimes used to describe Shiva's partner is *shakti,* power, and that is what the goddesses wield over Varanasi's presiding deity. Shiva is indeed subordinate to the goddesses. They limit, frighten or control Shiva. Most Goddesses are worshipped in the non-Brahminical, Tantric tradition, which means they must be propitiated with offerings of meat and wine. According to the Devi-mahatmya, the most famous and revered of the *sakta* texts, Durga is said to underlie or pervade the cosmos: to create, maintain, and periodically destroy it according to the rhythmic cycles of Hindu cosmology. Varanasi also has its own city-goddess, Varanasi Devi. She can be found in a shrine within the Trilochan Temple. Some say that Varanasi , the city itself, is a goddess that embodies Shiva's *shakti.*

Annapurna

Annapurna is the Goddess of Plentiful Food. Her legend goes thus. One day Shiva, who was a mendicant priest, found no food and felt hungry. He asked the sage Narada the reason for his hunger. Narada told him: 'This is all because of your wife. An auspicious wife brings good fortune to her husband. Look at Vishnu. He married Lakshmi and has since been living in plenty'. Narada then went to Shiva's house, where he found a starving, disconsolate Parvati, who asked the wise sage why she was condemned to poverty. He replied: 'This is all because

Department of Sanskrit, BHU

Bharat Kala Bhavan

Sculpture Gallery

Jnana Pravaha

Carvings

Sanskrit Vishwavidyalaya

Ganga Aarti at Rajendra Prasad Ghat

Aarti at Dasashwamedh Ghat

Morning Prayers

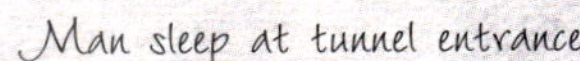

Man sleep at tunnel entrance

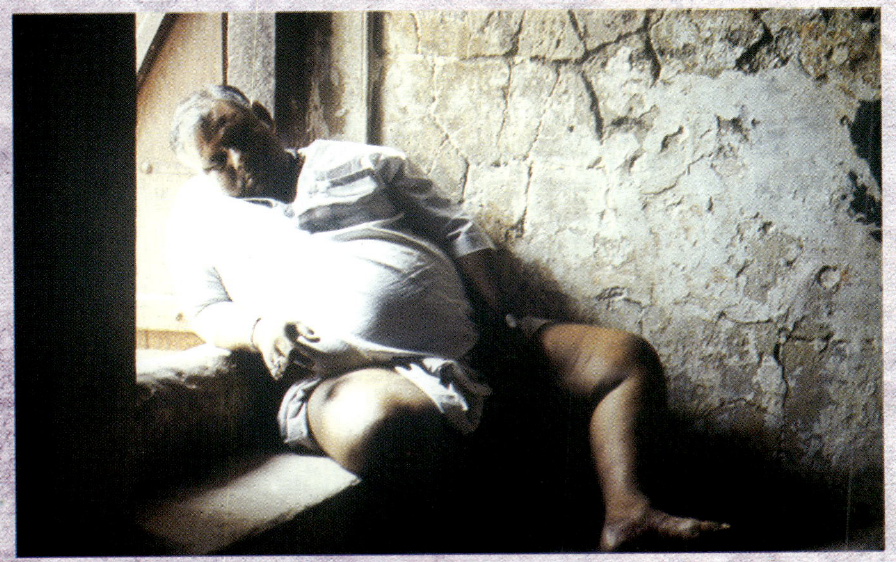

Bath

BHU Library

Roads

Concert Signage

Shehnai Players

Sarees (Doublespread)

Muria Tribals

Mithai

Resting after a wrestling bout

Ramlila Tableau

Kids dressed as Radha & Krishna, during Nakkataiya

Elephant leading procession at Rameshwar

Puja paraphernalia for sale

Offering prayers

Phirki – paper wheels

Priest – Ganga Dussehra

Durga on her way

Spinning

Ramnagar Gateway

Vashisth Temple

Close up of marble balcony

Flower Seller

Phoolmala Bazaar

Zarda Shop

God Images on sale

Colourful Joys

Chand Bhai shows off

Colourful Piggybanks

of your husband. A capable husband supports his family by earning plentifully. Look at Lakshmi. She married Vishnu and has since been living in heaven.' Parvati thought about what Narada had said. The next morning, when Shiva had left home, she left with her children, as she considered herself a complete failure. At that moment, Narada appeared once more and taught her how to persuade people to give her food. By evening, she had managed to collect baskets of food from many families, and returned home. When Shiva again returned empty-handed, she fed him till he was completely satisfied. This is how Parvati earned her other name : Annapurna.

She is the mother, and gives life to pilgrims and residents of Varanasi alike. Because of Her generosity, no one ever dies of hunger in the city. Beggars line the entrance to the temple. As Shiva's consort in Varanasi, and as the city's reigning queen, her temple is just a few metres away from that of Vishwanath, on the opposite side of the *gali*. It is said that, in Varanasi, the two made a pact: Annapurna fed the living, and Shiva offered them liberation at death. The temple of Annapurna was built around 1700 by the Raja of Poona. It is topped by a tower and an ornamented dome, held up by pillars. The Goddess bears no weapons, only a ladle and a pot, and her image is a new one, consecrated as recently as 1977 by the Sankaracharya of Shringeri Math. She stands in a small enclosure on a raised, pillared podium in the centre of the courtyard of the temple, giving enough space for devotees to circumambulate her shrine. That, however is not the 'real' Annapurna. That honour is reserved for an image of the goddess in solid gold, open to public viewing for only three days in a year – during the Annakoot Festival. In one corner of the temple compound is an image of the Sun God, seated on a chariot drawn by seven horses (One of the popular plays in contemporary Hindi theatre is called *Sooraj Ka Satvaan Ghoda*. It was written by Dharmvir Bharati, and made into a film by Shyam Benegal). In another corner is an image of Gauri Shankar. The other two corners have shrines dedicated to Hanuman, in bas-relief, and Ganesh.

After the autumn harvest, in the month of Kartik, the temple's premises fill up with mountains of food. Rich patrons donate enormous quantities of sweets, rice, pulses and other cereals, which are put on display in the temple compound. The food is later distributed among devotees, who throng the temple for a glimpse of the gold image of Annapurna. I sometimes wonder of Hindustan Lever Limited, which had branded its line of staple foods after the goddess, pays any royalty to the priests of the temple !

Durga

Once upon a time, in a grove of forests on the southern extremity of Varanasi was a shrine dedicated to the powerful Goddess Durga. The Goddess was created by the many Gods when they found themselves incapable of defeating the buffalo demon, Mahishasura. They decided to give her a share of their own tremendous energy, which they converted into matter – in the form of the different parts of their body. Shiva's energy became her face. Vishnu's became her arms, Yama's became her hair. Chandra's energy became her breasts, Indra's her waist. Brahma's became her feet, Surya's her toes, Agni's became her eyes, Vayu's became her ears, her teeth grew from Brahma. Kuber gave her a nose, Prajapati her teeth, and Bhumi her hips. Having created her thus, the Gods equipped her for war, giving her their most potent weapon or an ornament from their treasury. Shiva gave her his trishul (trident), Vishnu gave her his disc, Varun his conch, Agni a flaming spear, Vayu bow and arrows in a quiver. Indra gave the *vajra*, his thundering hammer, Yama his Kala-danda (Staff of Fate). Ambupati, the Lord of the Waters gave her a lasso; Prajapati gave her a rosary, Brahma a water jar for her daily ablutions. The Sun-God planted his rays on her skin so that she would glow, Kuber gave her a cup of wine, and Sheshnag, the snake God gave her a lion to ride on. Finally equipped, Durga set out for her battle, which is recounted in the Devi-Mahatmya, a poem of 700 verses, forming chapters 81-93 of the Markandaya Purana.

The antiquity of the Durga Temple is borne out by its mention in the Purana, which cite this as the spot on earth where the Goddess rested, on the banks of a tank – now called Durga Kund – after she slayed Mahishasura. As one of her ten weapons, a sword – given by the Gods who had themselves failed to kill the demon – fell to the ground, it scythed into the earth what is now believed to be the Assi river. How and when the shrine gained popularity is shrouded in the mists of history, but it is certain that the building of an impressive, free standing temple, in the typical North Indian style, by the Maratha Rani Bhavani in the 18th century, had something to do with it. Sherring describes it as 'one of the popular and most frequented temples'; and as a place where 'bloody sacrifices are offered to the goddess in great abundance, by persons wishing to obtain her aid in cases of sickness, under the impression that she will accept the life of an animal in exchange for the life of a human being'. He wrote that about Durga Temple in 1868, and little has changed since.

Durga Ji (as locals call it) is one of the busiest temples in the city. It rises tall next to a stone stepped water tank (Kund), and is identifiable by its distinctive deep red colour. A brass trident on top of the *shikhara* pierces the sky, and serves as a gymnasts' pole for the multitudes of monkeys that inhabit the temple's premises. Foreigners call this the Monkey Temple. Not allowed to step inside the precincts of the temple, they must be content to observe the goings-on in its corridors, and take a closer look at the spire from a balcony that runs around the temple. It is certain that many have suffered at the hands of a monkey, for the temple to earn its sobriquet. In any case, any pilgrim has to be careful about the monkeys, lest they snatch away the pilgrim's offerings even before he or she reached the goddess. On one occasion, I remember my mother return anguished from the temple. She had bought a woven basket on our recent trip to south India, and taken the *prasad* to the temple in the basket. Obviously, the bright colours were too much for a monkey to resist. He snatched the basket from her, quickly gobbled up and shared with his family the bananas and sweets inside, climbed the highest spire, and hung it from the brass trident.

Since the Durga Temple stands next to the main road, one is able to see the Goddess even without entering the temple, should there be a break in the mass of devotees in front of her image. Entering the temple, one comes across a courtyard, where shoes are taken off, and hands washed. Then, one climbs a few steps, and passes through a door that is guarded by two large brass lions. They are there to both protect the goddess, and to give her a ride whenever she wants to leave her home. On the left of the lions are two small shrines, one dedicated to Ganesh – in bas relief, and the other to Shiva, with a small marble *shivlinga* and Nandi. On the right, behind an iron grill, is another shrine in the honour of the golden-faced goddess Bageshwari (better known as Saraswati) and Lakshmi. The one descends and again steps up to the central platform, paved in marble. The main shrine of the goddess is at the eastern end of the platform. What one can see of the image is just a silver mask, and a pair of raised arms, bearing a sword and an axe. The rest of her body is draped in a red and gold sari, and covered with garlands, hibiscus being her preferred flower. All around, and above, there are bells. Four times a day, when the *aarti* is held, devotees and priests ring the bells, the toll and chime of which can be heard at my home, half a kilometre away. After paying one's respects to the goddess, one circumambulates the shrine, and rings the main bell. At the back of the main temple is a small shrine where women desirous of having children tie sacred threads.

Tuesdays and Saturdays are her holy days. Devotees throng the temple seeking *darshan*. Flower sellers and beggars line up near the temple's gate and all along the Kund. The shops selling ritual offerings like the red and gold scarf, coconuts, *sindoor*, bangles and packets of sugar balls, and *mithai* shops opposite the temple do brisk business. Traffic on the main road slows to a crawl. Friday is the preferred day for sacrifices, though today, it is only on important ritual days like Ram Navami, or the Durga Puja Navami that a goat might be sacrificed. A forked stake in the courtyard of the temple serves as the location for the grisly act. Most people are content with the token ritual of breaking a coconut.

Sankata

For a large number of women in Varanasi, Sankata ji is their patron goddess. She belongs to the folk tradition, as opposed to the tantric one, and is believed to be one of the *matrikas*, who are believed to be the protectors of children in life and their seizers in sickness. Every Friday, the women observe a fast, take a bath in the Ganga, pray to the 'Goddess Who Vanquishes All Dangers', and recite the *Sankata Vrat Katha* – stories of people whose troubles have been vanquished by the Devi after they observed the fast. Finding the Sankata Temple can be a challenge for those not familiar with the city. One needs to take a lane from Chowk, and find his or her way asking the locals. The temple stands next to the Ganga, above Sankata Ghat, in a large courtyard. At the centre of the courtyard is an old peepul tree, with many tiny shrines at its roots. The entrance to the goddess's chambers is through a large doorway flanked by the *swastika* and *shri yantra* symbols. The chamber is lit up with many *diyas* and the smell of incense permeates the air. The goddess, believed to be self-manifest, wears a silver mask, and is separated from her devotees only by a single rail. According to the Kashi Khanda, her first devotees were the five Pandavas from the Mahabharat, and their wife Draupadi.

Shitala

The Goddess Shitala emerged from the folk traditions of rural India. She, the Cool Goddess, is known to have control over fever and illness, and is especially invoked during small-pox. Now that the disease has been eradicated, I wonder if the Goddess has any work to do ! Her temple, next to the Dasashwamedh Ghat, is a hall of pillars. The steps to the ghat are flooded during the rains, and the walls of the temple re-painted after every autumn. In the temple, her image sits atop a throne. She wears a red and gold tinsel sari, and carries a bunch of reeds in her hand, which she uses to chastise her victims. As a *matrika* – an independent female power, she must be appeased, propitiated out of fear of illness and gratitude for its cure. Next to her is situated the *shivlinga* of Dasashwamedheshwar. Smaller images of Durga, Kali, Annapurna, Santoshi Ma, Uma Maheshwar and Bhairav surround the main shrine. Bengali widows from a nearby *ashram* sing devotional songs to the Goddess every evening.

Siddheshwari

The Goddess of Perfection (*Siddha*) is worshipped by Hindus oppressed by the trials and tribulations of life. The temple of Siddheshwari Devi lies close to the Sankata Temple, and is the site of the sacred Well of the Moon – *Chandra Kupa.* The temple has two quadrangles, one with the Chandra Kupa. The holiest day for worship here is the full moon day in the month of Chaitra (March); whenever the new moon occurs on a Monday, it is considered equally auspicious to pray here. The second quadrangle houses the main deity, Siddheshwari, as also a figure of Durga in a small niche at the base of the wall. The walls of a verandah on two sides of the quadrangle are covered with paintings of the various incarnations of Ganesh.

THE PROTECTORS

If a city is home to a pre-occupied God like Shiva, and his consort Parvati, it must have guards to ward of invaders and any kind of evil. Shiva's *ganas* fulfill this role, according to mythology. They have the ability to scare away those with ill intent, and are fearsome in depiction. Folk tradition considers the Bhairavas as a form of Shiva, in eight manifestations. They are Bhishana (horrific), Asitanga (with black limbs), Sanhara (destruction), Ruru (hound), Krodha (anger), Kapala (skull), Rudra (storm) and Unmatta (raging).

Kaalbhairav

The origin of Kaalbhairav goes back to a frenzied fight between Shiva and Brahma in Heaven. In his rage, Shiva is believed to have assumed his terrible form, Kaal Bhairav, and cut off Brahma's fifth head – the ultimate in Brahminicide, but the head remained stuck to his hand. He was forced to take a vow that he would have to beg for alms, using the skull, till it fell from his hand. When Shiva came to Varanasi, horrified, remorseful and dancing in frenzy, the skull fell from his hand and a beautiful pond called Kapalamochana was created. In his Bhairav form, he assumed the role of protector of the city – he is called Varanasi's *kotwal.* Because of his fearsome form, even Death is afraid of him.

The temple of Kaal Bhairav, affectionately called by local residents as Bhairo Nath, is located in a lane near Maidagin.

The entrance to the courtyard of the temple is guarded by a dog, his mount. Kaal Bhairav rests in an inner sanctum made of brass, inside a sixty-foot high temple. His face is covered by a silver mask, and he sits upon his dog, bearing a trident. His body is covered with an apron, and garlanded with flowers. Devotees ring the four bells in the temple porch, and are blessed by the priest who wields a club of peacock feathers. Those who are desirous of invoking his powers and warding off evil wear a woven black thread, after offering it to him at the temple. I myself wore one, for a long time when I had been ill !

Shani

Shani, the God of Saturday, is known to be malevolent or benevolent, depending on whether the devotee has propitiated Him. His shrine lies only a few metres before the entrance to the Vishwanath Temple. For six days in a week, an iron grill is pulled across the shrine. Come Saturday, and throngs of locals flock to Shani to pay their respects. His image is a forbidding one – a silver mask peering from a black shroud, but He is easily propitiated with a *diya* and small change. I've had the opportunity of experiencing His mystic powers. On one of my trips to Vishwanath Gali, when there were no devotees, I decided to take a picture of the shrine. No sooner than my flash went off, local priests began berating me – "Whoever told you that you could take a picture of Shani?" I beat a hasty retreat. When I developed the film, every picture came out perfectly – Shani's was a blank.

HANUMAN

In the mythic version of Hanuman's birth, his paternity is ascribed to Vayu, the God of Wind. Vayu was accused of surreptitiously impregnating Anjana. Acknowledging his paternity, but in recompense for undermining Anjana's moral fidelity, he bestowed a boon of windlike speed and strength on Hanuman, his unborn son. Hanuman's relationship to Vayu is significant on a symbolic level. Since it is associated with *prana* (vital breath), vayu is regarded as the purest of all elements. It is the root substance from which fire, water, and earth are derived.

Hanuman is commonly regarded as the incarnation of Shiva's Rudra form. Rudra is the manifestation of both creative and destructive cosmological forces and is often associated with fire. In this regard, Hanuman is often associated with the colour red. Hanuman is similarly associated with fire and the colour red in various mythic contexts: by trying to eat the sun, being a student of the sun, burning Lanka, and through the radiant brilliance of his own fiery body. The following story explains the nature of Hanuman's supernatural power:

Once when he was young, Hanuman flew into the sky to catch and eat the sun which he mistook for a piece of fruit. The sun only just managed to escape from Hanuman's grip and asked Indra the sky god for help. Indra agreed to help, and when Hanuman tried again to catch the sun Indra hit him on the chin and broke his jaw. Hanuman fell wounded to the earth. Angered by Indra, Hanuman's father Pavanadeva (or Vayu), the wind, stopped all life by making it impossible for anyone to breathe. To appease the wind, Brahma used his power to heal Hanuman, and in addition gave him a boon of immortality and divine knowledge. On account of breaking his jaw, Indra gave Hanuman his name: *Hanu* meaning chin or jaw. Indra also gave Hanuman a boon of incomparable strength. In his turn the sun bestowed on Hanuman a boon of unsurpassed wisdom, radiant brilliance and the ability to change form at will. Yamraj gave to Hanuman a boon of perfect health. Kuber bestowed on him victory in all battles. Varuna promised that Hanuman would never suffer any harm from water. Vishvakarma gave Hanuman the boon of long life and protection against all kinds of dangerous weapons. In his turn Shiva gave Hanuman immunity from his trident. Yama bestowed on Hanuman a boon of unchanging youth. One of the most striking features of Hanuman's character is that he appears to be the essence of all divine power manifest in one form. He has the speed of the wind, the radiance of fire and immunity from water. As the essence of virility, he is able to bestow fertility on barren women and potency on men. He can tell the future and cure diseases. He is a master musician, a sage interpreter of the *shastras*, and a great grammarian He is a warrior par excellence: immortal, tireless, and strong beyond compare. He is also capable of fervent and absolute devotion. Essentially he is all-powerful and all-loving. Each of his manifold abilities is regarded in different instances as more or less important than others. It is together, however, that they constitute an aura of generalized supernatural power. This generalized aura of shakti—inclusive of *bhakti* and *brahmacharya*—is an essential component of Tulsi Das's poetry.

One important event presages Hanuman's role in the Ramayana. While growing up, Hanuman enjoyed playing in a garden near a sanyasi hermitage. He played tricks on the hermits by spilling their holy water, pulling their beards, and disturbing them while they tried to meditate and perform yoga. Frustrated, the hermits cursed Hanuman by making him forget that he possessed phenomenal strength. Only when reminded of his abilities by someone else is Hanuman able to exercise his divine mandate of strength, speed and changing form.

The majority of stories about Hanuman derive from one or another version of the Ramayana. In summary Hanuman's role is as follows. As a devout Ram-bhakta, Hanuman goes in search of Ram's princess bride, Sita, who has been abducted by Ravana, a demon king from Lanka. Hanuman finds Sita in Ravana's garden where he gives her Ram's ring as a sign of good faith. He is captured by Ravana's guards and after engaging in a lively debate with the demon king, an oil-saturated cloth is tied to his tail and lighted. Turning this torture into a weapon of destruction, Hanuman lays waste the city of Lanka by jumping from roof to roof setting every house on fire. Hanuman returns and tells Ram of the situation. Accompanied by Sugriva's army of monkeys and bears, Ram attacks Lanka. After numerous great battles in which Hanuman defeats many of Ravana's great warriors, Ram's brother Lakshman is mortally wounded. Hanuman is sent in search of a root which will cure Lakshman. Not being able to distinguish the correct root, Hanuman carries back the whole mountain on which the root is said to grow. Lakshman is cured and Ram finally kills Ravana and everyone returns to Ayodhya where Ram is crowned king. Hanuman remains at his side as servant, suppliant, and warrior.

In all stories about Hanuman, two features stand out as the most important aspects of his character: his strength, and his devotion to Ram. Although *brahmacharya* is not often mentioned with regard to Hanuman's epic role, it too is an integral aspect of his character, a requisite condition for both his strength and his devotion.

Although Hanuman is one of the most popular deities in North India there is very little written about him in the academic literature. Even in the commentaries on the Valmiki *Ramayana* and Tulsidas's *Rama Charit Manas,* little attention is paid to an analysis of Hanuman's epic role. In contrast to the academic literature, which seems to be biased towards incarnate gods like Ram, Lakshmi, Krishna, Shiva, and Kali, there is a wealth of popular and folk literature elaborating Hanuman's exploits. The fact that there is a considerable market for many religious "self-help" manuals on Hanuman is indicative of the fact that the monkey-God remains a folk-deity in a modern context. He is accessible not only by virtue of his practical appeal but also because his worship is not regarded as esoteric or privileged. It is populist, available for mass consumption. The implications of this are significant. Publication of detailed manuals in Hindi effectively makes anyone who is able to read, an expert religious functionary. The publication of knowledge also serves to personalize the nature of one's interaction with Hanuman. By no longer being dependent on ritual specialists with esoteric knowledge, one can appropriate for oneself the methods and means for worship.

Sankat Mochan Temple

On Tuesdays and Saturdays, Varanasi's residents can be found lining up to seek Hanuman's blessings at the Sankat Mochan Temple. When it is examination time at the university, the crowd suddenly turns young, as hundreds of students seek His divine intervention in helping them improve their academic performance. At the University Multipurpose Hall where we took our papers, the number of examinees with the trademark orange *teeka* on their forehead was substantial. Even the senior surgeons at the university can be seen at Sankat Mochan in the early mornings of the days when they might have a particularly tricky surgery to perform !

The temple was originally built by Tulsidas between 1661-1666. Tulsidas prayed very hard for Hanuman to appear before him, and suddenly, the earth caved in. He dug deeper with his bare hands, and uncovered a stone image of Hanuman in the earth. This he placed under a peepul tree, and began worshipping, before building the temple. For more than three centuries, the Sankat Mochan Temple was in the middle of a forest, and devotees would travel in groups to have a *darshan* of Hanuman. The old temple was destroyed in 1850, and was rebuilt. It was only after the road from the city to Banaras Hindu University was built in 1920, that the path to Sankat Mochan became an easy one. The current temple is a simple structure set in a grove of trees populated by monkeys. Opposite Hanuman's temple is a Ram temple – He must always face and protect His Lord. The Hanuman Chalisa is written on a marble plaque next to the altar. A platform between the two shrines enables devotees to have a better view of Hanuman's image. They must, of course, be careful of the well in the middle of the platform. Small groups of worshippers sit in a courtyard on the side, swaying and singing *bhajans.* Every now and then, the cry of 'Bolo Bajrang Bali Ki Jai' goes up from the assembled crowd.

Tulsi Manas Mandir

Even though Hanuman remains the more worshipped deity in Varanasi, one cannot but mention the temple that has been built to glorify the object of his devotion, Ram. The marble edifice attracts a large number of awe-struck pilgrims from rural India, who come here to marvel at the mechanized puppets – notably the one of Hanuman tearing apart his chest to reveal the images of Ram and Sita - displayed on the second floor of the temple. The temple was built in 1963 by Ratanlal Sureka, a businessman from Calcutta, after he lost his only son. The walls of the temple are inscribed with every stanza from the Ramcharit Manas. The second floor also has on display a collection of old editions of the Ramayana. On the ground floor, successively from left to right, are the images of Annapurna, Shiva, Ram, Lakshman, Sita, Hanuman, Lakshmi and Vishnu.

Jagannath Temple

Near Assi Ghat lies the 17th century temple of Jagannath. It is believed that the chief priest of Puri's Jagannath Temple, Swami Brahmachari, had a disagreement with his king, and came away on a self-imposed exile to Varanasi in the year 1790 A.D. One day, in a dream, Lord Jagannath appeared to him in a dream and asked him to set up a temple and feed His devotees. With no resources, Swamiji approached the minister of Bhonsala estate, Beniram Pandit, and the Diwan of Cuttack,

Vishwambhar Pandit who were visiting Varanasi. Both readily agreed to Swamiji's request, and resources were immediately made available. Swami Brahmachari built the Jagannath Temple in 1802, and Beniram Pandit began managing the affairs of the temple. The temple lies in a compound some two hundred metres from the Assi Ghat, and is deserted for much of the year.

Swamiji and Beniram Pandit started the Rathyatra Festival four years later, on the lines of the Puri Festival. For three days of the festival, the images of Jagannath, Balarama and Subhadra are taken out in a chariot, along a festive route to Rathyatra. The festival received an impetus in 1965, when a prosperous businessman by the name of Rao Prahlad Das Shahpuri donated a large sum of money for the ceremonies and the upkeep of the ancient temple. During the festival, people from surrounding villages converge to the city. Sweetmeats, especially *nankhatai,* toys and flutes, bamboo baskets and trays, utensils, lacquer boxes, *bindis,* bangles and *sindoor* are sold in the fair. Giant wheels and merry-go-rounds come up, and every night there are *birha* and *kajri* performances. Prahlad Das Shahpuri's sons Deepak and Alok Shahpuri keep up the tradition today – I must admit that without their patronage, the Jagannath Temple would have crumbled by now, and the festival forgotten.

SIGNIFICANT PILGRIMAGES IN VARANASI

It is believed that the circumambulation of a sacred shrine is one of the best ways of absolving oneself of all sins committed during one's lifetime. At the holiest city in Hinduism, Varanasi provides the best opportunity for the pilgrim to cleanse herself or himself. While the scriptures provide many options, we shall discuss three of the most popular, perhaps most redeeming, of all the yatras, here.

The Panch Koshi Yatra

The sacred realm of Kashi is represented by the *kshetra* (region) that is encircled by the Pancha Koshi yatra - a circuit that some eight hundred years ago became the outermost pilgrimage in the city. This *yatra* (journey) encircles a sacred field with a radius of *panch koshas,* (17.6 kilometres), with the temple and *lingam* of Madhyamesvara – about a kilometre north of Manikarnika - as its centre. Over time, Vishwanath became the central object of worship for the pilgrim taking this *yatra.*

The route of the Panch Koshi yatra, according to the *Kasi Rahasya,* is punctuated by 108 stops, a number which reflects various aspects of the cosmic order. The dedication of the 108 places refers not only to the Great Tradition of Hinduism but also incorporates the gana (protectors) associated with local tradition. Almost every second place has a *linga* as object of worship. Others are devoted to Devi, Durga or Gauri and a few to Bhairava and Vishnu. Also worshipped en route are two sacred fields (*bhumi*), six water tanks and wells (*kunda, kupa, sarovara*), confluences of rivers and *ghats.* The sequence of the 108 places do not convey any specific order. They probably represent places, which were already there when the Panch Koshi yatra was established. The route probably took advantage of an existing infrastructure and shaped it into a meaningful sequence and order. Today, each of the 108 stops are marked with a small stone plaque (thankfully, I must admit, since local villagers remain blissfully ignorant about their names beyond saying 'It's a Shiva Temple'); and rest houses serve pilgrims undertaking the five day pilgrimage. There are several rules governing the yatra. Pilgrims must not wear any footwear, nor carry cooked meals with them. Sexual intercourse is prohbited while on the yatra, and menstruating women are not allowed to undertake it.

The yatra begins with a ritual bath at the Manikarnika Ghat, followed by a *sankalp* (statement of intention) at Gyanvapi. Here they recite all the 56 names of Ganesh, the 13 names of Narasimha, the 16 names of Keshava, and the more common ones of Shiva, who is referred to by an infinite number of appellations. After paying obeisance to Vishwanath and Annapurna, they seek the blessings of the city's guard, Dhundiraja Ganesh, before heading south towards Assi Ghat. Then they turn westwards, pass the gates of the Banaras Hindu University, and take a route that abuts the university's boundary walls for about five kilometres. En route at the village Adityapur is a pond, with a Hanuman temple next to it. Just a hundred metres later lies the first cluster of temples on the right side of the road, enclosed within an ancient compound. Near the entrance gate is the temple of Nilkantheshwar, the blue-necked Shiva. Some lovely carvings, including one of two fish, can be seen at the door of the shrine. The Devi temple of Kunwari Dakshini 'the Southern Virgin' is in the same compound, and a flight of steps on the right of the temple takes you up to a small image of Durga on the roof. Behind the temple of Nilkantheshwar lie the ruins of a once stately home; the ruins of whose pillars can only suggest what might have been.

Pilgrims carry on for about two kilometres before arriving at the village of Kandwa, where lies the first stop: Kardameshwara. This is a beautiful temple, the only one in Varanasi that dates back to the Gahadavala period. Set amidst a thicket of trees, the temple remains in a state of good repair, thanks to generous contributions from devotees like Kashinath Seth and Vinod Chandra Srivastava, who in recent times have paid for paving in marble the platform from which rises the temple. Recently, 200 students from Sunbeam School cleaned up the temple and its surroundings to fulfill their pledge of preserving their city's heritage. Carved *apsaras* flank the doorway to the main shrine. While the main temple is dedicated to Shiva, keeping in mind the non-sectarian character of Indian temples, there are images of the four-armed Vasudeva, Vamana, Varaha, Narsimha, Balarama and Shakti in niches in the façade of the temple. Outside the temple is a delightful little sculpture of a brahmin performing his penance earnestly, next to him another is engaged in preparing *bhang,* (cannabis). It is a classic Tantric depiction of *yoga* and *bhoga* (nourishing enjoyment). Opposite the door is a recent temple dedicated to Hanuman. Nearby lie smaller temples – those of Virupakshangan, Chamunda Devi, Nagnatheshwar and Somnatheshwar. On the gates of the last is carved a 9" image of Krishna playing the flute. There is a large *kund* next to the temple, where pilgrims take their ritual bath. They offer *pancha-anna* (a mixture of five grains) to the *shivlinga* here, and look into and draw water from the Kardam Kunda, a well, in the memory of the great saint Kardama. The following morning, they set off for the shrine of Unmatta Bhairava.

On the way are several *lingas* and *gana* (guardian) images, at which they may not stop but just throw Gangajal and bow. The first is a trio of shrines set amidst an open field – Mokshadeshwar, Chamunda and Karuneshwar, the last renovated in 1883 in memory of Lala Duloram Chopra, a businessman from Varanasi. This is followed by the shrine of Moksheshwar, lying under two *neem* trees in front of a row of shops. This temple was rebuilt by a devotee, Smt Rukmani Keshari of Delhana village. Up next is Birbhadreshwar, and at Delhana village, the temple of Vikataksha Durga Devi. The locals call it Ashtabhuja Mandir (after the eight-armed Goddess). Inside the temple are two small stone figures daubed in vermillion, one of them of a woman bearing a pitcher. The shrine of a holy man, Gujarati Baba, lies next to the temple under a fig tree. It was built by Vedantacharya Swami Hanumandas Ji and Shri Jankidas Maharaj. Carrying on, the pilgrim passes through Delhana village where he or she passes by Karuneshwar Mahadev – the Shivalinga here has an image of Hanuman right behind it. The temple of Unmatta Bhairava rises beside an algae-filled pond; fifty metres later is the small shrine of Neelkantha Gana. A placid buffalo chews cud next to the shrine. An image of Kalakuta Gana precedes the Vimla Durga Devi temple at Kashipur. The Mahadeveshwar Temple, up next, is framed by the smokestacks of two brick kilns. That is followed by the shrines of Nandikeshwar, Mriga Kirit Gana Dev and Gana Priyeshwar (these two on either side of a small settlement), Virupaksha. Pakshewshwar Mahadev comes next; here there are three small temples, one with a marble image of Devi inside. The Vimleshwar temple, next to a pond, is a bigger structure. One passes Gyan Deveshwar Mahadev and Amriteshwar Mahadev, before arriving at Bhimachandi, the second stop on the pilgrimage route. The first temple here is Gandheshwar, standing beside a *kund* that has four *chhatris* at its corners, and a primary school close to its left bank. The temple of Bhimachandi Mahadevi, the Fierce Great-Goddess, quite unusually, is topped by a dome, and is set in the middle of a courtyard. Pilgrims offer vermillion and hibiscus to the goddess, and perform a *shringar aarti* (decorative obeisance) in her honour at night. The main temple is flanked by those dedicated to Sri Ganesh on the right and Saraswati and Chanda Vinayaka to the left. Opposite, one goes through a doorway into the shrine of Parasuram; there are also images of Ravi Raktaksha Gandharva and Nara Karnava Taraka Gana.

On the third day, the pilgrims carry on past the shrine of Narakarini Awatar Mahadev, and cross the Grand Trunk Road at Raja Talab. At the crossing here lies a temple of Kaal Bhairav. After passing by the temple of Ekpad Shivagana and the incongrously named Yoga Convent School, they stop to pay respects at the Bhairavi Devi Temple at Bhairo Talab. Next to the *kund* here is a post-graduate college established by that maverick politician, Raj Narain. The Maha Bhingan temple next is festooned with bells; nearby lies the relatively new Radha Krishna temple. More shrines follow – Bhoothnatheshwar Mahadev, Somnatheshwar Mahadev; and Somnath Mahadev next to a pond that goes by the name Sindhu Sarovar. Two non-Shaiva temples are next, they are dedicated to Langotiya Hanuman and Ram Janaki; one passes the Pracheen Shiv – Parvati Mandir before crossing the highway that links Varanasi with the carpet-producing centre of Bhadohi. Then, appear the shrines of Kalnatheshwar Mahadev and Kapdirshwar Mahadev, and on the left of the road – the new Brahma Baba Mandir, where newly-weds can be seen being blessed by the priest. Now the pilgrim is heading towards the western border of the city, where Dehli Vinayaka stands guard. Again, they find a large *kund* here, as will they see a *mukha linga*, a *linga* with Shiva's face on it. On the way they pass Ganeshwar, Veerbhadra Shivagana, Charmukh Shivagana and Gananatheshwar. The road after Dehli Vinakaya is a shady one, flanked by fields of *jowar* and *arhar*. More shrines follow – Udand Vinayaka, Utkaleshwar Mahadev and so does the temple of Rudrarani Devi.

The third night's stop is at the village of Rameshwar, considered a representation of the southern pilgrimage centre of Rameshwaram. Lord Ram is associated with this spot, and locals will tell you that he visited it during his exile. The temple stands on the bank of the Varuna river, and a flight of steps leads down to the river so that devotees can take a bath before paying their respects. There are several shrines dedicated to Dhyavambhishwar, Someshwar, Agneshwar, Nhushasheshwar; as well as *lingas* honouring Rama, Lakshman, Bharat and Shatrughan. In the middle of a courtyard facing the main temple is a carved image of Sakshi Vinayaka; within an enclosure called Pavitra Dham beside it stand (from left to right) Vishnu, Lakshman, Ram, Janaki, Hanuman, Ganesh, Narasimha, Kal Bhairav and Surya. The chief priest of Rameshwar is Vashishta Narayan Tiwari, and he is quite willing to spend time explaining the intricacies of the Panchakoshi Yatra. The Ramachandraji Hariram Goenka Pathshala imparts Brahminical education to young students; and several members of erstwhile royal and business families like Baldeodas Birla and Rani Yogeshwari Devi Birla have set up *dharamshalas* where pilgrims can rest. Across the Varuna, in a *peepul* grove, is the shrine of Asankhyat Shiv Lingeshwar, where the spirits of all holy places are supposed to live; then a long walk till Dev Sandhyeshwar one kilometre before the yatra path bisects yet another highway at Harhua. One crosses that to reach the shrine of the Panch Pandava after the village of Shivpur. Erected to commemorate the stay of the five brothers immortalized in the Mahabharat, there are five *lingas* in their honour. The brothers' consort Draupadi has her own shrine and a well – the Draupadi Kupa – across the road. Eleven kilometres later lies the final stop at the Kapildhara, near the northern end of the city. This is one of Varanasi's most ancient temple sites. The *kund* was named after the saint Kapila, and this is another spot where Ram and Sita are said to have stopped by. The temple of Vrishabhadvajeshwara stands next to the *kund*. One cannot but be struck by the image of the dancing eight-armed Ganesh at the shrine of Chhappan Vinayaka here. On the final day, pilgrims visit the Adi Keshav Temple at Rajghat, salute Kharva Vinayak, before following the river's course. They take a dip at the Kapiladhara Kund, and pray at the shrine of Brisha Bhadwajeshwar Mahadeva. They take another bath at Manikarnika, and finally honour and thank Vishwanath for helping them make the pilgrimage.

But Hinduism allows its believers to do things symbolically. To serve that purpose, there is a temple that goes by the name of Pancha Koshi Mandir at at Gola Gali, near Chowk. The temple represents much more than the 108 places along the circuit. It incorporates, beyond the 108 places of the *yatra*, that provided the name for that temple, the complexity of Varanasi by adding 164 other places. The frame of the temple's entrance, the side and rear walls bear altogether 272 niches in which stylized reliefs symbolize Kashi's sacred places in their entirety. If sculptures in the lintels and beside the main door's jambs are added, the number adds up to 289 representations of gods, goddesses and places. A circumambulation of the temple encompasses Kashi as a whole. The essence, however, is found in the womb chamber. It houses a *linga* that is named Dvadaseshwar - Shiva as manifested by 12 *lingas* - of which the central one represents Vishwanath and eleven miniature *lingas* carved out of crystal the remaining eleven of the *Jyotirlingams.*

The Antargrihi Yatra

As mentioned earlier, the old city of Kashi was divided into three sections: Kedar, Omkar, and Visheshwar. The circumambulation of the Vishweshwar Khanda is referred to as the Antargrihi Parikrama. Being widely eulogized in the Puranas, this yatra is very popular among pilgrims. The Kashi Khanda fixes its boundaries as the Ganga in the east, Brahmeshwara in the south, Gokarneshwara in the west, and Bharabhuteshwara in the north. It is possible to complete within a few hours, and the texts recommend its undertaking at least once a year. Monday, Shiva's auspicious day, is when the journey should be preferably undertaken; most benefits can however be accrued by completing it on the occasion of Maha Shivaratri, in the month of Phalgun (February-March).

The yatra begins at the shrine of Manikarnika Devi, and spirals successively towards Vishwanath. The important shrines visited en route are those of Sakshi Vinayak, Annapurna, Abhimukteshwar, and Dhundiraja Ganesh, in addition to the ones at the extremities cited above.

The Panch Tirthi Yatra

The Kashi Khanda describes the Panch Tirthi yatra, taken along the river Ganga, as one which converts the pilgrim into the five-faced Shiva. It is one of the most popular pilgrimages taken in the city. Beginning at the southern ghat of Assi, the route takes pilgrims to Dasashwamedh Ghat, and on to the northern end of the city where the Varuna river meets the Ganga. The five stops 'tirthas' are Assi, Dasashwamedh, Manikarnika, Panchganga and Adi Keshava – pilgrims bathe and worship the important shrines at these ghats. Finally, from Manikarnika, they head inwards to the city, to worship Vishwanath, Annapurna and Sakshi Vinayak. At every stage of their pilgrimage, they make a *sankalpa,* a statement of intent to complete the pilgrimage, either merely to please Vishwanath, or in the anticipation of a boon.

Mediators and Enablers : The Pandas of Varanasi

The pilgrim who arrives in Varanasi for the first time is quite likely to be confused about how to fulfill his or her desire for communion with God. As in every major Hindu religious centre in India, Varanasi's *pandas* step in to mediate between God and humans. The *pandas* are facilitators of Hindu rituals. They have been assigned the religious authority, and provide the service with quite a vengeance. One often hears stories of how *pandas* keep on hiking the amount of money that has to be paid at every stage of a ritual. The *pandas* earned notoriety by robbing unsuspecting pilgrims of all their money and jewellery, and sometimes even murdering them, but this has been brought under control through better policing in recent years.

While the word *panda* is broadly applied to all categories of ritual mediators in Varanasi, there exists a clear class distinction among the *panda* community based on their ancestry, nature of service provided and ability. The *Naukul* (nine family) *pandas* are the priests at the top of the hierarchy. They have a regular client base of families belonging to different parts of the country, and a battery of assistants who help clients find accomodation and information in Varanasi. All are Kanyakubja Brahmins, and can be identified by their surnames : Chaturvedi, Dwivedi, Mishra, Pandey, Pathak, Shukla, Trivedi and Upadhyaya. It is believed that only four of the original nine families remain. The *Jatrawals* are employed by the *Naukul pandas* to act as guides for the pilgrims on their pilgrimage to different temples and shrines in the city. Most pick up their clients near the entrance of Vishwanath Gali and help them have an easy access to the deity. The *Ghatiyas* are the priests who sit on wooden platforms at the main ghats, under giant reed umbrellas. They help pilgrims with rituals such as the *pinda daan* and accept gifts in return. Calling themselves *Ganga Putra,* son of the Ganga, they perform the sacred worship of the Ganga. They are a community that numbers about 150; only five are women. Yet another specialized group, the *Karmakandis,* performs Vedic rituals like *yajna, abhisheka* and *samskara.* Finally, there are the *Bhaddars*, who accost pilgrims at railway stations, to 'help' them visit temples and offer the 'right kind' of prayers. Numbering about 2500, and belonging entirely to the Joshi Brahmin community, their main duty is to bring the pilgrim to the *ghatia* or the *tirthapurohita.* They are derisively called *'Sadak Chhap'* (Street Brand) by the other *pandas*, and might be the most irritating, latching on to visitors new to the city with promises of accomodation, the best deals in shopping, besides easing the way into temples. It is the naïve faith which the devout Hindus attach in their priests, the detailed prescriptions laid down in the religious texts for the performance of rituals, and the desire for fulfilment of vows that allow the *pandas* to prey upon pilgrims and operate with impunity.

ଓ

Sadhus and Cults

In the final phase of their lives, *Vanaprastha*, good Hindus must seek liberation from all earthly desires and become *sadhus*, loosely translated as 'holy man'. (Just to remove any doubts of gender bias, a holy woman is referred to as a *sadhvi.*) The word *sadhu* itself is derived from the Sanskrit *sadhana,* meaning preparation for self-realization. The common image that most have of a sadhu is either of an ash-smeared, long haired, bearded naked or loincloth clad man, or of an ochre robed, shaven headed (or long haired) ascetic with his forehead smeared with *tilak.* They might be the stereotypes that television and print images from the Kumbh Mela have relayed to the world, but there is much more to it. Today the ochre robe has become an insignia for a fanatical display of revivalism, as have the cannabis smoking, *bhaang* drinking, and outlandish appearances of the *sadhu* become symbols of religious sensationalism.

Militancy among the *sadhus* is nothing new. It began (as it is seen today) as a response to Muslim invasion. The Dashanamis fought the troops of Aurangzeb at Gyanvapi in 1665. The Nagas, though, were mercenaries who sometimes fought the Hindus, and sometimes the Muslims.[1] On the other hand, it is indeed the ideal of sober, ascetic renunciation that enjoys the highest social esteem among the masses. Ascetic orders insist on the greatest religious discipline. Centred around the *mathas,* these orders are about propounding a particular school of thought in philosophy or religion. They run schools for teaching Sanskrit and philosophy and help followers in the learning and observance of rituals. They offer shelter to pilgrims, because devotion is also expressed through helping the poor and needy.

In this section, I shall describe three of the fascinating and diverse sects that have mystified observers of and visitors to the city. These sects are the Dandi sanyasis, The Nagas, and the Aghoris.

The Dandi Sanyasis

Recognized by the *danda* (staff) they carry, the Dandi ascetics are devotees of Shiva. In Varanasi, they account for nearly twenty percent of all ascetics, and number between two and three hundred. The sect was founded in the ninth century, by Adi Shankaracharya. Its members are staunch defenders of the orthodox Hindu tradition, thus the four Shankaracharyas – the high priests of the most important Shaivite shrines in India – always belong to this sect. Their presence at Hindu religious festivals is seen by traditionalists to enhance the prestige of the event. The Dandi tradition is about strict adherence to the teachings of one's Guru.

When a person (usually a man) is ready to join the sect, he attaches himself as an apprentice to a Dandi swami – a religious preceptor – for a period of training. This could last for several months. When he is ready to be initiated, an elaborate ritual follows. On the first day, the initiate has to go through the *Krichchan* ceremony to attain bodily purification. On the following day, he has to perform *shraddha* and *tarpan* (offering of oblation to forefathers) at the Tulsi Ghat on the banks of the Ganga. After these tarpan ceremonies, he undergoes the ceremony of Panch Bhadra, when his head is shaved, barring a lock of hair on his scalp. In the next step of initiation, his sacred thread and the scalp lock are removed by the Guru. The scalp lock is thrown away into the river Ganga and the sacred thread is tied on top of the Danda (ascetic staff) under the cover of an ochre-coloured cloth. After this, the initiate is given a *Kopin* (loin-coth), his *Danda* (ascetic staff) and a *Kamandalu* (water pot made of dried gourd) with the chanting of Vedic hymns. Next, the Virja Homa (purificatory sacrifice) is performed with the appropriate *mantras* (hymns) after which the initiate is again taken to Tulsi Ghat where in knee-deep water in the river Ganga, he recites the Gayatri Mantra in the presence of his preceptor. In the end, the preceptor whispers the mysterious mantra called the *Praisha* or *Shiva Mantra* into the right ear of the initiate. This is the climax of the initiation ceremony. The Dandi will now carry his staff without it touching the ground for the rest of his life and will be buried with it. Ascetics are buried because they are already pure. Most Dandis cover their staff with a cloth lest it be polluted by the touch of some lower-caste person.

The matha of Swami Bhumananda, founded as recently as 1986 at Kedar Ghat is the wealthiest Dandi matha in Varanasi; while the Mumukshu Bhavan in Assi, established by Swami Ghanshyamananda in 1929 the largest. Other prominent mathas are the Muchhali Bandara Matha at Nagwa, Dharam Sangh in Durga Kund and Chausatti Matha at Chausatti Ghat.

The Naga Ascetics

No sect arouses as much curiosity as the Nagas. At the Kumbh Mela in Prayag, they provoke some kind of a mesmerizing fascination among foreigners, partly because of their appearance, partly because of their seemingly superhuman feats, partly because they seem to be always in a drug-induced state of trance. The Naga sect is headquartered at Hanuman Ghat in Varanasi. It takes its name from one of the three possible sources: a man from the hills, or the snake God, or the state of nakedness. While the Nagas are allowed to cover themselves with a piece of unstitched cloth, they do not wear anything on special occasions. They wear their hair and beards long and matted. Their bodies are covered with an even coating of ash, which gives them a ghostly Shiva-like appearance. They are impervious to heat and cold. Years of meditation up in the Western Himalaya have made sure that their bodies are free from 'wear and tear'. Some Naga sadhus are known to live as long as 150 years. As part of their initiation rites, the nerve attached to their penis is broken, which leaves them with no sexual desires and capable of performing improbable feats such as lifting bricks and pulling cars with their organ. Such displays are not part of their regular routine, but shows during events such as the Kumbh Mela. In Varanasi, on certain festival days, they walk in a silent procession to the Vishwanath temple, two Nagas side by side holding hands, and led by a Naga on a horse beating a *nagara* (kettledrum).

The Cult of Aghoris

Ask most Banarasis about Aghor *sadhus*, and you will be met with a look of disgust. You will be told that Aghors are *sanyasis* who eat flesh including that of humans, drink liquor and have sex. For them, indulging in carnal pleasures is part of their meditation. But, as this section on a feared yet misunderstood sect will tell you, the Aghor cult is not only about eating flesh and mating with corpses.

The word Aghor literally means "that which is not difficult or terrible". The words Aghor, Kapalik, Aghori, Aughar, Avadhoot mean the same. They indicate one which is simple and in the natural state of consciousness. Spirituality does not require any special knowledge, faith, worship or ritual. All it requires is inspiration, determination, perseverance and patience. There is no place for fear, hatred, disgust or discrimination in the eyes of an Aghor. Constant practice of these virtues makes a person an Avadhoot, regardless of the path. An Aghoreshwar is an Avadhoot who goes through various penances and then devotes himself to the cause of humanity.

It is absolutely a carefree state where the aspirant gets totally detached from the external world. He becomes desireless and doesn't demand anything. He doesn't care for or complain about anything. He has no worries, no constraints, no bondage and no obligations whatsoever. He is totally free. He is happy no matter where he is. He attains a state of indifference, for him all living creatures are equal. His heart becomes pure; no evil can touch him.

Following the principle of actionless action, they remain blameless and firm in their austerity, respecting everything. They may be cheated by others, but they never cheat others. Remaining prideless, they show respect to others. They use discarded pieces of cloth as their clothing, whether that cloth has holes in it or not, whether thrown away in the trash or even having been used as a shroud for the dead. They want to use only such things that are of no more use to any other person.

Aghor began with the existence of life on earth. It has been present in all the times. In Indian culture, the Ultimate or Supreme Being is worshipped as 'Shiva'. Shiva inculcates Shakti (spiritual power), without Shakti Shiva is 'Shav' (dead or lifeless). Aghor is Madhya-Marga (middle path) which represents a union of Shiva and Shakti. Aghor is Shiva by appearance and 'Kali' (Shakti) by activities.

After the prehistoric association of Aghor with Lord Shiva, another legendary being was not only considered by the ancients to have realized the state of Aghor but was believed to have propounded and taught the knowledge of it to others. This was Lord Dattatreya. In the sixteenth century, a great saint called Baba Kinaram came to be known as Aghoreshwar, the pre-eminent Aghor.

The story of Baba Kinaram tells of his wandering for years until he attained complete knowledge by having the *darshan* of Bhagwan Dattatreya, who appeared to him in the Girnar mountains, a holy place in Gujarat state. Baba Kinaram travelled far and wide across India. Upon witnessing the suffering of people, he engaged himself whole-heartedly in alleviating their suffering. Finally on the bank of the river Ganges in Varanasi, he established his *dhuni* (sacred fire) and continued his *sadhana* of service. The *akhand dhuni* (continuous burning fire) of Baba Kinaram fed by the leftover wood from the nearby cremation grounds, and the *samadhis* (tombs) of all the *siddhas* of the lineage in the same compound, are witness to the continuum of this intact lineage of Aghor Siddhas. Today, this *yogabhumi* (land of sadhana) of the Aghor Siddhas of Varanasi is called Krim Kund. He initiated many social reforms during the tumultuous times of the Moghul invasion when the Indian people were being persecuted.

Later in his life Baba Kinaram wrote a book called *Viveksar*, said to be the most authentic treatise on the principles of Aghor. In his book he wrote that when he understood what Bhagwan Dattatreya was saying to him, he saw that the whole world, the whole universe, is situated in this human body, a vast world perfect in all respects, which was called Maya. Maya and its every transformation was present inside his body. The other books by him are *Geetavali, Ramrasal* and *Ramgeeta.*

The direct lineage of the twelve Aghoreshwars that began with Baba Kinaram extends from the sixteenth century until the present. A new era dawned in 1958 with the incarnation of Aghoreshwar Bhagwan Ram Jee, who after completing penance and attaining enlightenment turned his attention towards masses. In this lineage of Aghor Siddhas of North India, Baba Bhagwan Ramji emerged as an Aghoreshwar for the modern times. Aghoreshwar initially founded an Ashram - Shri Sarveshwari Samooh Sansthan Devasthanam, in Varanasi, to emphasise that work is paramount. It was also meant to provide social aspect to the spiritual devotion, to help helpless and needy people and for other welfare works. Shri Sarveshwari Samooh Sansthan Devasthanam is the centre of Aghoreshwar's services to the mankind.

Bhagwan Ram discouraged drinking, flesh eating and sexual perversions and wanted his trust, which is the parent body of the Samooh as well as the Aghor Parishad Trust, to carry out various social programmes. He gave a new dimension to the Aghor tradition by eradicating the myths associated with it. Aghoreshwar also simplified it so that it appealed to the masses. That is why he is known as *'Ek Aughar League Se Hat Kar'* (a reformer among saints).

Heeding to the call of our time, Bhagwan Ramjee gave a new turn to this safeguarded tradition of Siddhas and expanded its field of activity. He opened up and availed of the teachings and practices of Aghor to the all-sincere seekers whether a renunciate or a householder. Bhagwan Ramji passed away in 1992. About 1 km from Shri Sarveshwari Samooh Sansthan Devasthanam and towards the eastern side of Rajghat bridge lies the Aghoreshwar Bhagwan Ram Maha Vibhuti Sthal. This is the place where Aghoreshwar's body was consigned to fire according to his wishes. The work of construction of shrine is in full swing. The devotees and loved ones of Aghoreshwar visit the ashram throughout the year, pray for his blessings and get spiritual inspiration by meditation.

ʗ3

Sarnath

While Hinduism is the predominant religion of Varanasi, Sarnath, in the city's northern suburbs attracts Buddhist pilgrims from the world over. The historic site, where Gautama Buddha delivered his first sermon to his followers, who thereupon spread his message across the world, is over 25 centuries old. After attaining enlightenment under the Bodhi Tree in Bodh Gaya, Buddha set off for the deer park at Isipattana, eight km north of Varanasi. There, at the age of thirty-five, in 528 B.C., he found his former ascetic companions and preached his first sermon. He explained the way to end suffering in the world and gain supreme enlightenment. The small audience was stunned by the brevity and clarity of his speech, by the manner in which the Four Noble Truths had been expounded. Within three months of his sermon, the core monastic order comprising some sixty monks 'The Sangha' was formed, and Buddha found converts among the laity from Varanasi. No doubt he found stiff opposition among the orthodox Hindu scholars in the city, but the simplicity of what he advocated – addressing the current condition of the world, taking an objective view of reality and understanding the place of man in the universe – earned him a large following. The members of the Sangha then set forth to all parts of India and neighbouring South and South-East Asia to spread the word.

For nearly two hundred and fifty years, Sarnath was but a hermitage. Emperor Ashoka changed all that. After he embraced Buddhism around 260 B.C., he constructed the magnificent buildings and monuments in Sarnath and elsewhere, as his imperial patronage transformed a local sect into a nationwide religion. The lion capital, which today functions as the seal of the Indian government, was carved in his time. So were the Dhamekh and the Dharamarajika Stupas. Between the 4th and 6th centuries A.D. – the Gupta period, Sarnath was the centre of Buddhist Art. During this time, the Dhamekh stupa was encased in beautifully carved stones. The glory of that age was documented by the Chinese travellers Fa-Hien and Hiuen Tsang. They describe the images of Boddhisattvas, and monasteries which accomodated as many as 3000 monks. Sarnath prospered till the invasion by Mahmud Ghazni, in 1017. Many monuments were destroyed, and by the middle of the next century, when Qutub-ud-Din Aibak raided the place, Sarnath's importance as Buddhism's living centre had been erased.

It was in 1793 that the ruins were first uncovered during some erection work ordered by Raja Jagat Singh. But systematic excavation was first carried out by Alexander Cunningham in 1836. Cunningham's team excavated sixty statues and bas-reliefs that now lie in the collection of the National Museum in Calcutta. Markham Kittoe, who was also involved in the construction of the Queen's College, made the next round of excavations. By 1907, most of the ruins of Sarnath, as we can see today, had been uncovered. Dr. J.H. Marshall, the Director-General of Archaeology, ordered the construction of a museum at the site, for the display of the artefacts that had been found. James Ransome was the architect of the red sandstone museum that we see today – it was thrown open to the public in February 1912. In the museum, and sprawled outside, over lush green carefully manicured gardens, one can see the remnants of a past era.

The **Dhamekh Stupa**, 33.5 metres high and 28 metres in diameter, towers above the entire landscape. The upper portion is built in brick, while the lower is encased in stone. The borders have geometrical and floral designs carved on them. On the other hand, one can see only the remains of the **Dharamarajika Stupa,** which was built by Ashoka at the site of the first sermon. It was razed by the workmen of Jagat Singh (not to be confused with the Raja mentioned earlier), who were in search of construction material for a bazaar nearby. Behind the stupa are the remains of the **Ashokan Pillar**, which was once crowned by the Lion Capital. Discovered in 1905, only a 2.03 metre stump of the original 15.25 metres remains today. The pillar, smooth to touch, bears inscriptions warning monks and nuns against creating a schism within the Sangha. The **Mulgandhakuti** 'always filled with fragrance' **Vihara** marks the spot where Buddha used to meditate in the rainy season. Hiuen Tsang recorded it as 61 metres high. The modern temple we see today was built between 1922 and 1931, at a cost of Rs 150,000. It is a true example of people from different religions coming together for a noble cause. Sir Harcourt Butler, an uncle of the Governor of the United Provinces, laid the foundation. Hindu noblemen like Raja Udai Pratap Singh, Raja Moti Chand and Raja Shiv Prasad were among the top donors. The priest Anagarika Dharmapala supervised the construction of the temple. The Japanese mural artist Kesetso Nosu painted the interior walls of the vihara between 1932-35, and the Mahabodhi Society of Japan donated the giant bell in the corridor that leads up to the temple.

The visitor to the **Sarnath Museum** is greeted by the Lion Capital, standing 2.31 metres tall, carved in buff-coloured Chunar sandstone. The four lions, carved in heraldic fashion, sit atop a bell-shaped base resembling an inverted lotus, with the Chakra (wheel) engraved on it. In an attempt to portray their benignness, the claws of the lions' feet are retracted. Richard Lannoy puts it rather well when he says, 'The Lion Capital … gathers archaic elements, such as the Indra Pillar, kingly emblems of sovereignty and the non-culture-specific solar wheel, and blends them with the Ashokan ideal of moral sovereignty'. In the central Sakyasimha hall is placed an immense statue of Buddha, seated as if in a posture of imparting security. The sculpture was made during the Kushan period, and was originally protected by a giant umbrella. This lies in ten pieces today, eight of which have been joined and kept on one side of the hall. To the left lies the Triratna Gallery, where the main attraction is a standing figure of Tara from the 5th century. The other antiquities one might see here are a seated Bodhisattva – Padmapani, an image of the pot-bellied Jambhala, the God of wealth and prosperity, and an inscription of Kumaradevi, the queen of the Gahadavala king Govinda Chandra. There are more Boddhisattva images in the northeast gallery, Tathagata, with the image of Buddha in Dharma Chakra Mudra (Turning the Wheel of Law) being most striking. It shows him in a serene, compassionate and introspective mood. On the southern side lies the Trimurti Gallery, which mainly houses Brahminical figures, including a Trimurti – the Trinity of Brahma, Vishnu and Mahesh. There are more Brahminical figures, and a massive image of a ten-armed Shiva killing the demon Andhaka, dating back to the 12th century in the Ashutosh Gallery. Of about the same antiquity is a figure of Nataraja, of which the head and feet have been broken. The wild Shiva holds a trident in the left hand, and wears a garland of skulls. Other architectural remains are exhibited in the two verandahs in the north and south of the main building.

Over the recent years, Sarnath has regained its prominence and received the patronage of Buddhists in Japan, Tibet, Sri Lanka and Burma, all of whom have built their temples in the area. The Tibetan Temple is home to the largest Buddha image in Sarnath. Followers of all the four sects of Tibetan Buddhism revere this temple, which contains about 150 rare Buddhist scriptures. Sarnath is a safe haven for the refugee Tibetan population, and there is an institute of higher learning here. The Burmese Monastery, Maha Wijitawi Sima, was built in 1934 by two Burmese ladies Daw Ryu and Daw Goom; while the Chinese Temple built in 1939 by Te Yu, a disciple of the Abbot of Beijing, His Holiness Tao Kai. Both contain marble images of the Buddha. The most recent addition is a Japanese temple, opened in 1991. Built in the Japanese style at a cost of a hundred million rupees, with material brought from Japan, it highlights the prosperity of Buddhists today.

The main festival that is celebrated at Sarnath is the full moon night in May, Buddha Purnima, when Buddha was born. Prayer meetings, group meditation and processions mark the occasion. On the first full-moon in November, scholars and monks celebrate the founding of Mulgandhakuti Vihara.

Life & Death on the River

THE GANGA & HER GHATS

Jab dil mila dayal so, tab kachhu antar naahi
Paala gayi paani bhayaa, jyon harijan Hari mahi

If the heart mingles with the Lord's,
there is complete union
As the melting ice mingles with water,
you find God in the man of devotion

Kabir

ও

It is impossible to think of Varanasi without the Ganga. It is said that all the great cities of the world lie next to a river, but never has a river changed its course to touch the banks of a city. It is probably the holiness of Varanasi that makes the Ganga, so long flowing eastwards, suddenly veer north, as if reminded of her origin in the mountains where Shiva lived. *Uttarvahini,* is what the Ganga becomes, in Varanasi. When seen from the Malaviya Bridge, it is not uncommon to be reminded of the crescent moon on Shiva's matted locks.

Ages ago, Ganga was a river that flowed in the Heavens. She came to earth only after the penance of King Bhagirath, sixty thousand of whose ancestors had been burnt to death, and their only route to salvation was, if Ganga came down and washed their ashes. Brahma agreed, but King Bhagirath had to appeal to Shiva to catch her raging torrent in his matted locks, lest the entire earth be swept away by the fierce waters. On earth, Ganga followed Bhagirath from the Gangotri in the Himalaya to Ganga Sagar in the Bay of Bengal, thus charting out her current course.

To the Hindu, the Ganga is a mother – she nurtures, gives life, dispenses grace, must be worshipped, and ultimately takes you back in the form of your ashes. Banarasis call her Ganga Maiya. Ganga provides salvation to the dead and purifies the living. Even if one cannot be cremated on her banks, it is deemed a privilege for one's ashes to be scattered in the river. Even the Beatle George Harrison wished that to happen. Pilgrims from far away wai* for the moment when they can immerse themselves in the river and drink its waters. Her waters are called *amrita* – the nectar of immortality. Newly married couples garland her with the *Aar Paar Ka Mala* – by weaving a string of flowers right across the width of the river, in anticipation of marital bliss and the offspring that she might grant them. The couple, accompanied by close relatives, arrives at the *ghat* where the *Ghatiya* applies sandalwood and turmeric to their foreheads. The couple then performs a *puja* at an image of Gauri Ganesh – this *puja* is necessarily performed by a boatman. Then they ride his boat to the opposite bank, stringing a garland whose composition varies according to the family's economic status – mango leaves, flowers or even cloth.

It is said that watching the sun rise over the Ganga is one of the closest experiences you could have to being in Heaven. Ever since I was given a camera, I have kept coming to the river to photograph that scene, in different seasons. Ganga changes colour every season, and her levels rise or fall depending on how much snow melts from the Himalaya and the monsoon unleashes torrents into the all-encompassing river. In winter, she is a shade of calm, aquamarine blue, reflecting the cloudless sky. In summer, she slows down to a narrow, sluggish, muddy-green stream, yet cools all around her. A few months later, she is a raging, muddy torrent, as the ghats disappear under the water. Sometimes she enters the city itself, submerging all that lies in her path.

Every morning, it is part of the daily routine of many Banarasis, especially the priests, to take a bath in the river. They are joined by countless pilgrims, the numbers of who swell to a crush on special bathing days. On an average day, sixty thousand bathe in the Ganga. Women wearing saris in vivid colours and prints jostle with widows in white. There are men in the briefest of *langots* – loincloths, others who are fully clothed, even as they are chin deep in the water. As the sun rises, they join their hands in prayer : *Surya Namaskar*, and murmur prayers in praise of the Sun God. Then there are the priests – called *ghatias* - who sit under large woven reed umbrellas, and help pilgrims offer prayers to Ganga herself, or to their ancestors – *pinda daan*. They perform rituals like *namkaran* – the naming of a newborn baby, and *mundan* – the shaving of the head.

Every year, some fifty-thousand bodies are cremated on the banks of the Ganga, and their ashes consigned to the waters. Pregnant women, holy men and children are considered to be clean – needing no purification by fire, they are simply weighted down with stones and dropped into the river. To a scientific person, or a foreigner, it boggles the imagination how the murky water, in which so many perform their ablutions, into which are cast away half-burnt dead bodies, can ever be considered pure? The answer lies in the ritual of purification. Cleansing waters have always been part of religious tradition from the time of the ceremonial tanks of Mohenjodaro. Running waters, like those of the Ganga, are especially effective, since they absorb pollution, and carry it away.

Dusk turns the river bank into an enchanting place, as the wondrous Ganga Aarti is performed at the Dasashwamedh Ghat. A wooden platform is laid out on the ghat, and the priests take their positions. As they chant *mantras* and trill a bell, several young men begin playing cymbals and drums. The river is first worshipped with flowers, incense, milk, *sindoor* and sandalwood. Then a camphor lamp is set albaze, and the head priest arches the lamp towards the waters, over and over again. He then lights a lamp that has many a flame, and repeats the ritual, as the music rises to a crescendo, and lights are reflected in the river's dark waters. Finally, all who have assembled on the ghat rise and sing, together, hymns in praise of Ganga Maiya.

This is a ritual that has been repeated every evening, for hundreds of years. As I watched it yet one more time in February 2002, with my friends and colleagues (who had come from places as diverse as Rajasthan, Mumbai, Wisconsin and Oregon), I could not help observing that, barring the electric lights, everything here was just the same as it had been a thousand years ago. Of course, there were no flashbulb-popping tourists on boats in the river then !

☙

THE GHATS, THEIR HISTORY AND SIGNIFICANCE

For most to-be visitors to Varanasi, the first picture that they possibly see of the city is of the ghats on the riverbank. Elders in the city describe the city , as it lies stretched by the river, as having five bodily parts. Assi is its head, Dasashwamedh its chest, Manikarnika its navel, Panchganga the thighs, and Adi Keshava its feet. Tall stone buildings, minarets and gateways rise high above the sandstone steps that line the Ganga for a length of 6.4 kilometres. It is the ghats that give the city as much of its character as do its temples or its narrow lanes. Compared to the city's antiquity, the ghats are a recent innovation, going back to three hundred years. Many of the ghats that one sees today were built in the eighteenth and nineteenth centuries by the Maratha rulers; others by saints and rich traders. Some, like the Assi Ghat, was paved as recently as the early 1990s. In all, there are eighty-three ghats along the river, and it is possible, on a winter day, to traverse their entire length. For the city's residents, the *ghat* is not just a place to take a dip in the Ganga. It is a place to sit down in the evening and chat about the day's happenings over a cup of tea, and maybe a small ball of *bhaang.* In the morning, it is the setting for exercise and body-building, at one of the many *akhadas* along the ghat. The young play cricket and *gulli-danda* on its steps, and fly kites taking advantage of the breeze that blows across the river. The ghats also provide a splendid backdrop for the classical and folk music performances that happen during the different seasons. Most visitors, whether foreign or Indian, take the token boat ride from Dasashwamedh Ghat to the burning ghats of Harishchandra and Manikarnika, but that is rarely enough to appreciate the true majesty of Varanasi's ghats. As a Banarasi, I believe it is my duty to take you, my reader, on a trip to every one of the ghats, beginning at the southern end of the city.

Saamne Ghat

The furthermost ghat upstream is the Saamne ghat. For much of the year, local residents and those visiting the Ramnagar Fort on the opposite bank use a pontoon bridge to cross the river. The bridge is barely wide for a single four-wheeler to pass. Guards at the two ends of the bridge use a primitive signalling method to control traffic: they flash a red or green traffic sign to each other, and let the vehicles pass. When the bridge is dismantled during the monsoons, a ferry takes them across the swollen river. The ghat has little religious significance for most Banarasis, but it was important to me as long as I was a student. After the Saraswati Puja, we would take the idol of the Goddess to the middle of the pontoon bridge, and immerse her in the river with a cry of 'Jai Saraswati Mai ki'.

Assi Ghat

Assi is one of the important ghats situated in the south, at the *sangam* of Ganga and Assi. The Assi, described as dried stream in Puranic literature, is all but a narrow drain today. The 17th century temple of Jagannath (One of the *Char Dham Yatra)* lies close to the ghat, and at the summit of the steps leading up from the ghat is the Pancha Ratna temple. The Kashi Khanda says "All the other *tirthas* that girdle the earth are not equal to a sixteenth part of the *tirthas* at Assi confluence" . This is one of the famous sites for celebrating Surya Sasthi ("the sixth day of the sun" as mother goddess) festival held on fifth and sixth light- half fortnight in the month of Kartik. The ghat was paved as recently as 1988, even though the Queen of Sursund, in Bihar, had attempted to do so at the turn of the century.

This is a ghat that seems to be designed for the western tourist, especially the low-budget kinds who populate this part of the city. A small bookshop called Harmony sells books on religion and spirituality, and picture post-cards. Another sells trinkets: bells, cushion covers, statuettes from different parts of India, and next to it is a cybercafe. In the evenings, they gather to watch the Ganga Aarti, sip tea out of earthen cups – *kullarhs* – and smoke *ganja* or *hashish*. One of the tea-shop owners on the ghat has been alleged to make enough money peddling narcotics to be able to go to Europe and North America on holiday every summer ! Students from the Visual Arts Faculty of BHU can be spotted sitting on the steps sketching ghat scenes for a class assignment. The Ganges View Hotel, converted from an old building, is a beautiful little property at Assi Ghat. Each room is decorated in the traditional way; every week, there are classical music concerts on the terrace of the hotel. When they visit Varanasi, Sir Mark Tully, and Khushwant Singh choose to stay here, rather than in one of the five-stars in the cantonment area. Next to it is the newer and grander Palace on Ganges, where each well-appointed room is done up in the style taken from one of India's various states. On the way to the Jagannath Temple lies Hotel Temple on the Ganges, a square four-story very un-temple-like building, but a favourite among backpackers.

When I was twenty-eight, I had been ill for a while, and decided to spend some time at my home in Varanasi. Every evening, I would walk to Assi Ghat, two kilometres from home, just before the sun set. I found immense peace sitting on the ghat for an hour, watching the *Ganga Aarti,* and watching the boats go by. As it would turn dark, I would take a rickshaw back. It was a routine that I believed helped immensely in my recovery.

Ganga Mahal Ghat

Made in 1830 by the patronage of Maharaja Banaras, this is an extended part of the Assi Ghat. The palatial house is now maintained by the Kashi Naresh Maharani Trust, and has been converted into a guest house for visitors who come to Varanasi to study the arts and music.

Rewa Ghat

Like the preceding one, this is also an extended part of the Assi Ghat and was originally called Lala Misir Ghat after the eponymous priest of the King of Punjab Ranjit Singh. The Maharaja of Rewa, in Madhya Pradesh, built a palace here in 1879, and the ghat took its name after his kingdom.

Bhadaini Ghat

This is the renamed Ghat of Lolarka, known after the most famous sun shrine and the sacred tank – Lolarka Kund near by. Lolarka ("trembling sun") is one of the most ancient sacred sites in Varanasi. In a niche on the stairs of the Lolarka Kund is a disk of sun, Lolarkditya ,while at the top exists the Lolarkeshwer Linga. In the *Bhadra* month (August/September), the people of Varanasi celebrate an important religious festival celebrated on *Shukla Sasthi.* It is believed that by bathing in the Lolarka Kund on this auspicious day, childless women will be able to conceive. Wife and husband bathe together, her *sari* tied to his *dhoti,* and they release some vegetable – usually a phallic cucumber – into the Kund, to signify the fertility they have prayed for.

Tulsi Ghat

Once part of the old Lolark Ghat, this ghat became famous because of its association with Tulsidas (1547-1623),the great Bhakti poet who wrote the *Ramcharit Manas.* On the top of the ghat is the house in which the poet lived and died, and a gymnasium – Akhara Swaminath - established by him. Among the artefacts preserved are his wooden clogs, his pillow, the idol of Hanuman which he worshipped and a piece of wood from the boat used by him to cross the Ganga. A temple of Ram stands on the ghat.

This is an important ghat for cultural and religious activities as during the month of *Kartik* (October – November) for about a fortnight. Krishna Leela, a theatrical performance based on the life of Lord *Krishna,* is performed every year at the Tulsi Ghat. Its most important day is the show of *Naga Nathaiya* (putting rope in the nose of snake demon) in the second light-half of *Kartik.* Residents of this area believe that the Krishna Leela was initiated by Tulsi and has been continued for nearly four hundred years. The annual Dhrupad Mela is also held at the Tulsi Ghat, and attracts the leading Dhrupad singers from all over the country. The ghat has a mansion built by the Maratha Balajirao Peshwa, and houses the office of the Clean Ganga Foundation.

Janki Ghat

The next ghat was first constructed in 1860 by Rai Girdhar Lal. It was subsequently made pucca by the Queen of the Sursund in 1917. It is believed that the people of Sursund were ardent devotees of Sita (Janki), and that association gave the ghat its name. There are four Shiva and Vishnu temples with gilded pinnacles at this ghat.

Anandmayi Ghat

This ghat was formerly known as Imiliya Ghat, possibly after the tamarind trees here. Paved by Shiv Prasad Gupta in 1945, is was renamed after Mata Anandmayee, a woman saint who died in 1982. A peaceful cluster of buildings – her ashram - stands behind a small, sunny garden. A retired Army Brigadier called A.K.Ganguly chose to turn down a promotion in the defence service, and run one of most frequented charitable hospitals in the city here. The ashram also runs a *gurukul* – Anandamayee Ma's Kanyapeeth - for girls, who are provided free education and residence, but lead an austere life in seclusion, cooking on coal fires, doing their own laundry and cleaning. Some of the girls stay on at the ashram, others go back to a wordly life.

Vachcharaja Ghat

At this ghat, one can see the image of Ganga, riding a crocodile, in a small shrine, along with images of Shiva and Ganesh. Above the ghat are temples dedicated to the Jain tirthankara Suparsvanath, and Akrureshwar, as also the Gopal temple built by Ma Anandmayee in 1960. The ghat is named after a merchant who paved it in 1790.

Jain Ghat

This is an extended part of the preceding ghat, and was built by the resident Jain community in 1931. At the top of the ghat is a Jain temple built in 1885 and dedicated to Suparsvanath. The northern part of the ghat is home to a community of fishermen, who tend to make their part of the riverbank dirty by defecating here and putting out their garbage!

Nishadraj Ghat

Nishad was a mythical hero of fishermen, in the Ramayana.This ghat – a congregation point for fishermen and their boats, was built to honour him, in 1942 along with the Nishadraj temple.

Prabhu Ghat

This was built by Nirmal Kumar, a rich Bengali businessman, in the early 20th century. The huge palace on the ghat was also constructed by him. The ghat is used by washermen to wash clothes.

Panchkot Ghat

This ghat is named after Raja Panchkot of Bengal, who made the ghat in 1915. The palace on the ghat has a beautiful garden inside, along with two shrines dedicated to Shiva and Kali. The large stone platform above the ghat is a favourite spot for local children to play *gulli-danda*.

Chet Singh Ghat

Formerly known as Khirki Ghat, this was the site of a fierce battle between the Maharaja of Banaras, Chet Singh, and the British troops of Warren Hastings in 1781. The fort-palace herewas built in the mid-18th century, in the Rajput style of architecture, by Raja Balwant Singh under the guidance of Baijnath Mishra. It is indeed an impressive building, with turrets flanking a giant gateway. There are three Shiva temples inside the palace.

Niranjani Ghat

This ghat was made pucca by the Raja of Panchkot in the early 20th century. It is home to the wrestlers and Naga sadhus of the Niranjan Akhara, which was established in 1897. Within the compound of the akhara lie the Kartikeya, Gauri Shankar, Durga and Ganga temples.

Mahanirvani Ghat

Another ghat made pucca by the Raja of Panchkot, this ghat has the Mahanirvani Akhara. During the Kumbh Mela, the Naga sadhus stay at the *akhara*. There are four small Shiva temples built by the King of Nepal inside the akhara. It is believed that Lord Buddha had taken a bath at this ghat. Mother Teresa's Missionaries of Charity has its destitute home here.

Shivala Ghat

This ghat was built by Raja Balwant Singh, the Maharaja of Banaras from 1738 to 1770. The Brahmendra Math, established by him here, today is a popular place for south Indian pilgrims to stay. The King of Nepal, Sanjay Vikram Shah also built a small palace above the ghat in the 19th century.

Gularia Ghat

Named after a huge *gular* (fig) tree, this ghat was built by a rich businessman called Lallooji Agrawal in 1820. Today, it is a place where the milkmen of the city bring their cattle in order to bathe them.

Dandi Ghat

This ghat takes its name from the Dandi ascetics who live in the neighbourhood above the ghat. This ghat was also constructed by Lallooji Agrawal, in 1812, with the help of Babu Sagarmal, and rebuilt by the Uttar Pradesh government in 1958.

Hanuman Ghat

Here lies a temple dedicated to Hanuman, built by Tulsidas, and shrines honouring the nine planets. There is also a temple of Rameshwar, an incarnation of Shiva worshipped by south Indians. The devotional teacher of the Krishna Bhakti cult, Vaibhav, lived here during the fifteenth century. The neighborhood above the *ghat* is populated with south Indian residents. The famous Juna *akhada* of the Naga *sadhus* is located above the ghat. Its chief priest Hariharnath got the ghat paved in the mid 19th century; subsequently, the Raja of Mysore rebuilt it.

Prachin Hanuman Ghat

This ghat is associated with the Bhakti saint Vallabha, who

lived in the 15th century. His birthday is celebrated at the ghat in the month of Baisakh. Both the old and new Hanuman Ghats were built by a priest called Mahant Hariharnath around 1825.

Karnataka Ghat

Built by the Maharaja of Mysore in 1920, this ghat houses a Sati shrine. There is also a small temple dedicated to one of the Bhairavas, Ruru (the Dog). Above the ghat lies a dharmashala built by the maharaja.

Harishchandra Ghat

Named after the legendary King Harishchandra, this is an ancient ghat, and one of the two cremation ghats on the Ganga in Varanasi. Harishchandra was the twenty-eighth king of the Solar dynasty, and famous for his piety and scrupulous adherence to justice. Challenged by the Gods to prove his truthfulness and charity, he not only subjected himself to all trials and tribulations, but lost all his wealth and kingdom; finally selling his wife, son and himself into slavery to a greedy slave dealer called Chandala, the keeper of the cremation ghats. When his son was bitten by a snake and died, the dead body was brought for cremation to his ghat. Not wishing to favour his family, he asked a cremation fee from his wife, who had barely any clothes to cover herself. She proposed that they join their son on his funeral pyre. The Gods, moved by his honesty, restored all his belongings and his kingdom to him. Indra created a special city in heaven for him, and it is said that on a clear night, the city is just about visible.

My memories of Harishchandra Ghat are painful, as they would for any Banarasi whose loved ones pass away. This is where, on an early October evening, my father was cremated. I remember my elder brother and I, hand in hand, lighting his pyre amidst the chanting of mantras, and then sitting on the stone steps watching, tearfully, the fire rise against the setting sun. Today, there is an electric crematorium on the ghat to prevent the river from being polluted by half-burnt bodies cast into the river because the relatives of the dead did not have enough money to buy firewood, but the Doms do not allow it to operate.

This ghat was built by Narayan Dikshit, the religious guru of the Peshwas, in 1740. However, it was made pucca only in 1988. The ghat has a temple dedicated to Kashi Kamakotishwar, built in the south Indian style. There are a vast number of images of different Gods and Goddesses at this temple.

Lali Ghat

This ghat is named after a saint called Lali Baba of Champaran in Bihar who lived there. The Gudardas *akhada* established by him has its headquarters here. The ghat was paved by the Maharaja of Vijayanagaram in the 19th century, and has small shrines of Shiva, Ganesh and Hanuman on its steps.

Prabhu Ghat

One of the few unpaved ghats, this is where the washermen of Varanasi bring their bundles of clothes to wash. A series of stone slabs jut into the river, and at any time of the day, the *dhobis* can be seen pounding the cotton garments against them to clear the dirt.

Vijayanagaram Ghat

This ghat was built by the Maharaja of Vijayanagaram, and is another favourite of pilgrims from South India. In the early 20th century, his succesor gave away the palace above the ghat to the saint Swami Karpatri, and his ashram is located in the palace today.

Kedar Ghat

This ghat is meticulously eulogized, in the Kashi Khand. At the top lies the temple of Kedareshwar, the patron deity of the southern sacred segment of old Kashi. The ghat is easily recognised from the river, by its red and white stripes. The shrines of Tarakeshwar and Bhairav can also be found at the ghat.

Kedar Ghat built by the Maharaja of Vijayanagar and is named after Shiva's shrine in the Himalaya. Two brass figures and four armed *dwarpals* - door keepers - guard the entrance to the temple from the ghat. A little below is the Gauri (Parvati) Kund whose waters are said to have healing properties. It is a favourite haunt of Bengali and South Indian pilgrims, and is especially crowded with bathers during the solar and lunar eclipses, *Nirjala Ekadashi, Ganga Dusshera* and *Makar Sankranti* festivals.

Chauki Ghat

Built in the 19th century by the Kumara Swami Math, this ghat is known for the giant *pipal* (ficus) tree, which has a number of stone figures of the cobra – *naga* - at its base. The snakes are worshipped as symbols of the Earth Goddess, especially during the festival of Nag Panchami in the month of Shravan (July – August). The Naga Kupa (Snake well) lies nearby. Scribbles Café today offers American, Continental and Chinese food to visitors.

Ksemesvara Ghat

Earlier called Nala ghat after a drain nearby, this ghat was built in the early 18th century.The neighbourhood is dominated by Bengali residents. A monastery built by the followers of Kumara Swami can be seen on the top of the steps.

Mansarovar Ghat

This ghat was built by Raja Mansingh of Amer, the Rajput state near Jaipur. At the top of the ghat was once a sacred pond, said to be a replica of the famous, sacred lake by the same name high among the mountains in Tibet. The pond was flanked by some sixty temples. Pilgrims visiting Mansarovar carry water from this tank all the way to the Rameshwaram temple in the Tamil Nadu: great merit is believed to accrue from this offering.

Narad Ghat

The old name of this ghat was Kuvai ghat. The ghat was constructed by Dattatreya Swami in 1788, and takes its name from the temple of Naradeshwar built here in the 19th century. There are temples dedicated to Dattatreyashwar and the Dattatreya Math above the ghat.

Raja Ghat

This ghat was first built by the Maratha chief Balajirao, in 1720, and subsequently repaired by Amrita Rao Peshwa in 1807. There is an Annapurna Math and a palace on the ghat. At present different cultural activities are organised by Intach (the Indian National Trust for Arts and Cultural Heritage) and Hotel Clarks on a boat, for their foreign visitors.

Khori Ghat

One of the most impressive collection of temples lies above this ghat. The ghat was made pucca by Kavindra Narain Singh.

Pandey Ghat

In 1805, this ghat was built in honour of a famous wrestler who established a wrestling academy – akhara – here. His name was Babua Pandey. Earlier, the ghat was part of Sarveshwar Ghat.

Sarveshwar Ghat

The ghat was erected by Mathura Pandey in the late 18th century. An image of Sarveshwar, and the Ganga Keshava Tirtha are nearby.

Digpatia Ghat

This was built by the Raja of Digpatia, in East Bengal, in 1830. The palace above the ghat is a magnificent example of the architecture of Bengal, and is currently the location of the Kashi Ashram.

Chausatthi Ghat

This ghat is described in the Kashi Khanda with respect to two notable pilgrimages : the Yogini Tirtha and the Agatsya Tirtha. There is a temple of Chausatthi Devi above the ghat, on 12th dark-half of *Chaitra* (March /April), and shrines dedicated to Kali, Shiva, Ganesh and Kartikeya here. Many pilgrims pay a visit to the Yogini Temple and take a ritual bath at this ghat on the occasion of *Shukla Ekadashi* in the month of February/March. The ghat was home to the Sanskrit scholar Madhusudan Saraswati in the 16th century. It was paved by the Raja of Bengal, Pratapaditya, in 1670, and subsequently repaired by the Raja of Digpatia.

Rana Mahal Ghat

This is an extended part of the preceding ghat, and was built around 1675 by Rana Jagat Singh of the Udaipur state in Rajasthan. The palace at the ghat is a good example of Rajasthani palace architecture, with three prominent turrets and fine stonework balconies. At the top, there is a shrine of Vakratunda Vinayak, one among the 56 protector Gods of the city.

Darbhanga Ghat

This is another ghat with a magnificent palace, built by the Raja of Darbhanga in Bihar, in 1920. The Neelkanth Shiva temple and a shrine dedicated to Kukuteshwar lie above the ghat.

Munshi Ghat

The finance minister in the court of the Raja of Nagpur, Sridhar Narayan Munshi, built this ghat in 1812. The ghat was thereafter named in his honour.

Ahilyabai Ghat

This is a ghat named in the honour of Ahilyabai Holkar, the Maratha Queen of Indore who was responsible for rebuilding the Vishwanath Temple, as it exists today, in 1777. She built a vast palace above the ghat, as well as a Hanuman temple in 1785. Near the entrance of the Hanuman temple are several lesser shrines; below the palace there are three verandahs for pilgrims to take rest. These have now been taken over by boatmen and local priests. In the evening, Bengali women from the neighbouring part of the city sing devotional songs at the ghat.

Shitala Ghat

Named after the famous Shitala temple here, this ghat is a place for special worship by newly married couples and their close family members. It also takes the spillover of bathers and devotees from the neighbouring Dasashwamedh Ghat. In the monsoons, the steps to the temple go underwater, and visitors to the temple must take a boat. The ghat was built by Narayan Dikshit in 1740.

Dashashwamedh Ghat

Quite simply, Dasashwamedh is the busiest and one of the oldest ghats in Varanasi. The origin of the ghat's name – Ten Horse Sacrifice – goes back to the legend of King Divodasa. According to the story, Shiva could not come to Kashi because it was occupied by the incorruptible Divodasa. Among the many schemes that were hatched was a plan wherein Lord Brahma came to the city disguised as a brahmin, and asked Divodasa to help him perform the great sacrifice. The money required was large, the list of essential ritual items long, and the Gods assumed that Divodasa would get things wrong. No such thing happened, Divodasa made flawless arrangements for the sacrifice, and the ten *ashwamedha* sacrifices were carried out by Brahma on the banks of the Ganga. The spot hereafter came to be known as the Dasashwamedh Ghat.

The Dashashwamedh Ghat built by the Maratha, Peshwa Balaji Baji Rao I in 1735. The temples of Sultankesvara, Brahmesvara, Varahesvara, Abhay Vinayak, the Ganga (goddess),and Bandi Devi are close by, at the top of the Ghat. These shrines are linked to several important pilgrimages. On tenth light-half of *Jyestha* (May-June.) Ganga is worshipped on a grand scale in the Ganga temple. The sacred bath on the occasion of solar and lunar eclipses, and also on the starting day of bath-ritual period in the month Pausa and Magha (December-January) are important festive occasions. There are two alternate routes to reach the ghat, from the main road from Godowlia and the main entrance to the Vishwanath Gali. Two hundred years ago, this road was the path taken by a stream called the Godowlia Nala, which connected the lake at Beniya, and the river Ganga. Locals consider Godowlia to be the corrupted version of Godavari, hence the confluence of the two rivers at Dasashwamedh was an auspicious place.

The road forks in front of the Dasashwamedh Lodge – the right one goes to the main bathing ghat, and is flanked by beggars and vendors selling flowers, vegetables and fruit. Cows amble by, trying to grab a bite of the greens on sale. As one nears the steps of the ghat, the small shrine of Ganga Ma can be seen on the right. The left road leads to the ghat from where boats are hired. Anyone carrying a camera is immediately surrounded by boatmen offering rides, speaking in tongues that try to place the person in the state of their origin. On one such occasion, I was there with my wife and sister-in-law, who conversed in Bangla, my nephew who spoke English with an American accent, and my brother who spoke with me in native Banarasi boli. A boatman who came after us blurted out, exasperatedly, "Will you tell us where you folks are from? Are you trying to confuse us on purpose?"

Prayag Ghat

This is a ghat that takes its name from the holy *sangam* – the meeting place of the Ganga and the Yamuna rivers at Allahabad. There are shrines dedicated to Prayageshwar, Shooltankeshwar, Brahmeshwar and Prayag Madhav, all incarnations of Shiva at the ghat. A tall but disused temple, in ochre, stands prominent above the steps. The temple and the ghat were built by the queen of Digpatia state in Bengal.

Rajendra Prasad Ghat

Formerly known as Ghora Ghat, this was once the landing spot for horses after they'd crossed the river on boats. Horses would also be bought and sold at this spot. It is believed by some that in the 2nd century A.D., after the Ten-Horse Sacrifice was performed, a stone statue of a horse was erected at this ghat. Above the ghat lie recently built shrines dedicated to Shiva, Durga and Ram Panchayatan. In 1979, the ghat was renamed in the memory of Dr. Rajendra Prasad, the first President of India, and a bust erected in his honour. It is the site of the annual classical music festival, which takes place in the month of November every year.

Man Mandir Ghat

This ghat takes its name from the beautiful mansion built by Akbar's general Raja Sawai Man Singh in 1600. There is a large courtyard paved with marble in the centre of the building, and the spacious rooms have windows of stained glass overlooking the Ganga. The balconies are intricately carved in stone, and a cool breeze blows into the rooms no matter how high the thermometer registers. In 1710, Sawai Raja Jaisingh of Jaipur built an observatory here around the same time that he built the better known observatories of Jantar Mantar in Delhi, and Jaipur. The inscription, on a marble plaque, makes for interesting reading:

'Originally constructed by Maharaja Sawai Jai Singhji of Jaipur in AD 1710. Was restored in AD 1911 by the order of Major

General His Highness Saramad-i-Rajah-i-Hindustan Raj Rajinder Sri Maharajadhiraja Sir Sawai Madho Singh Bahadur Knight Grand Commander of the Most Eminent Order of the Indian Empire, Knight Grand Cross of the Royal Victorian Order. Donat of the order of the Hospital of St John of Jerusalem. Doctor of Laws (Edin) of Jaipur. Conveyed by Mumtazuddoulah Nawab Sir Mohomed Fyazali Khan Bahadur Minister K.C.I.E, K.C.V.O, C.S.I through Rai Bahadur Khwas Bala Baksh. Under the Superintendence of Lala Chaman Lal Darogha Imarut Jaipur, Chandulal Overseer, Pandit Gokul Chund, State Astronomer, Bhagirat Mistri.'

A long flight of stairs from the river takes you to the entrance of the mansion that leads to the observatory. In the morning, wrestlers from the nearby akhara can be seen going about their strenuous exercise regimen. The terrace of the mansion is replete with fascinating, giant stone instruments to study the movement of the sun, stars and other heavenly bodies. The first instrument that one sees after entering the observatory is the Mural Quadrant, or Bhittiyantra. It is used to measure the sun's altitude and zenith distance at noon, and consists of a wall eleven feet high and nine feet one and a quarter inch wide in the plane of the meridian. Two large circles, one of stone and the other of lime, and a large square follow. They were used to measure the degrees of the azimuth. The giant sundial tells the time accurately, nearly three centuries after it was built. A huge instrument, called the Yantrasamrat (the King of Instruments) allowed the astronomer to measure the distance from the meridian, the decliation and ascension of any star and the sun. Another giant instrument here is the Digansayantra, which measures the degrees of azimuth of a planet or star. It consists of a pillar four feet two inches high around which is a circular wall of the same height and at a distance of seven feet three and a quarter inches, and yet another wall of exactly double the height, at a distance of three feet two inches from the first wall. The upper surfaces of both walls are marked with the points of the compass and divided into three hundred and sixty degrees.

Close by, at the top of the ghat are the shrines of Someshvara (after which the ghat was once named), Rameshvara and Sthuladanta Vinayak. The Someshvara linga is said to be a representation of the linga at the Somnath Temple in Gujarat. The temple is believed to be a hospital as Someshvara is thought of as a powerful healer, and devotees pray here in the anticipation of cure from disease of every kind.

Varahi Ghat

This ghat takes its name from the temple of Varahi, one of the mother Goddesses, in the lane above the ghat. This is where the Dom Raja, the King of the Burning Ghats, has his garish mansion. The ghat was made pucca by the Uttar Pradesh government in 1958.

Tripura Bhairavi Ghat

Named after the shrine of Tripura Bhairavi, the female consort of Tripureshwar, this ghat was built by the Maharaja of Banaras, Mahip Narain Singh and Pandit Dayanand Giri in the late 18th century, who set up a *math* here. One can see shrines of Shiva, Vishnu, Shakti, Ganesh and Surya below a giant peepul (ficus) tree at the top of the ghat.

Meer Ghat

Built by Mir Rustam Ali in 1735, this ghat represents the two old sites of Jarasandhesvara and Vriddhaditya, and was formerly referred to as Jarasandh Ghat. Pilgrims throw flowers and raw-rice in the Ganga and remember them here. Bathing here on the occasion of *Krishna Chaturdashi*, in the month of Kartik (October-November) is considered to be auspicious. The steps lead to the sacred well called Dharamkoopa, which is surrounded by five temples and also the Devdaseshwara linga. One of the temples, Dharmesha, is associated with the myth of Yama's (Lord of death) power over the fate of dead everywhere on the earth, except in Kashi. Yet another temple, that of Vishalakshi Devi, was built in the south Indian style. The temple houses images of the nine Gauris, whose sight is believed to rid devotees of all troubles associated with a worldly existence. The Bhajan Ashram at the ghat, built by the businessman Ganpat Rai Khemka of Calcutta, is home to widows from Bengal. The centre of the Sikh religious order of Nanak Panthis stands above the Meer ghat. They distribute free food and ayurvedic medicines to the needy everyday.

Phuta Ghat

This was formerly known as Yajneshwar Ghat, and made pucca by Swami Maheshwarananda in the 19th century. The Vishala Gaja (Great Elephant) Tirtha lies nearby.

Nepali Ghat

Patronized by the Nepalese of Varanasi, this ghat was built in 1902 by Nanhi Babu.

Lalita Ghat

Though this ghat is named after the famous goddess Lalita Devi, there are a number of important shrines here. The well-known Vishnu temple of Ganga Keshava and the shrine to the Ganga, called Bhagirathi Devi are located on this ghat. But what attracts attention the most is the 'Nepali' temple – which is said to house a replica of the famous Pashupateshwara of Kathmandu. Built in wood, with double sloping roofs in the Nepali style, the walls of the temple are replete with erotic sculpture, which makes local tourist guides salaciously call it 'mini-Khajuraho'. The area above the ghat is home to several *maths.* Notable among them are the Siddhgiri Math, Umraogiri Math, Moksha Bhavan and the Nepali Kothi.

Amroha Ghat

Formerly called Raja Rajeshwari Ghat, this ghat was built

by a rich merchant Babu Keshav Deva in the early 19th century. The Brahmanala Tirtha lies nearby.

Jalasayi Ghat

The ghat takes its name from the ritual of putting a dead body into the water, before it is cremated. This is part of the upcoming cremation ghat, Manikarnika.

Khirki Ghat

Named after a window from which attendants can watch a body burn, this ghat has a pilgrims rest house, built by Baldev Das Birla. There are five Sati shrines under a pipal (ficus) tree here, indicative of the widows who must have committed Sati here.

Manikarnika Ghat

If on one hand Varanasi enjoys the morbid reputation of a cremation ground, on the other nothing can be more auspicious than being cremated at the Manikarnika Ghat. From the river, it is easy to spot – smoke rises from the burning pyres, and blackens all the stone buildings around even as the grieving relatives of the deceased hover around to complete the rituals. Those bodies that have just arrived lie swathed in red or white cloth at the edge of the ghat, as the funeral pyres are prepared. A tall soot blackened tower with a clock that has stopped, and spires of several temples rise above the ghat. Firewood stands stacked around the steps of the ghat, in the spaces between the turrets of a great, four postered, disused temple built by Rani Ahilyabai Holkar, and in the boats nearby. The flames can be seen from across the river, and it is said that the fires have never, ever stopped burning here.

The Doms are the Lords of Manikarnika. No one knows their origin, but even Raja Harishchandra was sold in slavery to a Dom. They control every part of the cremation ritual – from selling the firewood, to collecting the taxes for every corpse, to keeping the fire from which every pyre is lit burning. Depending on how prosperous the family of the dead are, the body could be burnt on a pyre of sandalwood costing Rs 20000, or a pyre of *sal*, for Rs 1500. The eldest son of the dead, clad in a white *dhoti*, head shaven, walks anti-clockwise around the pyre after lighting a bunch of twigs of dried *kusha* grass, and lights the pyre as an offering to the God of Fire, Agni. Then comes the agonizing wait for the corpse to completely burn, as the Doms stoke the fire. Curiously, there is no stench. It is believed that the ritual of dipping the corpse into the Ganga purifies it. Finally, the mourner cracks the skull with a stick – in a ritual called the *Kapalkriya*, to release the soul and let it go to Heaven.

But Manikarnika is as much associated with life as it is with death. Bathing in the ancient Manikarnika Kund is one of the goals of pilgrims during their circumambulation of the city. It is said that Lord Vishnu carved the Kund with his discus, hence its older name was Chakrapushkarni – the Discus Lotus-Pool. He filled the hole he had dug, with the sweat of his limbs to create the pool, and proceeded to perform severe austerities for 500,000 years. Shiva appeared to him and asked him for a boon, upon which Vishnu asked him to always live in Shiva's presence. The delighted Shiva shook so hard in pleasure that one of his jewelled earrings fell into the pool, giving it the name Manikarnika – jewelled earring. Vishnu's footsteps are set in a round marble stone, and can be seen on the ghat – pilgrims touch the Lord's feet and leave flowers. The kund is said to be older than the time when Ganga came to Varanasi at the heels of Bhagirath. It is situated north of the cremation ground, in a depression some twenty feet square at the bottom, and sixty feet square at the top. During the monsoons, water from the Ganga fills the Kund up, and deposits a load of silt when she retreats. The steps are cleared annually, and the walls whitewashed.

At the ghat lies the dramatic temple, half sunk into the river. The local legend has it that a nobleman decided that he would build a temple to repay the debt that he owed to his mother for giving birth to him and for bringing him up. He built a grand temple in stone, which everyone around admired in awe. But on the day of the temple's consecration, the temple tilted and half sunk into the river – since no son can ever repay his mother's debts.

The ghat houses shrines to Shiva, Vishnu and Manikarni Devi. Shiva takes the form of Tarakeshwar, the manifestation which whispers into the ears of the dead the mantra that liberates them from the cycle of birth and rebirth. The image of Vishnu can be found in the northern wall of the Kund, in a small shrine. Manikarni Devi is shown sitting cross-legged next to the Kund, with Shiva and Parvati on one side and Vishnu on the other. The temple of Manikarnikesvar is located at the top, slightly into the city and approachable from the ghat by taking a steeply ascending lane south of the Kund. The *linga* of this temple, set dramatically underground at the bottom of a deep shaft, could at one time be reached by a tunnel originating from the ghat itself.

Bajirao Ghat

Also called Dattatreya Ghat after the scholar saint who was supposed to be the incarnation of the Holy Trinity, this ghat was built in 1735 by Bajirao Peshwa. In 1830, the queen of Gwalior, Baijabai, got the ghat repaired.

Scindhia Ghat

Formerly known as the Vireshwara Ghat, after the temple of the same name at the top, the ghat was paved in stone in 1780 by Rani Ahilyabai Holkar of Indore. In 1829, Queen Baijabai, wife of Daulatarao Scindhia of Gwalior, had to get it repaired and remodelled after part of the ghat sank into the river. This had to be done again in 1937 by their successors, and the ghat now takes its name from the Scindhias.The shrines of Vashisth, Vamadev and Atmavresvara are at the top of the ghat. Its broad steps are a favourite for young boys and men to dive from for a swim when the waters of the river rise in the monsoons.

Sankata Ghat

This is one of the ghats along the Ganga which bears a profusion of temples. The ghat itself is named after Sankata Devi, who is found in a lane right above the ghat. Near the top is a new shrine to Santoshi Ma, the Goddess of Satisfaction. There are shrines of the Goddesses Katyayani and Siddheshwari, and three Vinayakas – Harishchandra, Chintamani and Mitra. The ghat was made pucca in 1825 by the widow of Pandit Vishwambhar Dayal, called 'Panditain' by the local residents, and his nephews.

Ganga Mahal Ghat

This ghat is an old part of the Yamesvara Ghat. The Raja of Gwalior, Jiyaji Rao Scindhia built the majestic palace here in 1864, and paved the ghat. The turreted palace has two gateways for entry, and a temple of Radha-Krishna inside. The ghat was later repaired and rebuilt by Govinda Bali Kirantankara.

Bhonsale Ghat

The Maratha king Bhonsale of Nagpur built this ghat in 1780, and later in 1795 made it pucca, establishing the temple of Laksmi Narayan and building a majestic, turreted palace with elaborate balconies. Three important shrines near the ghat are those of Nageshwara, Yameshwara and Yamaditya. This part of the city is home to Maharashtrian and Gujarati communities.

Naya Ghat

Formerly called Gularia Ghat, this ghat was made pucca recently, in 1960.

Steps leading down to Lolark Kund

Sculpture at Mahadev Temple, Kedar Gali

The building housing a Power Plant, Bhadaini

Sadhu on the Ghats

Closeup of ghat architecture

Doorway at Nilkantheshwar

Flooded Nai Sarak

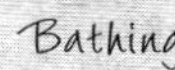

Bathing

Rani Barahi Mandir, Gurudham

Singh Vahana at Bhimachandi

Lawn for Meditation, Gandhian Institute

Omkareshwar, with graves in the foreground

Sadhu Bathing

Fish iconography at Nilkantheshwar

An image of Ma Ganga

The Temple at Kardameshwar

Swami Narayan Mandir at Machhodari

St. Paul's Church, Sigra

Krishna, from a panel at Kardameshwar

Sakshi Vinayak at Rameshwar

Periwinkle Offerings

Worshippers

Virupaksha

Dharamshala at Kardameshwar

Sunken Temple at Manikaranika

Scindia Ghat

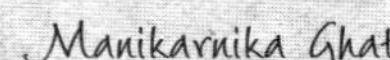

Manikarnika Ghat

Lal Khan ka Mauza, Rajghat

Nagari Pracharini Sabha Library

Manikarnika Kund

Manikarnika : Cremation Ground

Rope Climbing

Akhara

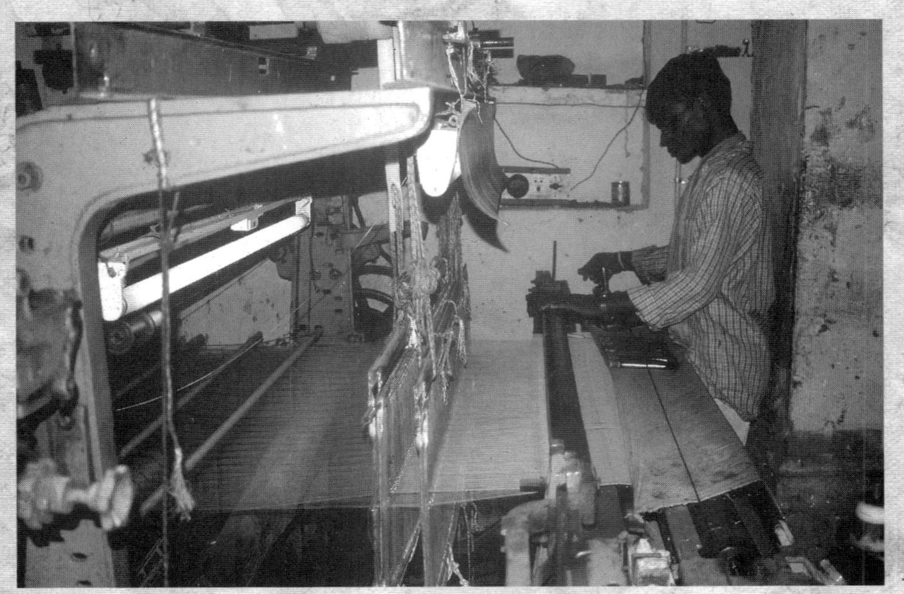

Weaver at a powerloom

Observatory at Sanskrit Vishwavidyalaya

Roadside Vendors

Chatwallah

Hot Kachoris being fried

Wooden Stuff

Rewri

Piles of Flattened Rice

Potter

Flute seller

Stoneware

Stretching and colouring Yarn

Palace Gates, Ramnagar

Offices of the Raja

Birla Hostel

Thandai

Pickleseller

Ganesh Ghat

This ghat was named after the temple of Ganesh here. There are shrines of Bhadreshwar and Nagesh Vinayak, and the water tirtha of Iksavaku at this ghat. The ghat was built by Amritrao Peshwa in 1807, and he also set up the temple of Amrit Vinayak. The older name of the ghat was Vighneshwara Ghat. The ghat is the site for a fair in the month of Bhadra (August-September), on the occasion of *Shukla Chaturthi.*

Mehta Ghat

Formerly part of the succeeding Ram Ghat, this ghat took its name from a hospital built by Vallabhram Shaligram Mehta, a rich businessman from Calcutta, in 1962. The ghat was made pucca by the Varanasi Municipal Corporation in the 1960s, but unlike other stone flagged ghats, this one was paved with brick and mortar. The Sangved Sanskrit Vidyalaya, located above the ghat, imparts Vedic education to students.

Ram Ghat

This ghat is associated with the Rama Tirtha at the shrine of Veer Rameshwar, and the temple of Ram Panchayatan. The temple of Ram at the ghat was originally built by the Raja of Jaipur, Sawai Jai Singh, and destroyed by Aurangzeb, only to be rebuilt in the 18th century by the former's successor. The ghat is the setting for celebrating the Ram Navami festival in the month of Chaitra (March-April), as also the worship of Khandoba by the Maharashtrian community in November-December. Two other water tirthas, Kala Ganga and Tamara Varaha, can be found here.

Jatar Ghat

This ghat was built by Diwan Balaji Jatar, the minister in the court of Raja Jiyaji Rao of Gwalior, in the 19th century. The multi-storeyed palace above the ghat is home to the artistic Lakshminarayan temple, which has some fantastic mirrorwork mosaic on its walls. Interestingly, the ghat was earlier called

Chor Ghat, because pilgrims who would bathe here would return to find their belongings stolen!

Raja Gwalior Ghat

This is part of the earlier Jatar Ghat, and was built by Raja Jiyaji Rao Shinde in 1760. There are three small Shiva shrines at the ghat.

Mangala Gauri Ghat

This ghat is named after the White Goddess, Mangala Gauri, who shares the space above the ghat with images of Gabhatishwar, Raghavendreshwar, Charchika Devi and Mangala Vinayaka.

Beni Madhav Ghat

Part of the Panchganga ghat, the ghat is named after the famous 10th century temple of Bindu Madhava, which was demolished by Aurangzeb.

Panch Ganga Ghat

This is one of the most sacred of the riverfront sites. It is believed that five mythical rivers flow into the Ganga here - the Yamuna, the Saraswati, the Kirna (sun's rays), the Dharmanada (river of dharma) and the Dhutpapa (cleansed on sins). Once the site of the legendary Bindumadhava Temple, it is today one of the most impressive and incongruous of Varanasi's ghats, for the giant Dharahara Mosque rises high above the skyline at Panchganga. The ghat has many a legend associated with it. One of them is to do with the mystic Kabir. Kabir wanted the great teacher Vaidanta Ramanand to accept him as a pupil. Since he was a Muslim from a low caste, Ramanand turned him away. So Kabir lay down on the setps, on the path he knew the guru to take every day, for his bath in the river. As Ramanand trippped on Kabir, he uttered the words 'Ram, Ram', which Kabir considered as a blessing. Ramanand's ashram can still be found at the top of the ghat. Panchganga was also where the 17th century poet Jagannath composed the poem Ganga Lahari in praise of the river. In the tradition of true romantic tragedy, Jagannath was ostracised by the Brahmin community to which he belonged, after he fell in love with a Muslim woman from the court of the Mughal emperor Shahjehan. He and his lover sat on the fifty-second step of the Panchganga Ghat, and he sang the poem he had composed, all fifty-two verses of it. With each verse, the river rose, one step, finally forgiving, purifying, blessing and sweeping away the lovers. Then, Tulsi Das composed his famous writing about the Bindumadhav temple, the *Vinay-Patrika* here.

Today, the temple of Bindumadhav lies next to the great mosque. It was built in the 18th century by the Maharaja of Satara, Bhawan Rao; and it is a Maharashtrian, Acharya Muralidhar Ganesh Patwardhan, who is its officiating priest. The shrine of Mangala Gauri lies nearby. The ghat has many small stone cubicles, some empty, others with images of Vishnu or Shiva. One of the cubicles is in honour of the five rivers – Panchganga. It is considered most auspicious to bathe here in the month of Kartik, when Shiva is said to take his bath. There is a stone pillar, called Deep Hazari Sthamb, with a thousand sockets that hold lamps. It was built by Ahilyabai Holkar in the 18th century. These, when lighted on the night of full moon, look mesmerizing. In the southern part of the Dharahara mosque is the giant Kanganwali Haveli built by Raja Jaisingh of Amer. This building houses a *pathshala*, where students are imparted Vedic education. The ghat is home to two *maths* – the Gokarna Math, where stands a Lakshimi Narayan Temple, and the Tailangaswami Math.

The stone steps at the ghat were made by Raja Todar Mal in 1580, and repaired by Bajirao Peshwa, and again by Sripatirao Peshwa and Pant Pratinidhi of Andhra Pradesh in 1775.

Durga Ghat

This ghat derived its name from its association with the Brahmacharini Durga temple. In 1772, Narayan Dixit, a guru of the Maratha Peshwas purchased land from local resident fishermen and built two ghats: Durga and the succeeding one, Brahma ghat. Today, several Maharashtrian Vedic scholars are known to live in this area. At the ghat exist the Marakandeya and Kharva Narsimha Tirthas, and at the top of the steps is a shrine of Kharava Narsimha. On the full moon day of the month of Kartik, young men show their fighting mettle by participating in a *dangal* (wrestling bout).

Brahma Ghat

This ghat is named after the temples of Brahma and Brahmesvara. The legend goes that, when Lord Brahma visited Varanasi, and wanted a place to stay, Lord Shiva gave Him this piece of land. Pilgrims visit the notable shrine of Bhairava Tirtha at the ghat, which is also the seat of a monastery, the Kasi Math Sansthana Sudhindra Tirtha Swami. There are temples dedicated to Bindu Madhava and Lakshmi Narasimha at the ghat.

Bundi Parakota Ghat

The Raja of Bundi (in Rajasthan), Surajana Hada, made this ghat in 1580. The ruins of a grand palace constructed by him can still be seen today. In the 19th century, one of his successors, Rao Pritam Singh, rebuilt the ghat. At the top of the ghat are the shrines of Seshamadhav, Annapurna and Karnaditya.

Adi Sitala Ghat

An extension of the earlier ghat, this was repaired by Narayan Dikshit in 1772. The ghat takes its name from the temple of the elder Shitala, and has shrines devoted to Nageshwari Devi (the Snake Goddess), Narayani and Shankha Madhav (the Conch Shiva). A festival is held at the ghat on the occasion of *Shukla Navami* in the month of Chaitra (March-

April), and attracts bathers from all over the city. This part of the city is inhabited by people of Rajasthani origin.

Lala Ghat

This ghat was built by the Raja of Tijara, Rajasthan, around 1900. Thirty-five years later, Baldev Das Birla built a palace, a school and hostel for students, and a free pilgrim's rest house here. The two ends of the ghat were unpaved till 1988, and used by washermen, till the Varanasi Municipality made them pucca. The prominent temple at the ghat is one dedicated to Goprekreshwar.

Hanuman Garhi Ghat

Named after the eponymous site in Ayodhya, this ghat is appropriately home to the Ganga Akhara. The saint Baba Shyamaldas lived at the ghat, and one of his disciples, Tekchandra Sahu, built the ghat in 1972. There is a shrine dedicated to Gopi Govinda near the ghat.

Gai Ghat

This ghat gets its name from the huge image of a sacred cow (Gai) – this was a place for cows and buffalos to drink water from the river in medieval times. It is believed that if one has killed a cow, whether by intention, or by mistake, taking a bath in the Ganga here will redeem the killer of his sin. In 12th century, when the centre of Varanasi lay in Adi Keshava, this ghat was considered the southern limit of the city. At the top of the ghat, there are four images of Bageshwari Devi, Nageshwari Devi (the Snake-Goddess), Mukhanirmalika Devi (the Pure-Faced Goddess) and Samhara Bhairava. On the southern end of the ghat is a palace built by the King of Nepal. There are several temples at the ghat, dedicated to Gauri, Lakshminarayan, Hanuman, Shiva and Shitala. Several Shivlingas, and a three-foot high stone image of Nandi can be seen on the steps of the ghat.

Badrinarayan Ghat

Formerly called Balabai Ghat after the Raja of Gwalior who built it in the 19th century, the ghat is home to the shrines of Nageshwar, Nagesh Vinayak and Nara Narayan Keshav. The last is derived from the temple at Badrinath, and gives the ghat its name. The festival to honour Nara Narayan, a form of Vishnu, is celebrated here on the full moon day in the month of Pausha (December – January).

Trilochan Ghat

This ghat is named after the famous image of Trilochana (three-eyed) Shiva. His *linga* is known as Trilochaneswar. The Kashi Khanda contains several verses glorifying this ghat and its associate tirtha, the Pilatippala Tirtha. The ghat was repaired by Narayana Dikshit in 1772, and by Nathu Bala Peshwa of Pune in 1795. The shrine of Varanasi Devi lies above the ghat, as do the temples of Saraswatishwar, Shanteshwar, Bhimeshwar, Pranav Vinayak, and Arunaditya. The holiest day to bathe at this ghat is on *Shukla Tritiya* in the month of Baisakh (April-May), when the image of Trilochan is decorated , and devotional songs sung at the temple.

Gola Ghat

Since the 12th century, this site was used as ferry point and was known for a number of granaries (gola) in this part of the city – which gave it its name. Today, the ghat is used only by washermen.

Nandu Ghat

Built by Dwarkanath Chakravarti, a resident of Bhowanipore of Calcutta, in 1940, the ghat has a shrine dedicated to Nandrishwar. There is also an Akhara at this ghat. A small community of basket-weavers resides above the ghat.

Shukka Ghat

This ghat has an old water-front sacred spot, the Pranav Tirtha. At the top of the ghat is the Haridas Sevashram, where lies the Chandreshwar Shiva temple.

Telianala Ghat

This area was once populated by people belonging to the oil-presser caste, called Telis. The Hiranyagarba Tirtha is located at this ghat.

Phuta / Naya Ghat

This ghat was deserted in the 18th century, hence the name *Phuta*. After it was rebuilt by Narsingh Jaipal, of Bhabua in Bihar, in 1940, it was renamed Naya Ghat. Shrines dedictaed to Hanuman and Phutkreshwar Shiva can be found here.

Prahlad Ghat

This ghat is named after Prahlad, the great mythological devotee of lord Vishnu. The shrines of Prahladeshwar, Prahalad Keshava, Vidara Narasimha and Pichindala Vinayak can be found on the ghat. In the month of Baisakh, (April - May), a grand festival to honour the appearance of Narsimha ("Lion-Man", an incarnation of Lord Vishnu) is performed on a massive scale in the temple of Prahladeshwar.

Raj Ghat

Lying next to the Malviya Bridge (originally called Dufferin Bridge), this was the site of river crossings before modern engineering made it convenient. There are four water tirthas affiliated to this ghat: Sankhaya, Uddalaka, Hayagriva and Nilagriva. At the top of the ghat is a grand temple dedicated to the cobbler-saint Ravidas. Then rises a plateau, where excavations have revealed that this was once the heart of ancient Kashi. In the southern corner of the plateau is the tomb of Lal Khan, a minister of the Maharaja of Banaras. This is a fine Muslim structure ornamented with colored tiles and mosaic. Rajghat is also home to the Krishnamurthi Foundation School, one of the finest in the country and the Gandhian Institute, inaugurated by the late Jaiprakash Narayan in 1962.

Adi Keshava Ghat

This ghat is the oldest and the original (Adi) site of Lord Vishnu (Keshava) in Varanasi. It was prominent during the reign of the Gadhahavalas. The temple-complex of Adi Keshava has a pleasant pastoral setting on the bank above the confluence of the Varuna and the Ganga rivers. Of the oldest puranic listings of sacred sites in the city, this is one of them.

The *Charan Paduka* (foot print) of Vishnu in the Adi Keshava temple symbolizes the moment that Vishnu first placed his holy feet in Varanasi. Bathing at the confluence of Varuna and Ganga and paying visit to Sangameshwar (Lord of Confluence) is considered auspicious. An excellent *linga*, that of Sangameshwar, is believed to have been installed by Brahma at this confluence. The Purana says, "If a man shall become pure taking his bath at the confluence of these divine rivers and then worship Sangameswar, he need not fear rebirth". Close to Sangameshwar is the four faced Brahmeshwar Lingam. The cluster of temples that one sees today at Adi Keshava were constructed by the Scindia kings in the 18th century.

☙

Swatchha Ganga Abhiyan

The first reaction of many a western tourist, upon seeing the Ganga is, how can anyone consider this dirty river holy, and pure? For the millions of Hindu pilgrims visiting Varanasi to take a holy dip, their ancient ritual is threatened by untreated sewage dumped directly into the Ganga - along with the disposal of human corpses and animal carcasses, human and animal feces, and other pollutants.

The Swatchha Ganga Abhiyan (campaign) was launched in 1982 to increase public awareness about Ganga pollution, in keeping with their religious beliefs and lifestyles. It was the brainchild of Veer Bhadra Mishra, professor of Civil Engineering at Banaras Hindu University and Mahant (chief priest) of the Sankat Mochan Temple. Three years later, the Indian Government announced a clean-up plan for the Ganga: the 'Ganga Action Plan'. Unfortunately, sewage treatment facilities built between 1986-1993 did not led to effective relief of river pollution. Finally, the citizens of Varanasi decided to take matters into their own hands.

An ambitious three-year public awareness project in Varanasi, launched late in 2001, is making the causes of 'non-point pollution' better known and understood both locally and throughout India. These issues include open defecation, laundering activities (dhobi ghats) and removal of corpses and carcasses from the waterway. Pilgrims and citizens alike have been encouraged to adopt appropriate measures, including cleanup of the all the historic ghats. Boatmen and volunteers patrolling the 7 km stretch along the ghats are now removing human and animal corpses every day. They are transported to an island outside the town and buried with dignity. This removal program is conducted in liaison with municipal authorities. The boatmen engaged by the campaign are already removing plastic bags, floating sludge and litter every day from the river and the 84 ghats.

Dead bodies, including partly cremated corpses, are typically consigned to the river by next-of-kin who cannot afford proper cremation. Corpses do not contribute significantly to river pollution, but do entail public health considerations.

Numerous volunteers brief the public and pilgrims alike about pollution every day from three ghats that they have adopted-Assi, Rewa and Tulsi. This pilot project will be extended in stages to all of the ghats. A conference of pandas (priests) who conduct rituals along the ghats was held in February, 2002 under the auspices of the campaign. The priests discussed various ways of altering ingrained social habits that contribute to Ganga pollution.

In 1998 the Swatchha Ganga Environmental Education Centre was established at Tulsi Ghat. This is a joint initiative with Australian environmentalists, and aims at providing environmental education and heightened awareness in the community. A parallel effort funded by Sweden is also underway at Tulsi Vidya Niketan (a senior secondary school), led by Indian and Swedish volunteers. In January, 2002 a student mobilisation campaign was capped by a Chattra Sangha or student congress at Tulsi Ghat.

In 1999, Dr.Veer Bhadra Mishra, was nominated by Time Magazine as a 'Hero of the Planet' for bringing the plight of the Ganga to the attention of the world. He is also recipient of the UNEP Global 500 Roll of Honour and the subject of several films, including a Time Warner documentary hosted by American actress Jane Fonda.

ꟹ

Scholarship in Varanasi

FROM UNIVERSITIES TO GURUS

"The whole city (of Kashi) is a university. Unlike classes, departments and colleges, every house belonging to a Brahmin is a centre of education."

Bernier

ᏣᏰ

Varanasi has been a centre for scholars and pundits for as long as there have been historical records. Buddhist litera ture calls Varanasi *Brahma Vadhdhhana,* the centre of learning. Its religious tradition was accompanied by an equally prominent one of erudition. However, unlike the 'university centres' of Takshila, Vikramshila and Nalanda, education here was imparted by individual *acharyas.* Students who could not pay for their education would serve their teachers, with most education centred around the three Vedas and the Upanishads. It was in these early years that Dhanvantari wrote several books on Ayurveda, and the skilful surgeon Sushruta founded his school of medicine in Kashi. At the time of Ashoka, Sarnath was an important seat of Buddhist learning, with as many as five hundred students under some teachers. In the mid- fourteenth century, the Kashi Khanda, running into hundred chapters one of the most authoritative texts on life in ancient Kashi, was written. In the following centuries, Sant Kabir and Tulsidas emerged as the great proponents of the Bhakti tradition. The lamp of Sanskrit learning was kept burning from the 16th to 18th century by the Maharashtrian and Kannada Brahmin families that migrated to the city, later the pundits from Bengal and Mithila came to their support. In the 19th century, Bhartendu Harishchandra emerged as the great revivalist of the Hindi language.

Education in ancient Varanasi was a self-organizing system. Generally, schools had no buildings of their own. Education was imparted in temples, homes of teachers, private buildings donated by pious families, and even the ghats of the Ganga. A majority of the teachers were Brahmins who taught out of a sense of self-righteousness rather than for economic gain. Students did not race through examinations to pick up well-paying jobs; education was considered a lifelong pursuit.

With the arrival of the British in India, the education system began to gear itself towards the aim of technological and scientific advancement. In 1791, Jonathan Duncan established a Sanskrit pathshala. This was followed by the Banaras Anglo Indian Seminary set up by the East India Company in 1830. Later, the seminary and the pathshala were merged and renamed as the Queen's College.

The later half of nineteenth century witnessed cultural renaissance, in the hinter land cities of India. Varanasi was one of them. Annie Besant founded the Central Hindu College in 1898. But it was only in the early 20th century that Varanasi got its pre-eminent centre of learning – the Banaras Hindu University.

Banaras Hindu University: the historical perspective

The 1905 session of the Indian National Congress was held in Varanasi, and Pandit Madan Mohan Malaviya floated the idea of Banaras Hindu University at the session. He got overwhelming support, especially from Annie Besant, who came forward to help Malaviyaji in his plan of making Banaras Hindu University. In 1908, at the time of the Kumbh Mela at Allahabad the idea of a Hindu University was approved by Dharma Sansad presided over by the Shankaracharya of Kanchi. One only wishes that the current Dharma Sansad, which is pre-occupied with the building of the Ram Mandir at Ayodhya, were more farsighted. On December 15 1911, the Banaras Hindu University society was registered, and the Central Hindu College transferred to this society. Pandit Malaviya got the requisite funding of 1 crore rupees as per the requirements of 1904 University Act within no time.

Before 1911, when Malaviya wrote a letter to Hindus of India for contributing to the University fund, the idea of a Hindu University caught the imagination of prominent Hindus in all parts of India. Dated July 15th, 1911, Hindu University office, Allahabad, Pandit Malaviya addressed his letter to the Hindus of India. "It hardly needs saying that a large scheme like this (making of Banaras Hindu University) can succeed only with the hearty cooperation of thoughtful Hindus all over the country. I write you to kindly consent to be a member of the society and to ask other Hindu gentlemen of your district also to become members of it." The idea of a Hindu University paved way for the coming together of those who in the late 19th century in different parts of India were subscribing to new religious identities like the Arya Samaj, Sanatan Dharma, Brahmo Samaj, followers of Ramkrishna Mission, and the theosophists.

Pandit Malaviya chose Varanasi as a site for Hindu University with the purpose of having maximum appeal for Hindus from North and South to East and West. There had already been a tradition in all part of India among Hindus to pay at least one a visit to Varanasi, the city of Shiva. The Maharaja of Banaras, Sir Prabhu Narain Singh was magnanimous enough to donate not only a huge amount of money for starting a college of Indology devoted to the study of ancient Indian history and culture, but also granted 1700 acres of land to Hindu University Society. The magnificent structures that came into existence in the premises of Banaras Hindu University reflected the growing Hindu solidarity for a common cause. All the maharajas, zamindars, bankers, professionals, peasants and commoners vied with each other to record their contribution towards Banaras Hindu University. On February 4 1916, Basant Panchami day, the Viceroy and Governor General of India, Lord Hardinge laid the foundation stone of the university. The university began functioning from October 1 1917 with the Central Hindu College as its nucleus; the College of Oriental Learning and Théology was set up in 1918, and the Engineering College in 1919. In 1921, the Prince of Wales formally declared the university open, amidst huge celebration.

The ground of Hindu consciousness prepared by the movement for Banaras Hindu University was well capitalized on by Mahatma Gandhi when he came to address India for a political cause in the form of Non-Cooperation Movement in 1920. BHU was instrumental in supplying the men and ideas for the freedom movement in India. During the three great waves of the freedom struggle, i.e., the Non-Cooperation Movement (1920-22), the Civil Disobedience Movement (1930-33) and the Quit-India Movement (1942-45), the university made its mark by way of its Vice-Chancellor, Pt. Madan Mohan Malaviya (1919-1939), its teachers, students and *karmacharis* who took active part in the freedom movement and organized the masses to pose a stiff challenge to the British rule in India.

During the Non-Cooperation Movement, Pandit Malaviya invited Mahatma Gandhi to address the students of BHU. Malaviya Ji was opposed to students leaving their education and taking part in the Non-Cooperation Movement. While jointly addressing the students of BHU with Gandhiji on November 27, 1920, Malaviya Ji said:

"Mai kisi ko Chidia ki taraha pinjara me band karne par vishwash nahi karta. Jiska man Paradhi se hat gya hai aur jo vishwavidyala chorana chahata ho, woh awashya jay. Mere man me virodh ka bhav nahi hai. Jo rahana chahata hai, mehanet karke padhey. Isey Rashtra seva mane. Parmatma se puchiye ki

kya ap abhi desh ki seva layak ban gaye hain? Aapke liye adhyayan ka samay hai. Hamari peerhi ka kaam swaraj lana hai. Aapka dharam padhai me man lagana hai."

Gandhiji in his speech asked the students to leave the University for one year and take part in the Non-Cooperation Movement against the British rule. Gandhiji promised that he would get *Swaraj* – self rule - for India within one year. At the end of the speech the students were asked to raise hands in favour of the appeal of Gandhiji. Almost all the students raised their hands in favour of Non-Cooperation Movement and leaving the university for taking part in it. Malaviyaji who was presiding over the meet, allowed the students, with tears falling down his cheeks, to take part in the movement and assured them that the doors of BHU would always remain open for them. Some of the teachers also decided to take part in the movement. Acharya J. B. Kripalani was one of them who resigned from BHU and joined the Non-Cooperation Movement.

The Quit-India Movement saw an upsurge of the Indian masses under the leadership of teachers and students in different parts of India. When the political leadership was put behind bars, the students and teachers of Banaras Hindu University took charge of the leadership to make the movement most effective. BHU was considered by the British government as the source of the disturbances in Eastern Uttar Pradesh and Western Bihar. At one point of time the British government decided to convert BHU into a hospital for war purposes. The Vice-Chancellor of BHU, Sir Radhakrishnan persuaded the Government to desist from the scheme. He was successful in convincing them to withdraw the military from the premises of BHU, which they had entered in the middle of August 1942, to oust students who were launching a guerilla attack on the British installations. It seems a repetition of history when we find that many of the political leaders of Uttar Pradesh have been groomed in the Student Union elections of BHU.

Over the years, the university expanded. The first hostels - Ruiya, Broacha and Birla were established in 1921. The Law College and the Ayurvedic College were set up in 1923, and the Women's College in 1928. They were followed by the College of Agriculture in 1931, the Science College in 1935, the Department of Commerce in 1940, the Colleges of Music and Fine Arts in 1950, and the Medical College in 1960. In 1962, the museum Bharat Kala Bhavan was inaugurated by Pandit Jawaharlal Nehru. The college system was replaced by a faculty structure in 1966, when the Golden Jubilee of the University was celebrated. The College of Engineering was upgraded to an Institute in 1971, so was the Medical College in 1973. That year, a separate Faculty of Social Sciences was established and my father, Professor Madan Mohan Sinha appointed its first Dean.

Banaras Hindu University, today

The university family consists of about 15000 students belonging to all streams of life, castes, regions, religions and races, about 1700 teachers, and nearly 8000 non-teaching staff. Its sprawling 1300 acre campus stands in physical contrast with the city itself, with its exemplary, planned architecture and well maintained roads, extensive greenery, minimal traffic and sense of calm. The education infrastructure comprises 3 Institutes, 14 Faculties, 124 Departments, 4 Interdisciplinary Centres, a separate college for undergraduate women and 3 schools, spanning a vast range of subjects pertaining to all branches of humanities, religion, social sciences, technology, medicine, science, fine arts and performing arts. It has six centres for Advanced Study, and a large number of specialized Research Centers. Four degree colleges in the city are affiliated to the University. Bharat Kala Bhavan, the reputed museum of the university, is a treasure trove of rare collections. The 927 bed Sir Sunderlal Hospital of the university is equipped with all the modern amenities.

BHU lies on the southern end of the city. The university itself is laid out in a half-circle, with main roads running in consecutively smaller half-circles while other roads cutting across diametrically. A large gate, with the statue of Pandit Malaviya welcomes visitors and students alike. The straight road in is lined with *Ashok* trees on either side; the Chief Proctor's Office, responsible for security within the campus is right next to the entrance gate. The hospital lies on the right, and the Women's College on the left. Opposite the hospital is located the prestigious Institute of Medical Sciences. It is easy to navigate within the campus, since most faculties and institutes lie along one road, one after another, with a few exceptions that I shall just talk about. The same holds good for student's hostels, which follow one another for several kilometres at a stretch.

So, on to the faculties and institutes. Straight after the Institute of Medical Sciences, situated next to it with good reason, is the College of Nursing. From there, one takes a right turn for what I call the College Road. The residence of the Institute's director is followed by a landscaped but unkempt park called Madhuban. A favourite for young amorous couples, there are a few sculptures set amidst a lawn, and in the middle of a lily pond here. The Faculty of Ayurveda and Indian Medicine and the Faculty of Performing Arts lie face to face. The latter has the Pandit Omkarnath Thakur Auditorium on its premises. Next to the former is the Students Union Building. The University Guest House lies in the corner opposite the Students Union, and the International Students Hostel next to it. Next up are the Faculty of Management Studies on the right side of the road, and the Bharat Kala Bhawan on the left. Behind that lie buildings that house the Faculty of Visual Arts, and the Department of Sanskrit. One carries on to the Faculty of Social Sciences, a relatively new building, and the Hindi Bhawan; on the opposite side of the road are the Department of Metallurgy, somewhat displaced from its fellow technology departments, and the Arts Faculty. Carry on for another furlong, and there's the Faculty of Commerce and the massive buildings of the Physics and Chemistry departments on either side of the road. After that are the Departments of Zoology and Botany, and, appropriately, a Botanical Garden. The small Department of Journalism is tucked behind a mango grove, and then one reaches the centre of the university - the new Vishwanath Temple.

The Vishwanath temple is a massive temple complex consisting of seven temples. Its marble spire rises 252 feet high and is simply the highest structure in the city. The foundation stone of the temple was laid in March 1931 and it took almost three decades to complete its construction. Green lawns, stone and marble seats, rippling streams and tanks of water surround the main temple. The Shiva temple is on the ground floor and the Lakshmi Narayan and the Durga temples are on the first. The entire Bhagwad Geeta and extracts from the sacred Hindu scriptures are inscribed with illustrations on the inner walls of the temple. Devotees, pilgrims and tourists from all over the world visit the temple throughout the year. Religious discourses are held and hymns sung periodically in the central hall of the temple.

Opposite the temple lies one of the largest libraries anywhere in India - The Maharaja Sayajirao Gaekwad Library, named after the generous donor from Baroda in the state of Gujarat. Modelled after the British Museum in London, according to the wishes of Pandit Malaviya, the construction of the library began in 1927, and it was inaugurated in 1941. The total collection in the library today exceeds 1.1 million volumes including over 10,000 manuscripts in various scripts. Nurtured in its infancy by the renowned historian Sir Jadunath Sarkar, it had eminent scholars of the library science like Dr. S.R. Ranganathan, the father of Library movement in India, as its Librarian. The Library has a unique collection of rare books and journals dating back to the 18th century.

The Institute of Agriculture is next on the road. The minor gate of the Institute of Technology follows. Amidst the tall massive buildings that date back eighty years are the smaller, newer, flatter departments of biotechnology and computer science. At the extreme end of the university lies an airfield, probably the only one situated within a university campus anywhere in the country. The airfield of the campus was built for military training for flying during the Second World War. For the last fifty years, cadets of the National Cadet Corps train on vintage Pipers and earn their first sixty hours towards their Private Pilot Licence. In the year 2001, one of the vintage planes at the airfield, now no longer airworthy, was sold to a British publisher-cum-vintage car aficionado Peter Vacher. The aircraft was used for two years in the war between Britain and Japan in Burma in 1942. Just before Independence in 1947, the British government donated it to the university for study purposes. Vacher found immense nostalgia in the aircraft's Rolls Royce engine, and paid twenty-seven thousand pounds for it.

The semi-circular road parallel to the one just described has along it three important buildings, and the university stadium. The Faculty of Law comes first, a relatively modern building built with assistance from the Ford Foundation. Then is the massive sports complex called the Amphitheatre – containing football, cricket and hockey stadia, tennis, squash, basketball and volleyball courts and an athletics stadium. I spent many a gruelling, but enjoyable afternoon and evening here, first being coached in long jump, then playing tennis for hours on end during our summer vacations. After that lies the University Central Office, its administrative hub, housing the Controller of Examinations, the Bank and Registrar's offices. Further down the road is the massive auditorium, the Swatantrata Bhavan

(Hall of Independence), the venue of many a cultural program and conference.

One must return to the Institute of Medical Sciences to take a different path, one that goes past the many hostels where students spend their formative years. After the Institute is the small Medical Enclave, where doctors serving at the Sir Sunderlal Hospital live. The memorial to Pandit Malaviya, Malaviya Bhavan is opposite to that colony. The Vice-Chancellor's residence is next, replete with armed guards so necessary in today's times. He shares a boundary with important guests, who stay at the Lakshman Das Guest House next door. Then follow some four kilometres of huge hostels, that house and feed some five to eight hundred students each. I shall simply rattle off their names now – names that suggest power, nobility, leadership and wisdom. Some were named after the merchants and industrialists who donated money, others after leading academicians, social reformers and scientists. The massive Ruia, Baldeodas Jugal Kishore Birla, Sangi Das Shapoorji Broacha hostels with Dhanvantari, Rammohun Roy, Homi Bhabha, Jagadish Chandra Bose, Acharya Narendra Dev hostels behind them. Seth Doolichand Dalmia, and Dr. C.P.R. Aiyar Hostel follow, with Ram Kinkar Hostel behind the latter. Thereafter one passes hostels named after Dr. Sarvepalli Radhakrishnan, Bal Gangadhar Tilak, Dr. Bhagwan Dass, Dr. Iqbal Narayan Gurtu, Sri Ramakrishna, Dr. C. V. Raman, the Morvi and Dhanrajgiri estates. The Rajputana Hostel takes its name from its donors Seth Rameshwar Das Birls and Seth Shivratan Mohta, this is followed by Thakur Shree Jaswant Singhji Limbdi hostel, Vivekananda, and Dr Shyama Charan De hostel. The girls studying in the Institute of Technology live in the Gandhi Smriti Women's Hostel, behind Limbdi. Opposite the hostels are six massive playgrounds, with cricket pitches, football and hockey grounds, volleyball and basketball courts. An Olympic sized swimming pool lies behind Morvi Hostel. A gymnasium and the Jammu & Kashmir badminton stadium stand face to face in front of the Broacha Hostel. Tucked away within the walls of the Women's College are the Jyoti Kunj and Kasturba Gandhi hostels; more girls hostels behind the Vice-Chancellor's residence: Sarojini Naidu, Gargi, Ganga, Jamuna, Saraswati, Nivedita and the appropriately named Mother Teresa hostel for nurses.

Behind the hostels, along two roads shaded with sal, jamun, gulmohur and mahua are the numerous colonies where the teachers reside. They were all renamed in the late 1980s, but I somehow prefer the old names : Nizam of Hyderabad Colony, Jodhpur Colony, Principals Colony, where we lived, Ladies Colony, so named because teachers in the Women's College would reside there. The sprawling old bungalows were built in the 1920s and 1930s. Each has massive rooms, high ceilings and thick brick walls that keep the interior cool in summer and warm in winter. Shaded verandahs, many lined with fragrant creepers welcome the visitor; there are no walls between homes, only wire fences with trimmed hedges. Servant quarters for the little army that would be required to keep the bungalows and their gardens in shape abut the main house. In the sixties, the first apartments came up, in response to the need to accommodate a larger number of teachers on campus. The apartment boom took off in the eighties, but the university always had enough land to absorb the extra buildings. In any case, we were not talking about highrises here. Most apartment blocks were never built higher than two floors; they all had patches of garden in front of them. Almost in dread, I went back to my old home a year ago. Eight apartments had come up in the vacant area near the house. It was eight in the evening, and dark. I was simply amazed. The only sounds I could hear were those of crickets. The heady smell of *mahua*, and that of the fragrant jasmine mingled and hung in the cool air. When someone rang the bell in the tiny Hanuman temple next to where we lived, its sound carried a hundred metres away. The foxes were long gone, but not the peacocks. Every afternoon in summer, water tankers would go around the university roads, sprinkling water to cool things down. The Buddhist monks who lived in Sengupta Lodge nearby, went about peacefully, in their orange robes, but riding shining bicycles. It was on this road that I would see Ananda Shankar, musician son of Uday Shankar, walk past after his music lessons, every few days. It was on this road that we learnt to ride a bicycle, because there was never any traffic. I am sure that kids would still be doing that.

ଓ

There is one memory vividly etched in my mind, from my childhood days in the Principals' Colony. It had to do with the *nilgai.* It was an early evening, and we heard a commotion in the neighbourhood. My brother and Neera, one of our servants, rushed out. My father and I followed. At the neighbouring Hanuman Temple, we found a desperate, wounded *nilgai* (deer), chest heaving, and a group of young men with sticks and stones outside the temple. It figured that the *nilgai* must have strayed into the city, God knows from where, and these chaps were eager to make a meal out of him. Running across fences and fields, hurting himself, he had finally found refuge in the temple. My father and one of our neighbours, Dr Gupta asked the young men to leave. We brought Dettol and cotton wool and bandages, tended to his injuries. A cot was fetched, to improvise as a stretcher, and with much difficulty the *nilgai* was put on it and brought home. He was taken to an extra room that we had next to our house, gunny sacks spread on the floor, while Neera went off to find some grass and fig leaves to feed him. For the next one month, the *nilgai* was nursed back to health, even as our parents complaïned that we were turning our house into a zoo, since we would invite endless friends to come and watch. Finally, my father got in touch with the authorities at the Deer Park in Sarnath. Sedated, the *nilgai* was put on a jeep, and taken to Buddha's land, where he was placed in the company of others of his kind.

When one lives in the company of scholars and scientists, it is only expected that one would be enriched in their company. The many professors at the university, were for us, more than just storehouses of knowledge and erudition. They were the parents of our friends, and friends of our parents. They made academia accessible, interesting through the stories they narrated. When Professor Bhupen Kanungo visited our home, on his old bicycle, his stories about Kailash Mansarovar had me wide-eyed. When Professor Sultan Akhtar of the Aligarh Muslim University, and the president of the university's cricket association told me stories about the spinner in the Indian team, Mushtaq Ahmed, I was fascinated. When he presented me with a cricket bat, I was ecstatic.

Before I knew it, I had finished school, and entered the university where I had grown up, to study for a Bachelor's degree in Physics. I began to see things in a different light. The physics and chemistry departments were huge, mysterious places in the beginning, laboratories that seemed like wizards' chambers, with pipettes, burettes, bunsen burners and solutions of the most amazing colour. Gauges and spectrometers, torsion meters and dark rooms that made us play around with light and matter, sound and waves. Blackboards filled up with mathematical equations and diagrams, notebooks followed suit. Our books got thicker, our satchels heavier by the year. At examination time, we all filed into the giant Multipurpose Hall, and saw if our minds had absorbed it all. So great was our obsession with the subject of our choice, that I never even visited the wondrous Bharat Kala Bhawan as long as I was a student in the university. In my scientific endeavours, the arts lay shut out, unrecognized and unexplored. I gave up learning Hindustani Classical Music, even after passing the first examination with distinction, and made my guitar teacher angry. But this was also the time I discovered photography, probably more as a result of my fascination with the instrument – lenses and light, than with the image. As the images developed – naturescapes of the Ganga and the rising sun, close-ups of the myriad flowers that bloomed in spring, I veered right back into aesthetic appreciation.

If I had been enlightened in the company of several professors, one of them, Professor Anjan Bannerjee almost succeeded in quashing my career even before it began. When I got my admission in the Post Graduate course in Advertising at the Indian Institute of Mass Communication, no one in my family or elsewhere had any idea about the profession or knew why I had decided to pursue such a course. My father decided to take the opinion of Professor Bannerjee, whose field – journalism – suggested he knew something about the institute. He returned quite upset. Professor Bannerjee had said, "Why on earth is a 'good student' like Kunal thinking of studying advertising? It is something only girls study !" Even though there were a large number of girls in my class, it did not hinder my career prospects in any way. My father let me have my way, reluctantly. My only regret today is that he never lived to watch me make a successful career in the profession.

Bharat Kala Bhavan

Once I entered in the advertising profession, it was inevitable that I would learn to develop my creative sensibilities. Twenty-four years after having been born barely two hundred metres away from the Bharat Kala Bhavan, I decided to visit it.

Bharat Kala Bhavan, the art and archaeological museum of Banaras Hindu University, is an internationally known institution. No university in India has a museum of this dimension. The collection exceeds 100000 objects that include historically important archaeological materials, paintings, textiles and costumes, literary materials, decorative arts and Indian philately. It was founded by the late Padmavibhushan Rai Krishnadasa, a well-known art connoiseur and writer, as the Bharatiya Lalit Kàla Parishad, on January 1 1920, near Godowlia. Gurudev Rabindranath Tagore was the first President of the Parishad. It then shifted to Central Hindu School, again to Kashi Nagari Pracharini Sabha, before becoming an integral part of Banaras Hindu University in 1950. Pandit Jawaharlal Nehru laid its foundation stone, and inaugurated the building in 1962. Rai Krishnadasa was inspired by his family tradition and by freedom fighters for salvaging and preserving the cultural heritage of the nation within the country itself.

The museum has twelve galleries where only 2 per cent of the total collection are exhibited at any given point of time. It organizes periodical exhibitions when the materials are taken out of the reserves. Research scholars and teachers of about a dozen academic disciplines visit the museum for study and research. A Masters degree course in Museology is conducted in this museum. The museum is also frequented by a large number of scholars in the related field from various parts of India and abroad and is visited daily by many tourists both national and international. It houses a well-organized library with rare books on Indian art and culture.

The **Paintings Gallery** on the ground floor exhibits works that span ten centuries, from the 11th to the 20th. The earliest are a set of palm leaf manuscripts depicting events from the life of Budhha, and male and female deities of Vajrayana Buddhism. Part of the 16th century collection of Rajasthani miniatures is the famous illustrated manuscript of Mrigavati, which has over 200 illustrations. A closer study of this collection reveals changes and improvements made in the treatment of faces, eyes, gestures, and costumes. The paintings from the Mewar School are remarkable for their varied subject matter – from the Ragamala to Panchatantra, from Ramayana to the Bhagvad Purana - and superb execution. The later paintings from the century belong to the Mughal School, of which Akbar was the chief patron. Illustrations of the Hamzanama, painted on cloth, and the exodus of Moses are worth a look. While these reflect the pomp and grandeur of the Mughal court, paintings from Jahangir's reign (1605-1627) evince a sense of delicacy, subdued colour schemes and a fascination for portraying animals and birds of rare species. The grandeur returns to the collection from the time of Shahjehan. Noteworthy paintings from his time, on display here, are his portrait, the Treaty of Kandahar, Lady Painter in Zenana and Bharatiya Sundari. The period from 17th to 19th century are represented by a rich collection of Pahari Paintings: folios of the Gita Govinda from the Kangra School, the twelve Mahavidyas by the artist Molaram, and a painting of Raja Siddhasen of Mandi incarnated as Shiva. The museum has a rich collection of Company paintings from the 19th century – portraits, means of transport, landscapes, daily life, birds, flowers, architecture and fairs. A few of these are on display. From the 20th century is a display of modern Indian paintings, particularly belonging to the Neo-Bengal School. A representative collection of the paintings of Jamini Roy, Abanindranath Tagore, Nandalal Bose and Sailendranath Dey is on view in the gallery.

The extensive **Sculpture Gallery**, on the ground floor, is home to nearly two thousand stone sculptures, spanning the period 3rd century B.C. to 14th century A.D. They have been excavated from sites ranging from Gandhara (in Afghanistan) to Bengal, mostly the Gangetic plain. Among the oldest is a collection of ring stones from the period 3rd-1st century B.C., carved in sandstone and collected near Rajghat and Kaushambi, in Allahabad. These are decorated with floral and vegetal motifs and animals, some have a hole in the middle, a few indicate a standing figure of the Mother Goddess. There are fragmentary pieces of Ashokan pillars from Sarnath, and sculptures from the Sunga Period (2nd-1st century B.C.). There is a large collection of sculptures from the Kushan Period (1st-3rd century A.D.) which depict Surya, Kuber, Agni, Harihara, Hariti and Mahishasuramardini, and an outstanding figure of the gracefully poised '*Prasadhika*' (toilet-bearer) in spotted red sandstone.

Fifty-four pieces of sculpture from Gandhara, some of them Bodhisattvas, are housed in the museum, as is a collection of classical art belonging to the Gupta Period (4th-6th century A.D.) unearthed in Varanasi and Bihar. Productions of the Mathura or Sarnath School, there are a number of Buddha busts, the head of Ardhanarishwara, a fascinating image of Kartikeya seated on his peacock, and a monumental image of Govardhanadhari Krishna, displayed in the Central Hall. A fine image of Indrani, the consort of Indra, comes from Shahbad in Bihar. The Goddess seems aloof in her bearing, as she bears a *vajra* (thunderbolt) and a pomegranate in her hands. Another image carved in schist stone, whose origins lie in the Ganganagar region of Rajasthan, blends the characteristics of Vishnu and Shiva – the left has emblems of crown, disc and conch, the right stone of matted hair, rosary and trident.

On the ground floor itself, we come across the gallery of rare objets d'art – **Nidhi** – where seven showcases exhibit gold repousse, crystal, coins, precious and semi-precious stones of historical significance and rare jewellery from the period 2nd century B.C to the late 19th century. There are nearly 550 gold coins struck by different kings – the Aswamedha of Samudragupta, Chandragupta II's Chhatra, Jahangir's coin with the 12 signs of the zodiac and his portrait, the Rama Siya coin issued towards the end of Akbar's reign. A large number of such items belong to the Mughal era – wine cups, dagger hilts, opium cups, archer's rings and hookah spouts made of jade, and gems inscribed with the names of Akbar, Jahangir, Shahjehan and Aurangzeb. A silver hookah base manufactured in Lucknow has elaborate enamel work in the form of flora and fauna.

Two special galleries, one dedicated to the painter Nicholas Roerich, the other to Madan Mohan Malaviya, are also on the ground floor. The **Roerich Gallery** has twelve canvases by the Master of the Mountains, and three by his son. Roerich's oils, with titles like Journey on Yak, A Scene of Compassion, Tibetan Stupa and Kalki-Avatara convey the songs of the wild, of lofty mountains, mystery and beauty in the brilliant colours of azure, green, ochre and reddish-brown. The **Malaviya Gallery** highlights important events in the Mahaman's life through correspondence, photographs, gifts and books on and by him. There's a letter from Mahatma Gandhi, dated September 7 1931, which says, "I am a devotee of Malaviyaji ... He is matchless in his patriotism."

Moving up to the second floor, the visitor comes across the **Archaeology-Terracotta Gallery**. This section possesses in its collection 235 stone tools from the Paleolithic, Mesolithic and Neolithic times, found in excavations. These include knives, awls, hand axes, cleavers, choppers and scrapers. One finds clay pottery from Harappan sites in Rajasthan and Maharashtra, these have human, animal and plant motifs on them. The museum has 1700 seals, mostly made of clay, in its collection. Discovered across north India, between Taxila and Bihar, they have images of Buddhist and Hindu deities and symbols – Avimukteshwara, Yogeshwara, Bhringeshwara, Tara, Garuda, Nandi, Trishul, Chakra, Shankha and Bodhisattva. These seals were issued by kings, courtiers, traders, teaching institutions and monasteries. A small number of copperplate inscriptions belonging to medieval times, signifying land grants during the dynasties of the Pala, Gahadavala and Chandela kings, can be found. The art of terracota is significant from the perspective of reconstructing cultural history. The earliest specimens here belong to the pre-Indus and Indus Valley sites. The female figurines from the Indus to the pre-Mauryan period were modelled by hand, and ornamental in design. Some of them are interpretations of the Mother Goddess. In the Mauryan Period, animal figures became popular – they can be found in one showcase at the gallery. The third showcase contains figures that were produced by the moulding process. This allowed the production of images of new and interesting themes, such as a toycart depicting a picnic party. One of the showcases contains terracottas from the Gupta Period. These are again divine figures – Ganesha, Ardhanarishwara, Mahishasurmardini, and a two-headed Shiva. On the floor of the gallery is a large storage jar belonging to this period, found at Rajghat.

It was in the 7th and 6th century B.C. that coins evolved as a medium of transaction, to replace barter. The **Coin Gallery** on the first floor, where only a part of the museum's 33,000 coin collection lies on display, is a numismatist's paradise. The earliest punch-marked coins, made in silver are in round, rectangular and sometimes irregular shapes. After the Greek invasions of the 4th century B.C., the art of coin-making improved by striking dies. The coins of this period, in silver and copper, bear legends in Greek and have pictures of deities and the issuing monarchs. It was the Kushanas who introduced gold coins during their reign in the 1st century A.D., emphasizing portraiture of the issuing kings. The coins of the later Gupta period record events, like Chandragupta I's marriage with the Lichchavi princess, and achievements, like Chandragupta II's expertise as a rider, archer and slayer of lions. Sultanate India saw a change in which human and divine figures were replaced by calligraphy. Sher Shah introduced a fiscal policy by abolishing bullion and introduced a standard copper currency, the paisa. From the Mughal period can be found gold and silver mohurs, as eminent artists and calligraphers were commissioned by Akbar, and Jehangir after him. Some of these bear beautifully executed portraits of the emperors.

The **Decorative Arts Gallery** on the first floor displays objects of daily use from a period spanning over three centuries. They include jewellery, glassware, metal crafts, ivory and weapons from the Mughal, Company and later eras. The Mughals set up royal workshops in Agra, Fatehpur Sikri, Delhi, Lahore and Ahmedabad for the production of decorative art objects. The gallery has a fair number of Bidri – black metal with gold and silver inlay – work artefacts: *paan* containers, spittoons, candlestands, hookah bases and plates. There are glass utensils fashioned in the factories of Europe, collected by the Mughals: rose water sprinklers, hookah bases, cups and plates. A small collection of arms, some elaborately decorated with gold and precious stones on their hilt and protective armour can also be seen here.

On the first floor also lies the **Banaras Gallery**, where some of the archival documents related to the history of the city, temple grants issued by kings, and old maps and charts have been displayed. There are rare paintings and sketches of kings and of the architecture of the city, notably its *ghats*. Some of the wooden toys for which the city is renowned, and masks used in the Ramlila can also be seen. The **Gallery of Literary Works** is currently under reorganization, and will display unique literary materials in the form of manuscripts, magazines and correspondence between some of the erudite leaders of the country. Painstakingly collected by Rai Krishnadasa, the collection includes six thousand Sanskrit manuscripts of the Vedic era, as well as a number of Arabic, Persian and Urdu texts. For someone interested in a study of the origins and evolution of Hindi literature, the library's collection is a veritable gold mine.

Kashi Vidyapeeth

It was set up in 1920 by Babu Shiv Prasad Gupta to provide alternate education arrangement, discarding that of the British. It soon became a centre of National education with Hindi as the medium of instruction.

Sampurnanand Sanskrit Vishwavidyalaya

In 1791, a gentleman named Jonathan Duncan put forward a proposal for starting a Sanskrit College in Varanasi to the Earl of Cornwallis, who was then the Governor General of Bengal. He wrote: *'A certain portion of the surplus revenue of the province or zamindari of Banaras should be set apart for the support of a Hindu college or academy; for the preservation of Sanskrit literature and religion of that nation, at the centre of their faith and the common resort of their tribes.'* Thus was born the Sanskrit College, with Pandit Kashinath as its first Principal. The College was run with governmental assistance and there was a provision for obtaining additional funding in case of a natural calamity or disaster.

Initially, a faculty was appointed to teach the *Vedas, Vedanta, Nyaya*, Philosophy, *Puranas*, Poetry, Astrology, *Ayurveda* and theology. Lord Cornwallis was the Visitor of the College. Duncan's idea perhaps was not only to support Hindu philosophy and an ancient language but also to train people who could assist the judiciary in litigation among the Hindu citizens on the basis of Hindu holy scriptures. On this score, theology was introduced as a multi-disciplinary subject comprising the entire gamut of *Vedic* and *Puranic* literature.

At the outset there was only one teacher for the classes of all the four *Vedas*. In the year 1800, the faculty strength rose to four. For some reasons, the teaching of *Vedas* was stopped in 1828. This provoked a lot of resentment among the elite. However, much later, *Yajurveda* was reintroduced in 1922 and still continues as a principal subject at the Sampurnanand Sanskrit University. Though the subject of *Puranas* was approved from the early days of the Sanskrit College, it enjoyed little importance in the curriculum. The College administration displayed a casual attitude towards the growth and development of the subject, possibly due to paucity of funds. Fortunately, one Gauri Shankar Goenka came forward in 1930 with a heavy donation. This facilitated the promotion of a course called *Puranic* Studies which brought some renowned scholars to the classroom. Since Persian language was widely used in the Indian judiciary, it was introduced as a subject at Sanskrit College in 1913.

The foundation stone of its magnificent main building was laid by the King of Varanasi on November 2, 1847. Actual construction began in 1848 and the whole work was completed in 1852. European Gothic architecture made the building unique and perhaps the only one of its kind in entire contemporary Varanasi and its adjoining districts. Its architect, Markham Kitto, built pointed arches, pinnacles and towers here, in the manner of an Oxford College. The entrance is inscribed with several famous quotes from Hindi, Sanskrit, Persian and English languages.

Earlier, the glory and progress of this College commenced in 1844 under the stewardship of the famous British scholar of Sanskrit, J. Muir. He organized the curricula in a scientific manner. His essays on a wide variety of subjects are still preserved in the College. However, Muir resigned in January, 1846, and Rind Wallis took over. He was an efficient principal although he knew little of Sanskrit. He was replaced by Dr. J.J. Ballantyne in February, 1846. He was a highly spirited administrator and a great scholar of Sanskrit who made his mark in the history of the College, working till 1861, and doing his best to enhance the status of Hindi. During 1846-48, the innovative discipline of English-Sanskrit had been introduced. This entailed the study of English literature to help analyze texts of great authors of

Sanskrit. It was not only language that was studied, but there was a comparative study of the thoughts of classical Indo-European authors considered to have contributed philosophically and otherwise to mankind.

German Indologist Dr. G. Thibaut who had a deep interest in Sanskrit, philosophy and astrology became its Principal in 1880. He authored a number of titles in various areas of philosophy and got recognition wherever Indology and Sanskrit were taught. Dr. Ganganath Jha, a great scholar of philosophy, was the first Indian to be appointed Principal of the College in 1918. He was there for five years till 1923. He is credited with publishing classical Sanskrit texts and their English translations. In 1937, Dr. Mangaldev Shastri took over. Incidentally, it was at this time that Dr. Sampurnanand was made the Uttar Pradesh government's Minister of Education. He was a reputed scholar who had high respect for Sanskrit and allied subjects. He, under the Chairmanship of Dr. Bhagwandas, another noted scholar, formed a committee to establish linkages of Sanskrit education with other areas of knowledge. The Committee drafted a brilliant report, which, though rather belatedly implemented in 1950-51, helped transform the curricula at the College into a highly progressive one. Following its implementation, Sanskrit was accepted as a modern and useful subject throughout the country.

On March 23, 1958, Dr. Sampurnanand, now the Chief Minister of Uttar Pradesh in independent India, visited Varanasi and elevated the College to a university - the Varanasi Sanskrit University. Dr. Aditya Nath Jha, the then Chief Secretary of Uttar Pradesh and son of Dr. Ganganath Jha, the first Indian principal of the Sanskrit College, was appointed the first Vice Chancellor. On December 1, 1974, after the death of Dr. Sampurnanand, the Institution was renamed Sampurnanand Sanskrit University in his honour.

The University has an impressive museum with sculptures that date back to 900-1200 A.D. It also has a pillar of Ashoka's period made of Chunar sandstone, brought to the Sanskrit College campus in 1853. For astronomical studies, the University has an impressive *Vedhshala* (observatory) which has the look of the *Jantar Mantar* in Delhi. It invites astronomers from across the country and abroad for research.

Sampurnanand University has come a long way by offering a platform to scholars of Sanskrit and Indology, inspiring them to help develop these areas of knowledge and learning. Today, as many as twelve Sanskrit colleges, and over 1500 schools are affiliated to this university. Festivals of Vedic chants organized here attract scholars and audiences from all over the country. Its current Vice-Chancellor is Professor Ram Murti Sharma.

☙

Krishnamurthi Foundation

" ...In our relationship with children and young people, we are not dealing with mechanical devices that can be quickly repaired, but with living beings who are impressionable, volatile, sensitive, afraid, affectionate; and to deal with them we have to have great understanding, the strength of patience and love... "

— J. Krishnamurti

The Rajghat Education Centre of the Krishnamurti Foundation India was founded by the well-known seer and religious teacher J. Krishnamurti in the year 1928. Located in a beautiful 250 acre campus full of trees, it overlooks the confluence of the rivers Varuna and Ganga, on the outskirts of Varanasi. The centre functions in the light of Krishnamurti's teachings and his vision of education, and is home to the Besant School, the Vasanta College and the Rajghat Study Centre and Retreat.

The Rajghat Besant School is a fully residential co-educational, English-medium school affiliated to the Central Board of Secondary Education, New Delhi. It has about 350 students ranging from 6 to 18 years, residing in twelve different houses spread over the campus. There are nearly fifty teachers of whom twenty-five also function as House-Parents and live with the students in the hostels. The classes range from Grade II to Grade XII, with about twenty-five students in a class. The overall ratio of staff to students in the school is 1:7, and there is one house parent for every fifteen children. The school aims :

- To help cultivate all aspects of the child — physical, intellectual, emotional and aesthetic with a holistic development of all the faculties.
- To motivate children without punishment or reward and without encouraging competition.
- Not to condition the mind of the child in any belief, whether religious, social or cultural.
- To encourage enquiry with an open mind, and a respect for dissent.
- To inculcate a love of Nature and a respect for all life.

The school offers a range of extra-curricular activities, like games and sports, yoga, gymnastics, art, music, dance, gardening, computers and literary skills. The noted mythology scholar, Joseph Campbell, after delivering a lecture here on September 22, 1954, observed, "My first lecture without shoes. The questions were cute: What is being done in America about the health and recreation of the students? What about military training? Have you been to Red China? What do American students think about Indian students? What about sport? Do you teach gardening? Are students interested in music? What do you think about Indian students?"

The Vasanta College was started by Dr. Annie Besant in 1913. The college is one of the oldest institutions in the state and has done pioneering work in the field of women's education in India. Affiliated to the Banaras Hindu University and offers the 3 years' B.A. (Hons) courses in Arts and Humanities (Social Sciences) and a one year B. Ed.(teacher-training) course in Education. It has 850 students ranging from 18-22 years, most of whom are day scholars living in the city. The college runs buses to transport them from their homes in Varanasi. There is a hostel on the campus called Vasanta Ashram with accommodation for 120 girls coming from other towns in India.

The Rajghat Study Centre and Retreat is located in the house in which Krishnamurti lived during his annual visits to Varanasi. Set on a high promontory overlooking the Ganga, the campus includes a guest-house and cottages to accommodate the visitors to the centre. A well manicured lawn is the site for early-morning meditation sessions, as the sun rises over the Ganga. Mr. Rajesh Dalal is its current rector.

The Krishnamurti study centre/retreat has no schedule or instructor; it is a place where people study the teachings without any organized programme and with only their own seriousness to guide them. The study centre has a range of materials:

- Books by Krishnamurti, translations of his works, copies of out-of-print materials, biographies, evaluative studies of the teachings and bulletins of the Foundations
- Video consoles and a catalogued video collection of Krishnamurti's talks and dialogues
- Audio players and a catalogued audio collection of Krishnamurti's talks
- A CD-ROM containing most of Krishnamurti's published works.
- A silent room for meditation

The Rajghat Study Centre also has a translation and publication cell for producing translations of Krishnamurti's books into Hindi and other North Indian languages. It brings out a quarterly bulletin called *Parisamvad* (Dialogue). The study centre exists for a serious purpose. In keeping with the ethos of the place, guests are requested not to smoke and drink on the campus, or treat the centre as convenient lodging houses or bases for sightseeing or transacting business.

ଓଃ

Panini Kanya Mahavidyalaya

In the backstreets of Mahamoorganj lies a unique institution whose aim is to impart Vedic learning to its girl students. Traditionally, the Vedas have been the domain of male scholars. Twenty seven years ago, in 1975, two sisters – Prajya Devi and Medha Devi – set up a *gurukul* where education is imparted in Sanskrit, the key to learning the Vedas. Medha Devi explains, "Sanskrit that is taught in most schools is *bhasha* – a language. What is taught here is *gyan* – knowledge that helps one understand the Vedas". It was their belief that unless the Vedas are studied in the language they are written in, much would be lost. "Translation results in footnotes, not understanding", says Surya Devi, Medha Devi's former student and her right hand in running the institution. The 70 girls who live here at any point of time receive training in the conduct of ceremonies marking the sixteen *sanskaras* – rites of passage from birth to death – that traditionally require the services of an officiating priest. In the true *gurukul* tradition, parents leave their daughters here at the age of eight, and the girls only return home after their education is complete. In order to break the popular belief that the Vedas are only accessible to Brahmins, the *gurukul* takes students from all social backgrounds. The student remains under her teacher's watchful eye all the time. She wakes up in the morning before sunrise and practises yoga, before the morning *havan*. They take turns cooking, cleaning – and the older students often teach the younger ones. The students master the texts so well that they play *antakshari* with the 4000 sutras of Sanskrit grammar! The women priests emerge from their training with tremendous self-discipline; many – like Dharna Yajaki of Shivgang in Rajasthan - have gone on to start their own *gurukuls*.

Jnana Pravaha

The appeal of Varanasi as a centre of education and culture motivated Smt. Bimla Poddar to set up a campus for cultural studies in 1996. Jnana Pravaha aims at 'rediscovering and highlighting the basic elements and ethos of Indian culture of universal appeal and salubrious to the posterity'. This is done through the in-depth study and interpretation of the scriptures by learned scholars and students. The institution is engaged in the preservation and dissemination of the varied forms of visual and performing arts of the country, aspects of classical literature, traditional wisdom and metaphysics.

The centre is located at the southern extremity of Varanasi, on the banks of the Ganga, across Ramnagar Fort. The beautiful building, set amidst sprawling, manicured lawns and gardens, was designed by B.B. Doshi of Ahmedabad, and represents the union of male and female aspects – Ardhanarishwara. Its takes its inspiration from early Indian rock-hewn architecture, and houses a library, conference room, exhibition hall, museum, documentation and archival room, conference facilities, conservation laboratory, hostel and cafetaria. The centre organizes academic debates *'Sastrarthas'*, lectures, discourses, workshops, lectures and demonstrations on music and dance.

Seminars on Samskaras, Dhvani (sound), the Ganga, Jaina, Sakta and Vaishnava contribution to Kasi, Meghaduta and Sakuntalam (including staging of the latter in Sanskrit), appraisal of the cultural spectrum of Varanasi, and cultural gleanings from the Puranas have been held in the last six years on the premises of Jnana Pravaha. Among the special projects undertaken are periodic classes and deciphering of old and obscure scripts, recording and documentation of musical recitals and folklore, and building a computerised archive on art and culture. Notable scholars in Varanasi, just as Professor Anand Krishna, Bishwanath Bhattacharya, Vidya Niwas Mishra, Dr. Bhanu Shankar Mehta and Manjula Chaturvedi are associated with the centre; with Professor R C Sharma as its honorary director and acharya.

The Great Scholars of Varanasi

Kabir

Known for his *dohas* (couplets) and *bhajans* (devotional songs), the most outstanding saint-poet of the Bhakti (devotion) cult was born in Varanasi in the year 1389. Legend has it that he was left abandoned by his mother, a Brahman widow, after his birth on a giant lotus leaf in the Lahartara Lake, on the outskirts of the city. A Muslim couple, Niru and Nimma noticed him. Being without a child, they picked him up, considering him as God's gift, and raised him as their foster child. Young Kabir did not take up any formal education, believing that all he needed to know were the letters that made up the word 'Rama'. I have already written about his initiation rites on the banks of Panchganga Ghat.

Having been born at a time when Islam was spreading in the country, Kabir was deeply disturbed by the communal clashes and feuds between followers of both religions. By his innate talent, he was able to bring about a synthesis of the best of both faiths; at the same time deriding their weaknesses. His *dohas* and songs helped alleviate the misunderstanding between the communities to a great extent. Soon, Kabir had a large following.

Kabir composed his songs effortlessly, in the language of the common people. He recited them to the accompaniment of the *tanpura*. While some of the verses were deeply spiritual, others contained words of wisdom, and showed how people could lead a pure and happy life. His metaphors and similes were earthspun and natural, and appealed to the common people. I only wish more people read him in today's communally charged times – every word he wrote six hundred years ago makes sense. The Kabirchaura Math on Sant Kabir Road that runs from Maidagin to Lahurabir in the north of the city was the original seat of discourse, and today is the headquarters of his band of followers, the Kabirpanthis.

Goswami Tulsidas

Tulsidas was born at Rajapur, in the Banda district of Uttar Pradesh in the year 1497. He is said to have been a Sarwaria Brahman. His father's name was Atmaram, and his mother was named Hulasi, and his own name being Rama Bhola. His parents abandoned him immediately after his birth, and it is assumed that he was probably one of those unfortunate children known as *abhuktamula*. Such a child is said to be destined to destroy its father, and the only remedy is to abandon it on its birth, or, at best, so to arrange that its parents shall not look upon its face during the first eight years of its existence. Rama Bhola was given over to a wandering sadhu. The sadhu renamed him Tulsidas (Servant of the tulsi plant) in honour of the sacred leaf used in the ceremony of purification of the infant, and by this name he was henceforth known. With this sadhu, who was probably also his guru, Narahari Das, he wandered all over Northern India. Narahari Das could see that this young boy was very special indeed, so he decided to instill in him all of his own knowledge and love. From his guru Tulsidas learnt the story of Ram, but owing to his ignorance of Sanskrit, he could not at first grasp its importance.

Tulsidas began to learn Sanskrit, the scholarly language of the scriptures. Listening to his Guru recite in Sanskrit the story of Ram's life, the *Ramayana*, young Tulsidas was filled with devotion for the great Lord Ram. At Narahari Das's ashram, he vowed to make the Ramayana available to all people by translating it from Sanskrit into a language they could understand. On a pilgrimage to Varanasi in 1509, Tulsidas and Narahari Das stopped at the ashram of the renowned scholar of Sanskrit and the ancient scriptures, Sheshnathji, at Panchganga ghat. Though he loved Tulsidas like a son, Narahari Das did not want his own affection for the boy to hold Tulsidas back. He could see it was time for Tulsidas to study with a different master and encouraged him to continue his studies in Varanasi.

Fifteen years passed, by which time Tulsidas grew up to be one of the most learned and respected young men in the land. Then he returned home, where in a grand wedding, he married the wise and beautiful Ratnavali. After a time, however, Tulsidas became so infatuated with his beautiful wife that he could hardly think about anything else! Even in meditation, his mind rested not on Ram, but on his wife's lovely form. Ratnavali herself was a great devotee of Ram. The last thing she wanted was to distract her husband from his path of union with the Lord. Because of her deep love for him, and her devotion to Lord Rama, she knew that she had to leave Tulsidas. She wrote him a letter of farewell and left for her brother's house. Finding Ratnavali's letter, Tulsidas went out of his mind with despair. Even though a huge storm was raging outside, he rushed from his house to find her. As he tried to cross a river, he was swept along in a fierce flood. Catching hold of a log, he managed to struggle ashore. Barely surviving the journey to Ratnavali's brother's house, Tulsidas climbed a rope onto her balcony. She was shocked to see him there and tells him that the log he caught hold of in the river was actually a dead body, and the rope he climbed onto her balcony was really a huge python! Ratnavali implored Tulsidas to focus his love not on her but on the Lord. Upon hearing these words, Tulsidas realized that in his mad infatuation for his wife, he had indeed forsaken Ram.

Tulsidas's one-pointed devotion to Ram was rekindled with Ratnavali's words. He decided to renounce his family and his home, and immediately set off on a pilgrimage to all places auspicious to Ram. Resting one day in a forest, Tulsidas helped a tree become free from an ancient curse. The tree spirit reminded him of the vow Tulsidas had made as a boy – to make the *Ramayana* available to all people. The tree spirit promised that Hanuman himself would come to listen to Tulsidas's tales of Ram. Tulsidas travelled to the nearest city, where he began to recite the *Ramayana* in the local language. He became lost in ecstasy as he narrated these stories of Ram and his brother Lakshman, Ram and his beautiful wife Sita, Ram and the wicked demon Ravanna – and so too did the people who come to listen. Each day, one old Brahman sat himself in the back of the crowd and listened to these tales. After some time, Tulsidas realized that this old Brahmin was none other than Hanuman himself! Throwing himself at Hanuman's feet, Tulsidas prays for Hanuman to grant him a glimpse of his beloved Ram. Together, Tulsidas and Hanuman travelled to the town of Chitrakoot, where Tulsidas spent his days meditating. So absorbed in meditation was he, that he didn't see Ram and Lakshman when they came to his very house. Enlightened by his love of Rama, Tulsidas began a pilgrimage across India to spread the Lord's holy name, visiting Vrindavan on his way.

His pilgrimage complete, Tulsidas returned to Varanasi. In 1574, he began writing down the exquisite love songs he had been reciting all these years: the *Ramcharit Manas*. The Ramacharit Manas was written between 1574 and 1577. The poem, written in Awadhi, an Eastern Hindi dialect, consists of seven cantos of unequal lengths. Although the ultimate source of the central narrative is the Sanskrit epic Ramayana, Tulsidas's principal immediate source was the Adhyatma Ramayana, a late medieval recasting of the epic that had already sought to harmonize the Advaita system and the Rama cult. The influence of the Bhagvata-Purana, the chief scripture of the Krishna cult, is also discernible, with that of a number of minor sources.

But not everyone agreed with Tulsidas' recitations. In fact, the scholars of the land were outraged that their Holy Scriptures were being recited not in Sanskrit, but in the language of commoners. Despite the scholars' objections, Tulsidas continued his recitations of the *Ramayana*. This raised the hackles of the traditionalists who attempted to steal his manuscript, and disturbed him while he was at work, making him decide to leave the city. It was only after Raja Todarmal intervened, and the great Sanskrit scholar Madhusudan Saraswati praised his work that the pandits accepted his Ramcharit Manas. Finally, Tulsidas' opponents became his devotees, and today his work is among the most beloved of India's treasures.

Eleven other works are attributed with some certainty to Tulsidas. These include Krishna Gitavali, a series of 61 songs in honour of Krishna; Vinay Patrika, a series of 279 verse passages addressed to Hindu sacred places and deities (chiefly Rama and Sita); and Kavitavali, telling incidents from the story of Rama. Through his work, Tulsidas attempted to bring the Shaivites and Vaishnavites together by arguing that Ram and Shiva were the same. Tulsidas died on the banks of the Ganga, at the ripe old age of 127. His songs are recited in Varanasi even today.

Bhartendu Harishchandra

The father of modern Hindi literature laid the foundation of a clear, systematized, modern Hindi as we know it today. Bhartendu was born in 1850, in the elite family of Gopalchandra in Varanasi. His father was a renowned poet. But his parents died young and adequate arrangements could not be made for his early education. He enrolled in Queens College, but did not find the classes interesting, and decided to drop out and educate himself. His efforts clearly succeeded, as he not only mastered the Hindi language, but also gained fluency in English, Sanskrit, Bangla, Gujarati, Marathi, Marwari, Punjabi and Urdu. At the age of 18, he started a monthly magazine, the Kavi Vachan Sudha, which he later turned into a weekly. The magazine provided him the platform to write about social problems, politics, delays in justice, women's status in society and religious intolerance. Five years later, he began publishing yet another magazine, 'Harishchandra Magazine', and then 'Barla Bodhini'. The language of Hindi became a forceful medium of expression, and gave a fresh dimension to the freedom struggle. When he was just twenty, Bhartendu was appointed as an honorary magistrate in the Varanasi courts.

In his short life span – he died at the age of thirty-five – Bhartendu published twenty-six plays, forty-one literary works and wrote thirty-five essays. His major plays are Bharat Durdasha (1875), Shri Chandrawali (1876), Satya Harishchandra (1876), Neeldevi (1881) and Andher Nagari (1881). His poetry collections include Prem Malika (1871), Prem Madhuri (1875), Prem Tarang (1877), Uttarardha Bhaktamaal (1877), Geet Govindanand (1878), Holi (1879), Vinay Prem Pachasa (1881), Phoolon ka Guchchha (1882) and Krishnacharitra (1883). He also translated Bengali works like the play Vidyasundar, and the Sanskrit plays Karpur Manjari and Mudra Rakshas into Hindi. Pratap Narain Mishra, Ayodhya Singh

Upadhyaya, Pandit Badrinarain, Lala Srinivas, Pandit Balkrishna Bhatt and Gadadhar Singh were the prominent authors who followed the traditions of Bhartendu Harishchandra.

Munshi Prem Chand

Prem Chand was born in a village 5 kilometres from Varanasi in the year 1880. He is quite simply the most famous novelist in the Hindi language. He started writing fiction at the turn of this century, giving Hindi literature its modern form, observing with a keen pair of eyes the changes occurring in the social fabric of India. He was also aware of the political aspirations of the Indian masses. He started his career as a government servant and was a teacher in several schools of Uttar Pradesh. He was later made the Inspector of Schools. He was never a prisoner of routine and chronicled the political and social turmoils in Indian life through the medium of short stories and novels. His first collection of short stories was published in Urdu and was entitled, *Soze-Watan* (The Love of Homeland). It was promptly proscribed and Premchand immediately saw that the government service would not allow him to function as a novelist of the people in the true sense. He continued in the government service but was not every happy at his situation. Ultimately he resigned from government service in 1921, and returned to Varanasi to write.

Literature was not mental luxury and a matter of word-play for Prem Chand. He was convinced that literature had a social role and it could remain significant only if it zealously guarded its relevance to life. He never believed in the theory of art for art's sake. And yet he believed that fiction could have an impact on the psyche of the reader only if it had a satisfactory 'form'. This was the reason why he was dissatisfied with the state of Urdu fiction which at that time had a penchant for narratives centering around mysterious adventures in the land of fantasy. Prem Chand wanted to bring fiction closer to reality and wanted literature to reflect the tensions of a changing society.

His first important novel *Seva Sadan* (The House of Service) narrates the story of a prostitute. She tries to come out of her predicament but her efforts to lead a respectable life are resisted by the orthodox quarters. Prem Chand depicts the hypocrisy of the so-called pillars of society who can sacrifice their orthodox principles if they can have a session with her in bed. These same people mouth moral platitudes in public. He portrays reality in a vivid manner but conceives of an ideal community which gives a new direction to the life of a fallen woman and allows her to live a meaningful life. This streak of idealism in the work of Prem Chand has been criticized by scholars but we should not lose sight of the fact that the book was published in 1916 when the nation was struggling to have a better tomorrow and idealism went with the mood of the people.

His next great novel *Premashram* (The Abode of Love) was published in 1920. In this novel he presented moving pictures of life in the villages and towns of north India. He wrote about the life of the peasants, their tears and smiles, struggles, despair, hopes and aspirations. The novel presents a gallery of characters who are a curious mixture of good and evil. Two brothers, however, dominate the entire fictional scene. Gyanshankar, the younger one is selfish, crafty and scheming. He is the symbol of evil and is absolutely indifferent to human suffering. His elder brother, Premshankar, is an idealist and a visionary. He wants to make the life of the peasants easier and establishes an *ashram* which recognizes the ideals of Mahatma Gandhi. Here too we find idealism giving resonance to a realistic portrayal of life.

Another of his great novels is *Rangbhumi* (Arena or The Stage). It has an epic canvas and depicts several themes. The villages and towns of north India form the backdrop for the activities of characters who represent humanity in its different hues. The central character is Surdas, a blind beggar who runs after vehicles begging for small coins. He owns a patch of land which is used for grazing the cattle of the village. Mr. John Sewak wanted to purchase his land because he wants to establish a cigarette factory. Surdas does not want to sell the land, wants to keep it for the village community and unconsciously develops into the leader of a challenge to the spirit of industrialism. He is unsuccessful in his efforts and ultimately the factory is established. The organic life of the village community is destroyed. The factory brings with it numerous evils like liquor, gambling, obscenity. For the first time, the village women are molested by outsiders. Surdas goes to the city and tries to rouse the conscience of the people against he injustice done to him and other villagers. He ultimately dies in a fire which destroys his hut. Here we find Prem Chand moving towards stark realism. All sections of society come to life on this broad canvas and dozens of memorable characters are created. It is truly a saga of Indian life.

His last great novel, *Godan* (The Cow-Offering) was published in 1935, a year before his death. It formed the apex of Prem Chand's work as a writer. It is a novel of epic dimensions. Hori is the central character of the novel but he is surrounded by a large number of characters who operate against a very broad background representing almost all aspects of Indian life. Village life with its struggles, its poverty and despair, oppression of the landlords, kindness and greed of various characters, are presented with vividness and élan. The city is also portrayed. The empty lives of rich people, their hypocrisy, love of luxury, their indifference to moral values are all presented with a great amount of vitality.

Prem Chand wrote about two hundred and fifty short stories. Some were admittedly pedestrian and were written in response to urgent requests from the editors of journals. Others, however were outstanding social documents informed by an artistic purpose. *Kafan* (the Shroud) tells the story of two idle and worthless poor villagers with stark realism. They are unmoved by the sad plight of a dying lady who is the wife of one of the characters of this moving short story. *Idgah* (The place where the prayers of Id are held) presents the tender feelings of a child for his grandmother. He goes to the fair on the festive occasion of *Id*, resists the temptation of purchasing sweets and balloons, and purchases, instead, a pair of tongs which may help his grandmother in the kitchen. *Bare Ghar ki Beti* (The Daughter of a Cultured Family) presents the picture of a home whose people believe in traditional values. Tensions gradually appear and there is a misunderstanding between a woman and her husband's younger brother. The basic humanity of the woman, however, saves the traditional family from collapse and the two are reconciled. *Mate Ram Shashtri* is a satire on quacks who are social parasites. *Poos ki Raat* (the Night of Winter), *Sawa Seer Gehun* (A Kilo and Quarter of Wheat) and *Thakur ka Kuan* (Thakur's well) present themes based on village life. Taken together, his stories present the vast panorama of North Indian life with vividness, strength and passion.

ꞵ

Nagari Pracharini Sabha

Several parallel events around the turn of the nineteenth century led to a movement to bring Hindi to the forefront of the nationalist movement. While the precocious fifth-standard students at the Queen's Collegiate School were enthusiastic to set up a debating society in the language, noblemen and judicial officers alike were offended when the British decided that the official language to be used in the courts of the United

Provinces would be Urdu. A delegation comprising Maharaja Sir Pratap Narayan Singh of Ayodhya, Raja Balwant Singh of Etah, Ghanshyam Singh of Aligarh, Rampratap Singh of Allahabad, Raja Lachhman Das of Mathura, accompanied by Pandit·Madan Mohan Malaviya and a collection of Rais and Munshis went to the Lieutenant Governor of the Northwest Provinces and the Chief Commissioner of Oudh's office in Allahabad to present their case. Theirs was a successful appeal, and it strengthened the cause of Hindi as a language.

On July 16 1893, Babu Shyam Sundar Das, Pandit Ram Narain Mishra and Thakur Shiva Kumar Singh established **Kashi Nagari Pracharini Sabha** at Varanasi to propagate and enrich Hindi. Their objectives were as follows :

1. Unearth and archive old handwritten Hindi texts
2. Prepare life histories of Hindi writers and editors
3. Hold examinations in Hindi literature
4. Document the history of the Hindi language
5. Prepare a history of the Hindi novel
6. Document India's history in Hindi
7. Collate accounts of travels in Hindi
8. Sponsor and document scientific explorations in Hindi
9. Publish ancient texts.

As a result, a large number of Hindi dramas, novels, essays, histories and books on criticism and science, and many periodicals were published. The sabha's journal was first published in 1953 with Shyan Sumdar Das as its first editor; the criteria for publishing articles were rigorous. In short, the sabha developed Khari Boli literature in all its variety and gave it a definite shape. Setting up a library was one of the key tasks facing the sabha. The first collection of about 2000 books came from the founders and was housed in the Hanuman Seminary School.

The current building – the Arya Bhasha Pustakalaya at Maidagin - came up in 1954, and literrateurs from various parts of the country contributed their collections. Among them were Kunwar Ramdeen Singh of Bankepur in Patna, Ramkrishna Varma – the editor of Bharat Jeevan Press, Raja Rampal Singh, Badri Narayan Chowdhary, and Radha Krishna Das, an industrialist from Bombay. Today, the collection has mounted to some 36000 titles in thirteen languages. Among these are the priceless handwritten manuscripts of notable texts – Chand Bardai's Prithviraj Raso, Nur Muhammad's Indravat, Matiram's Rasraj, Amrit Kavi's Chitravilas, Keshav Das's Jahangir Chandrika and Ram Chandrika, Surdas's Sur Sagar, Anant Das's Kabir Parichayi, Ratan Kavi's Anand Lahari, and Kabir's Bijak.

Culture & Folklore

LIFE AND THE ARTS

Kabira Lahari Samad Ka, Moti Bikhare Aai
Bagula Sama na Jaanad, Hans Chune Chun Khai

Says Kabir – Many gems are cast on the shore
by ocean waves,
They are relished by the swan,
but not noticed by the crane.

Kabir

Ꮚ

The resident of Varanasi believes, like Kabir's *doha* above, that he is endowed with intellect, conscience and wisdom that enables him to rise above the rest of humanity. He is the discerning swan. Ask a Banarasi the question 'How's life?' and you'll be sure to get the reply 'Mauj Masti hai!' – it's all about fun and relaxation. The residents know that they have the three essential ingredients that make life so easy: their faith in salvation, Ananda; their freedom from suffering and sin, Avimukta; and their happy temperament helpful to undiluted joy, Ashutosh. Living within the boundaries of Varuna and Assi provides the feeling of Ananda, because their path to Heaven is clear. They are free from suffering and sin, one bath in the Ganga ensures that. They are happy tempered because they do not really have to worry about their next meal - a trip to Annapurna will surely fill their stomach.

Of course, generalizations are dangerous, especially in 'his'tory. In spite of that warning, a typical male Banarasi's routine runs somewhat like this. He wakes up in the morning, and takes a bath in the Ganga, which is followed by a *darshan* of Vishwanath and Annapurna. On Tuesdays, this might be supplemented or replaced by a visit to the Durga Mandir, and Sankat Mochan. Breakfast is hot *kachoris* and *jalebis*, and a glass of milk. Thus fortified, he heads for the *akhara* for a few hundred situps, swinging the *gada*, and a wrestling bout. Though his appetite has been worked up by now, he enjoys a simple, but delicious vegetarian meal. A siesta in the afternoon is taken, and he leaves home to spend the evening with friends, first drinking tea and eating samosa, then maybe a glass of *thandai*, as they indulge in a bit of *dillagi baji* – poking fun at society and individuals in general. At any point in time, he may pop a succulent *paan*, purchased from one of the many shops on the roadside, into his mouth. For some time, his speech emerges out of his mouth impeded by the pulp and juices that roll about in his oral cavity. Then he takes aim at any little spot on the road that is unoccupied by pedestrian or vehicle, and unloads what's in his mouth. His speech resumes, unhindered.

Where is the famed celebration of the festivals – the Ramlila, Burhwa Mangal, Holi, and Deepavali in all this, you might ask? What about the mellifluous music that originates from the Banaras gharana, with Ustad Bismillah Khan, Pandits Rajan and Sajan Mishra, and Pandit Shivkumar Sharma as its exponents? What about the folk music – the Kajri, the Birha and the Phag – whose verses float in the Varanasi atmosphere in different seasons? Yes, there is much to describe, and in this chapter, I shall take up Varanasi's music, its folk tradition – manifest in the form of wrestling and the Ramlila, and its festivals.

☙

The Banaras Gharana and its exponents

Look into the biographies of some of the leading performers of Hindustani Classical Music, and you will find that Varanasi has played a defining role in shaping their musical destinies. Pandit Ravi Shankar was born here on April 7 1920. The santoor maestro Pandit Shiv Kumar Sharma considers himself a proponent of the Banaras Gharana, since his father and guru, Pandit Umadatt Sharma, received his *taleem* under Bade Ramdas Ji.

The Banaras Gharana was influenced by the folk tradition of the adjoining areas of Uttar Pradesh. It was evolved by the *Thumri* singers in Varanasi, Lucknow and Gaya, who used musical ornamentation to highlight their lyrics. The style takes after the *Bol Banav Thumri*, which creates certain moods through combinations of words and melody. Restraint in rendering is a feature of this style and the *taals* used are mainly *Dadra, Deepchandi*, and *Addha. Thumris* are composed of lighter *ragas* and generally simpler *taals*. The text of a *Thumri* is generally romantic and is based on the beloved. The text is normally pronounced very clearly during the performance and the emotions are expressed out musically.

Singers of the Banaras gharana are known for their *Khayal* singing. The word *Khayal* literally means "imagination," and this form demands improvisational flexibility as well as careful attention to nuances of intonation, phrasing and rhythm. Paradoxically, it is less known to audiences in the West, who have learned to enjoy Indian instrumental music unhesitatingly — and have even begun to absorb the intricacies of Dhrupad vocals.

Khayal is several hundred years old. Originating in the courts of the Moghul emperors as a less rigid alternative to the Dhrupad style, it has evolved into a remarkably flexible form that allows an artist's individuality considerable rein — while remaining within the steady, inexorable flow of Indian tradition. Even within the past five decades the form has undergone metamorphoses, and the tradition of innovation continues. An artist is expected to develop an individual style (albeit one that is demonstrably connected to the tradition), and those performers who restrict themselves to a mere imitation of their preceptors or of other famous musical personalities are firmly criticized for a lack of imagination.

Khayal texts draw freely from Hindu and Muslim poetic traditions, and are usually romantic or devotional — or a combination of the two. Generally composed in the archaic Hindi dialect known as Brij Bhasha, Khayal songs are also found in languages like Bhojpuri – which is the language that singers from Varanasi sing in, Punjabi, Urdu, Rajasthani, Marathi and occasionally, in Sanskrit. Many songs have unclear wordings, and in some cases the texts have become completely garbled through multiple generations of oral transmission. However, the primary focus in a Khayal performance is less on the textual or lyrical content of a song than on abstract musical values. Audiences respond with delight to nuances of ornamentation, to complex rhythmic improvisation, to intricate melodic patterns or to a vocalist's superb intonation.

Performances of Khayal often start with a song in a very slow rhythmic cycle, perhaps of 10, 12, 14 or 16 beats; often the pulse is so slow that each beat is further subdivided — for instance, a 12-beat cycle becoming one of 48. Each beat of the rhythm is marked by a specific stroke or combination of strokes on the tabla drums; by listening to their sound a singer can keep his or her place in improvisation. The tonal material of the raga gradually moves from a restricted melodic range to an extensive gamut; from a slow and relaxed pace to a quicker one. Improvisation is punctuated by the first few words of the song, which become a familiar melody leading up to the first beat of the rhythmic cycle. All extemporized melodic or rhythmic variations aim for this beat, and the gradual building of tension as it approaches is one of Hindustani music's great delights. Eventually, the singer switches to a faster song in the same raga, displaying his or her virtuosity and command over the material. Sometimes a Tarana is used to conclude — these pieces are rhythmic in focus, and make use of nonsense syllables; they are thus in a sense analogous to scat singing in Jazz. This music presented in a jugalbandi format, as the Mishra brothers do, surely should provide rapturous delight to the audience.

Bade Ramdas Ji

The doyen of the Banaras Gharana was Bade Ramdas Ji. Born in 1877, Bade Ramdas Ji was trained by his father Pandit Shivnandan Mishra, and later by his father-in-law, the famous dhrupad singer Pandit Jaikarna Mishra. His exposition and style of singing were exceptional, and it was only natural that some of the best musicians from Varanasi such as Siddheshwari Devi, Rajan and Sajan Mishra, Pandit Umadatt Sharma (father of santoor player Shivkumar Sharma) and the sarangi player Pandit Gopal Mishra followed his tradition.

Pandit Gopal Mishra

Pandit Gopal Mishra was born in 1920. It is also said, that the musical forefathers of Gopal Mishra came from the Balrampur state. His father Pandit Sur Sahai Mishra was himself a leading sarangi player of his time and Gopal Mishra was under his tutelage. He then learnt from the revered Pandit Bade Ramdas, who was acknowledged for his complex and difficult *gayaki*. Gopal Mishra mastered both solo as well as accompaniment techniques from this source. He accompanied all leading vocalists of his time. When he was in the role of an accompanist, he played in an extremely attractive manner. As a soloist, he touched the hearts of the listener with his music making. He was adept, unlike many other sarangi players, at the *tihais*; which he took before arriving at the *sam*. His raga development was marked by a sense of novelty, with many unconventional note patterns. Gopal Mishra's fame as a Sarangi-player began to spread even before he reached twenty years of age. In those days, princely courts were the main patrons of music. He was invited to perform by the Kashmir, Patiala as well as Baroda princes. According to Pandit Ram Narayan, Gopal Mishra could play any note with any finger and he had a remarkable sense of rhythm. He could play fast and complex rhythmical patterns with his bow. As an aside, he also did a small role in the popular film *'Jhanak Jhanak Payal Baje'.* Gopal Mishra died in 1998.

Rajan and Sajan Mishra

Gopal Mishra's brother Hanumanprasad Mishra was also a leading sarangi player. The leading exponents of khayal singing today, Pandits Rajan and Sajan Mishra are the sons of Hanumanprasad Mishra. Trained by their uncle and by Bade Ramdas Ji, they are now so popular that they always command huge audiences wherever they perform be it in India or abroad. Endowed with voices that are rich and well blended, their singing is characterized by unusual beauty, energy and imagination. Surely, the Mishra brothers have carved a niche for themselves with their unique style, which combines grace with the power of the male voice. In addition to Khayal, Mishra brothers also excel in rendering the light classical forms such as Tappa, Tarana and Bhajan. Pt. Rajan and Sajan Mishra must be acclaimed as the best in *jugalbandi* (duet) singing which requires immaculate coordination among other things. The aim of *jugalbandi*, the musical partnership, is to bring home the subtleties and refinements of music as naturally and as spontaneously, as in the solo performance. With their immense skills, imagination, and energy they have raised the status of *jugalbandi* music to the heights rarely heard before.

In 1979, the Mishra brothers received the coveted Sanskriti Award for musical excellence from the Prime Minister of India. They were honoured with the titles of Sangeet Nayak from Pracheen Kala Kendra, Chandigarh, the Sangeet Ratna from Allahabad and Sangeet Bhushan from Banaras. They are top ranking broadcasters on the All India Radio and on Doordarshan (the Indian national television channel) which conferred on them the title Pandit. Their voices have reached every part of India, and since the revival of Maharishi

Gandharva -Ved Music they have toured extensively on almost all continents.

Siddheshwari Devi

Born on 8th August 1903, in Banaras, Siddheswari traced her musical lineage to her maternal grandmother Maina Devi, a reputed singer of Kashi of nearly a century ago. She was the inheritor of great musical traditions from a family which produced several famous singers like Maina Devi, Vidyadhari Devi, Rajeswari Devi and Kamaleswari Devi. As Siddheswari lost her mother when she was barely 18 months old, she was brought up by her maternal aunt, Rajeswari, who was a famed disciple of Maina Devi, Mithailal, and of the great Moizuddin himself. Brought up in this musical atmosphere, Siddheswari absorbed a great deal of the art right from her infancy. Her childhood was an unhappy one as she lost her father also very soon. About this period of her life, she once said : "We did not have luxuries like the gramophone. But our neighbours had one. I used to go to them to listen to the records of popular singers like Janaki Bai, Gauharbai and several others. How their music used to captivate me!".

Noticing the talent and eagerness of the young girl, Siyaji Maharaj began to teach her. Siyaji's father Shyamacharan Misra, and uncle Ramcharan Misra had been good musicians. About her guru, Siddheswari used to say : "No one could possibly get a more generous and affectionate guru. Having no children of his own, he treated me like his own daughter. He taught me all the basic ragas and a large number of Khayals, Tappas, and Taranas. He taught me with all his heart, and I practised my music with intense concentration and devotion. Nowadays, alas! the students are all in a hurry to acquire a diploma or a degree; they have no *lagan*."

After the death of Siyaji Maharaj, she for a while learnt from Ustad Rajab Ali Khan of Dewas, and Inayat Khan of Lahore.

However, her greatest guru, the one to whom she attributes most of her musical training was none other than Bade Ramdasji of Varanasi. Her face glowed with pride and veneration whenever she spoke about this generous guru who taught the eager disciple magnanimously. Nostalgically recalling those times of close *guru-shishya* bonds, Siddheswari once remarked: "The age of such great and generous gurus seems to have gone. No longer does one come across the really devoted type of pupils either. Today they are all in such a hurry."

Later, in 1965, when she joined the Shriram Bharatiya Kala Kendra in Delhi as a professor, she earned the reputation for being a sincere and conscientious teacher. Siddheshwari Devi's music represented Banaras Gharana style, by laying more emphasis on the intensity of feelings and expression of emotions through musical notes and voice modulations. A stalwart of thumri, Siddheshwari's music also included khayals, dhrupads, dadras, tappas, kajris, chaitis, horis and bhajans. In thumris she specialized in *Poorabang thumri*, which is also known as the *Bol-Banav-ki thumri.* Reliance on ragas was a distinctive feature of Siddheshwari's thumris. She helped in raising thumri to a classical form. She earned the title of Thumri Queen and was presented the much-coveted Padma Shree award in 1967. Siddheshwari Devi strongly believed in the Guru Shishya Parampara, which has been kept alive by her daughter Savita Devi. Savita established Smt Siddheshwari Devi Academy of Indian Music in the loving memory of her mother in 1977, the year in which Siddheshwari passed away.

In her book of reminiscences and records *'Maa ... Siddheshwari'*, Savita Devi lovingly and painstakingly traces the journey of her mother's life. It describes in detail, Siddheshwari's rise from an uncared for orphan in her aunt's house in Varanasi to a famous classical singer and recipient of a Padmashree award. The book traces the birth and evolution of a glorious singer, the long years of riyaaz under her gurus, her performances that reveal nuances of thumri gayaki, hitherto unknown, and her many sorrows and successes in her personal and professional life. It also touches upon the rich and varied styles of music of the Banaras Gharana which she perfected and her interactions with other artists who gave shape and colour to Indian Classical Music. In this only exhaustive and definitive biography available of this great vocalist, the author shows us closely the angst, hardships, joys and sensibilities that are the core of a true artiste.

Savita Devi

Savita Devi not only inherited a rich tradition of classical music but is a vocalist of rare artistry in her own right. It will not be an exaggeration to say that she had her first lessons in the womb of her famous mother. Savita Devi, in her childhood, not only studied but also breathed music. From an early age, she underwent a long period of comprehensive training under her mother and specialised in Thumri, Dadra, Chaiti, Kajra and Tappa of the Banaras Gharana (Poorabang), a style made famous by her illustrious mother. Although Savita has a rich and varied fare of music to offer her audiences, she is a purist. Her thumri does not overflow into her khayal or vice versa. Likewise, her Hori, Kajri, Dadra, Tappa, Chaiti etc., are always separate and pure in content. When she sings bhajans, majestic cadences filled with devotion come forth. For her, music is an offering to God and is marked by melody and a sublime feeling.

After graduation in arts, Savita Devi studied classical music at the Banaras Hindu University and received a postgraduate degree. She later received the Sangeet Alankar from Poona. Carrying forward the legacy of music, Savita Devi is doing extensive research in the Thumri style of singing, the object of which is to develop new and more pleasing ways of presenting the old compositions. Besides being the Managing Director of the Sidhheshwari Devi Academy, she is also the Head of Department of Music in Daulat Ram College at the University of Delhi.

Ustad Bismillah Khan

In over thirty-four years of my life, I have heard him only twice. The first time, he was playing at the tiny Hanuman Temple, right next to our home in the Banaras Hindu University, on the occasion of the foundation day of the temple on Chaitra Poornima. I was only three, too small to understand the music, but felt privileged to be in an audience that numbered only a hundred. It was an intimate concert, and I am sure everyone felt that way. The next time I heard him was at New Delhi's Siri Fort Auditorium in the year 2001. The hall was packed with two thousand people, all mesmerized at the sight of the old man putting in a magical performance. He began by saying, *"Aaj hamaara mood hai"* (I'm in the mood to play today). And after playing one raag, he said, *"Abhi hamare Banaras mein Saawan ka mahina chal raha hai. Sab Kajri gaatey hain, main bhi Kajri bajaoonga".* (It is the month of Saawan in Banaras. They sing the kajri this time of the year, and I shall play it too.) I was sitting some twenty rows away from the stage, but I felt I was on stage, watching his lips weave magic out of the shehnai reed.

Ustad Bismillah Khan, the most outstanding and world-famous shehnai player, has attained astonishing mastery over the instrument. The legend was born on 21 March 1916. His ancestors were court musicians in the princely state of Dumraon in Bihar and he was trained under his uncle, the late Ali Bux 'Vilayatu'. He spent his childhood in Varanasi, on the banks of the Ganga, where his uncle was the official shehnai player in the famous Vishwanath temple. It was due to this that Bismillah became interested in playing the Shehnai. At an early age, he

Sadhu makes way for a cow

Malviya Bridge, the view from Rajghat

Filigreed Verandah at Satyanarayan Temple, Bansphatak

Wedding Iconography around a doorway

Ganesh painted on wall near Nai Sarak

Swami Bhaskaranand's Memorial at Durga Kund

Kurukshetra Kund near Ravindrapuri

The Biswas House in Sonarpura

Town Hall at Maidagin

Radha Swami Temple, Lohatiya

Narasimha

Swami Ramdheen, Head priest of Ratnakar Mandir

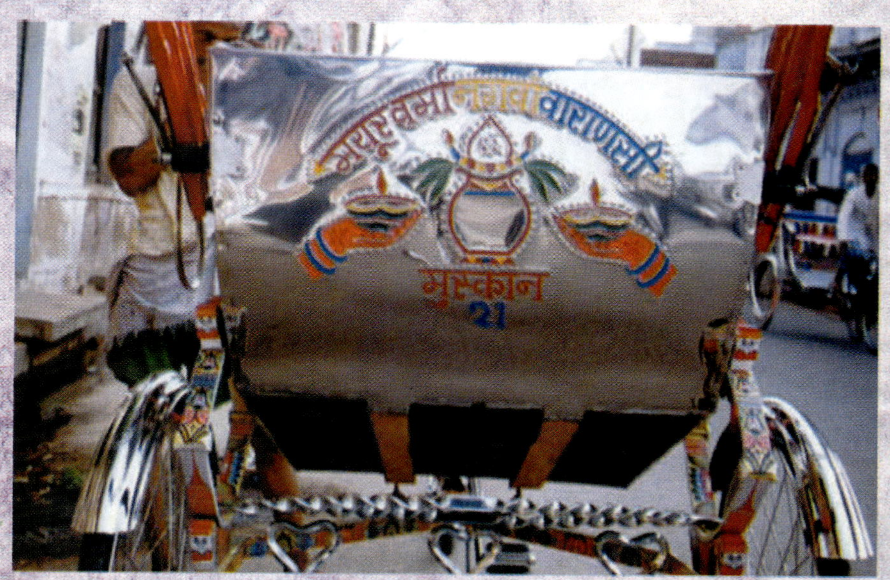

The back of a Rickshaw

Durga Temple

Tulsi Manas Mandir

Dandi swamis in conversation

Dandi swamis in procession

Baba Rajeshwar Prasad : Iconography at Shivala

The Buddha at Sarnath

Dhamekh Stupa

Mulgandha Kutir Vihara

Three Shrines : Mokshadeshwar, Chamunda, Karuneshwar

Ganesh Paduka at Chausatti Ghat

Ram, Janaki, Lakshman

Aghor Baba Kinaram and others

Temple at Bhairo Talab

Woman drawing water from Kardama Kund

Nepali Temple

Kardama Kund

Dev Deepawali

'Bajra' on the Ganga

Sadhu on a boat

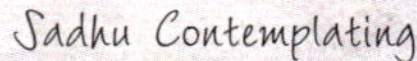

Sadhu Contemplating

Mansarovar Ghat

Manmandir Ghat

Observatory at Manmandir Ghat

Dharahara Masjid

Rameshwar

familiarized himself with various forms of the music of Uttar Pradesh, such as Thumri, Chaiti, Kajri, and Sawani. Later he studied Khayal music and mastered a large number of ragas.

The first public appearance of Ustad Bismillah Khan was at the Allahabad Music Conference in 1930 and the next in Lucknow, where he received gold medals for his performance. It was, however, after a performance in Calcutta in 1937 that he shot into limelight and started attracting the attention of connoisseurs and music lovers.

In his early days, his brother also played with him sometimes. Both the brothers were expert players, but the famous Urdu saying "*Bade bhai so bade bhai, lekin chhote bhai - Subhanallah!*" perfectly described the brothers. When they played together Bismillah Khan always played down his own part as he did not wish to overshadow his brother. "Even though I have the ability, I must always remember that he is my elder brother" he always said with humility and modesty. It was only after his brother's death that he allowed himself to break loose. On India's first Republic Day ceremony it was Khan Sahib who poured his heart out in Raaga Kaafi from the Red Fort. On a more popular level it was Khan Sahib who composed that magic film number *'Dil ka khilauna hai toot gaya'* for the film Goonj Uthi Shehnai. He has made money but spent it just as fast. He supports nearly 100 relatives, including 10 children.

"Music, *sur, namaaz*. It is the same thing," says the maestro. "We reach Allah in different ways. A musician can learn. He can play beautifully. But unless he can mix his music with religion, unless he strives to meet God, he will only have *kalaa* (art) but no *assar* (mystical union). He will always stand at the ocean and never reach the heights of purity."

Khan Saheb is soaked in religion. It is his sustaining life-force. But it is this same religion that damns music, condemns it as an act of rape. For the Shias, music is *haraam* (taboo). But for the man who took the shehnai out of the wedding processions and *aubatkhaanas* - the shehnai player, traditionally was to be heard and not seen - and who was able to weave patterns of dazzling intricacy into his music as he brought it to the centre-stage of classical respectability, his instrument is also his Quran. Where others see conflicts and contradictions between music and religion, he sees only a divine unity. Even as a devout Shia, Khan Sahib is also a staunch devotee of Saraswati, the Hindu goddess of music.

"When *maulvis* and *maulanas* ask me about this, I tell them, sometimes with irritation, that I can't explain it. I feel it. I feel it. If music is haraam then why has it reached such heights? Why does it make me soar towards heaven? The religion of music is one. All the others are different. I tell the *maulanas*, this is the only *haqeeqat* (reality). This is the world. My *namaaz* is the seven *shuddh* and five *komal surs*. And if this is *haraam*, then I say: *aur haraam karo, aur haraam karo* (if music be a thing of sin, sin on)."

His house in Varanasi, in Sarai Harha, is an ample but decrepit structure. His living room, which also serves as guest room, is sparsely furnished with creaky wooden benches and a large *takhat* on which, at a given time of the day, his children perform *namaaz*, oblivious of guests and visitors. Still in incessant demand as a player he travels by train regularly with his troupe, often by second class. He hates to fly. And when travel arrangements are being made, the house buzzes with activity as instruments are laid out, ancient steel trunks and torn British Airways flight-bags are packed with clothes and lunch boxes stuffed with rice and *samosas*. The shehnai player, whose name is familiar even to the international jet set as that of Ravi Shankar, travels by cycle rickshaw. And as he wheels down the city's streets at the head of a caravan of rickshaws, smiling at well wishers, he looks as happy as a British Lord in a Rolls Royce.

Each year, on the eighth day of Muharram, this devotee of the Shia faith who refuses to touch the reed of his shehnai with his lips unless he has offered his *namaaz* before sunrise, engages himself in his own private drama of religious apostasy. Dressed simply in white, he leads a procession, like a mischievous Pied Piper of rebellion, playing a silver shehnai reserved specially for the occasion. The procession winds its way through Varanasi's Byzantine lanes to the *mauzaa* of Imam Hussain. Here, just inside the gate, he sits cross-legged on the dusty ground in the fashion of a mendicant street minstrel and plays for hours, weeping copiously all the time, while the audience pitches coins into his lap. This is simple man. A man of tenderness, a gentle private man, yet given to unbridled display of emotion. When he laughs, the ground shakes. At 85, he is an immensely handsome man with a princely beard and eyes which glint with boyish mischief, his only 'bad habit' he apologises, is smoking Wills cigarettes which he puffs with obvious relish. There is nothing about him that bespeaks his fame - his honorary doctorates, his Padma Vibhushan, his concerts in almost every capital around the world, his dozens of best-selling record albums.

Girija Devi

As a performing artiste, Girija Devi has become a legend in her lifetime. There is no musical honour she has not received. Her brilliant renderings of light classical music have captured audience hearts worldwide. Born in 1929 in Varanasi, music lessons had started for Girija Devi at the age of five. The home of Pandit Sarju Prasad Mishra or Dadaji, as he was called, in the densely populated Kabir Chaura, must have been something of an eye opener. Kabir Chaura, in the thirties, was a stronghold of the Banaras gharana. Some of the leading tabla players, Kathak dancers and sarangi players belonged to this area. Her tutelage lasted for 10 years, until the guru's death, and he fostered in her the habit of practicing the alankars and other fundamentals for three or four hours every day.

The visage of a saint-singer, a stirring artiste and a serene devotee is the quintessence of her musical genius. But the journey to this rarefied pedestal has been an uphill climb where every step of the way has been washed clean by purgatorial fire. While most children are instilled into the art by the simple ceremony of tying a thread or *ganda* around their wrists by the guru, marking a symbolic acknowledgement of the responsibility of training shouldered by the guru, Girija Devi's ceremony was accomplished after years of rigorous pedantry under the late Guru Shambu Mishra. Her teacher held a musical trial for her before an invited audience of fifty learned musicians. Only when these musicologists had given the nod of approval for her did her guru acquiesce to formally consecrate the instructional process. Of course the question of making her debut before concert audiences was to come later in 1949 when she broadcast a recital from the All India Radio Station, Allahabad. "The idea was to assess whether I was progressing in the right directions in my music and get a feedback from listeners about my performance." This seemingly innocuous event turned momentous. It was as if the floodgates had opened and the very next year Girija Devi was invited to give her first live concert at Arrah in the state of Bihar and from the fifties, she was a constant invitee to concerts in India and abroad.

Not that there has been a lack of thumri singers before the advent of Girija Devi, but few had captured audience hearts to the extent that she has succeeded in doing. In a typical Girija Devi concert, there is music, which speaks to the audience "before the public one develops antennae for their responses," she apprises; and there is the thumri, which she has made her chief vehicle of communication, a kind of two-way traffic of emotive rapport. The parched hearts of musical audiences find succour when she sings the dalliances of Lord Krishna with female devotees or *gopis* in her innumerable thumris and this base is made the onus of a large corpus of human emotions expressed through technique and eloquent verse. "I loved decorating words with music," she explains. "Take for instance the line *'rasa ke bhare toreh nain..'* suggesting the Lord's eyes being a repository of emotions. I imagine a hundred gopis or devotees of the Lord seeking attention in His eyes. Some see in Him a tinge of jealousy. Others perceive a hint of pride or carefree abandon. Others see only a divinity; some the playfulness of Krishna. I use notes to suit the mood of the sentiment so that a single line can be sung to at least tweny-five different interpretations." The music thereby inspires listeners.

Today there is no musical honour which she has not received. A recipient of the Padma Shri and the Padma Bhushan from the President of India, she has been honoured by all the music academies of the states, the Sangeet Natak Academy Award and with the coveted title of 'Sangit Shiromani' by the Prayag Sangeet Samiti, Allahabad. She has also served at the ITC's Sangeet Research Academy for 12 years, and is now back in her beloved Varanasi, as a visiting professor at the Banaras Hindu University.

The Tabla Tradition

Varanasi has its own distinctive style of playing that percussion instrument, the tabla. The tabla *baaj* that is today associated with the city of Varanasi was developed over two hundred years ago by the legendary Pandit Ram Sahai. Born in 1780, he was a child prodigy in his native city. At an early age, he became a disciple of Ustad Modhu Khan (grandson of Sidhar Khan of Delhi) a musician in the royal court of Nawab Asafuddaula in Lucknow. During his twelve year apprenticeship with Modhu Khan, Ram Sahai amassed a prodigious repertoire of compositions and mastered the art of improvised elaborations on a given theme. When he was 21 years of age he made his debut performance at the court of Nawab Wazir Ali and accomplished the astounding feat of playing a tabla solo which continued uninterrupted for seven consecutive nights without repetition of a single piece.

In the middle of his career Ram Sahai retired from public life and turned his attention to the creation of a new style of tabla playing. Through major changes in the position of the hand on the drum and a more efficient use of the fingers he increased the tabla's range of tone and dynamics. In addition to composing numerous pieces in the existing forms he introduced several new types of compositions which have come to be associated exclusively with the Banaras *baaj*. The new style was eminently suitable not only for solo playing, but for any type of music from heavy classical dhrupad singing (usually accompanied by the pakhawaj drum), to the lighter forms of thumri and tappa, to all styles of instrumental music, and lastly, to Kathak dance. He died in the year 1826.

Ram Sahai's innovations and the devotion to musical excellence of his descendants has produced what is today one of the most respected and popular tabla styles in India. Later, two gharanas evolved within the Banaras gharana. One was the Kabirchaura gharana, and the other was the Ramapura gharana. Pandit Kanthe Maharaj, and Pandit Samta Prasad belonged to the Kabirchaura gharana whereas Pandit Anokhelalji, belonged to the Ramapura gharana. The names of Pandit Durga Sahai, Pandit Kanthe Maharaj and Pandit Anokhelal Misra are remembered with awe and reverence by Indian musicians as being among the greatest virtuosi of recent times. Since their passing, the high standards of the tradition have been preserved by the present generation of Benares players which includes such contemporary greats as Pandit Sharda Sahai, Padma Vibhushan Pandit Kishan Maharaj and the late Pandit Samta Prasad.

In the Benares baaj, the art of solo tabla performance is greatly respected and very highly developed. A tabla solo is traditionally played in a sixteen beat *taal*, a rhythmic cycle, known as *teen taal*. Throughout the performance, an aural outline of this *taal* is maintained by means of a cyclic melody known as a *lahara*. There are more than twenty forms of composition in use, many of them unique to this tradition. Some are theme and variation forms which require spontaneous composition by the performer, while many others involve sophisticated compositional techniques with finished pieces handed down from generation to generation. In addition, there is a well defined procedure for joining the various types of compositions to form a logical and pleasing performance.

ᏣᏍ

Folk Songs of Varanasi

All through the summer nights of my childhood, we would sleep on our terrace. The nights would be crisp, we would lie on our backs identifying the stars and the constellations we'd learn about in school. After nine o'clock at night, suddenly, the sound of the *birha*, amplified across the distance, would waft across from neighbouring Khojwan, or Lanka. The lead singer would sing out a phrase, a set of young boys would repeat after him. The harmonium and the dholak would suddenly rise in tempo and volume to emphasize a point, and then fall back into accompaniment. Many years later, when Ustad Bismillah Khan mentioned that he was going to play a *kajri*, at Siri Fort in New Delhi, I found tears welling up in my eyes even before he began playing. I was reminded of the hordes of village women who would pass by our home during the Saawan Mela, singing the folk song of the monsoons.

There are two versions of the origin of the Birha. One suggests that this is a song of separation; the other that it is a song sung in the memory of heroes – 'Birs'. Originally sung by women, it is now mostly the men who sing it to express their melancholy thoughts or to remember something sweet that happened to them. Through their lyrics, they express emotions like longing, heroism, satire and devotion. For example, the song 'Chunri Satrangi Chatkar', This is a song depicting all that is good on this earth. The woman, symbolic of a human being is asking her husband, symbolic of God, to put all the best qualities in her 'chunri', a symbol of life. She wants the virtues of Raja Harishchandra, the greatness of Ram-Sita, Krishna, Gandhi, Buddha, the purity of the river Ganga, presence of Gods of all religions, the courage of Razia Sultan, the beauty of the mountains and the essence of the creator - Brahma.

Traditionally, the Ahirs - the milkman caste – have performed the birha. Is that why the colourful Bihari, Laloo Prasad Yadav, occasionally turns so poetic, I wonder? One of the best known singers today is Jawaharlal Yadav, who lives in Ausanganj in Varanasi. Apart from performing regularly on All India Radio, he travels to sing for functions in other states as well. His loud booming voice, characteristic of folk singers together with the accompaniment, gives the audience a 'no holds barred' feel. Other well known performers include Munna Lal Yadav, another resident of Ausanganj, Gyani Yadav, Ramjanam Topiwala, and Ram Kailash Yadav, of village Lamahi in Allahabad. Performers use the opportunity to poke fun at the establishment, especially politicians. At a recent performance, singer and poet Danda Banarasi sang, *"Ram ko bhaganey wale desh kya chalayenge"* (How will those who chase Ram away run the country) making fun of Prime Minister Atal Behari Vajpayee. Saand Banarasi responded with *"Rat te Rat te Jay Siyaram, Kahan Ayodhya Kahan Ram"* (While chanting Ram's name, you seem to have converted a religious issue into a political one for your own gains). Of late, of course, the lyrics have turned somewhat obscene – if the cassettes available in the local markets are anything to go by. They have titles like 'Sainya Le Gaye Kotwaal' (The Policeman Took Away my Lover), and 'Harami Rickshawalla' (The Bastard Rickshaw Puller) !

One of the most popular and well known forms of folk music - Kajris are often sung by classical and semi classical musicians. The word Kajri is possibly a derivative of Kajal - meaning Kohl or Black. In a country of sizzling hot summers - the black monsoon clouds bring with them relief and great joy - with a need to sing out loud. This is the moment for the Kajri to be sung. Even though Kajri is sung all over Eastern Uttar Pradesh - neighbouring Mirzapur is considered the real home of the Kajri. According to a folk tale of Mirzapur - there was a woman called Kajali whose husband was in a distant land. The monsoon arrived and the separation became unbearable... she started crying at the feet of the Goddess. These cries took the form of the popular Kajri songs. The Kajri *'Kaune Rang Mungva'* is a simple conversation between two sisters-in-law. In the depictions of folk songs, a woman has a complex relationship with her husband's sister, *nanad* - in which she is sometimes a confidante, a friend and often jealous or antagonistic.

There are three forms of Kajri singing in Uttar Pradesh. One is sung on a performance platform, and is called 'Shastriya Kajri'. Another is a competition between two or more performers, called 'Dangali Kajri'; the third is sung by women on monsoon evenings, while dancing in a semi-circle- this is known as the 'Dhunmuniya Kajri'. Bhartendu Harishchandra and Ambika Dutt Vyas were among the famous Kajri composers.

The other forms of folk songs popular in Varanasi are the Chaiti and the Phag. They are sung in the harvesting season – the months of Phalgun and Chaitra – and are characterized by lyrics suggesting joy and plenty.

☙

My own brush with Hindustani classical music began when I was in Class Seventh. Our school introduced what was called 'Extra-Curricular Activity' classes on Saturdays, and I chose to learn to play the Hawaiian slide guitar. My father bought me a Gibtone guitar from Calcutta (probably named after the better-known Gibson that the pros use). Our teacher was a young Bengali gentleman called Gopal Das. I began by learning the *sargam* – and was soon playing some old Hindi film songs, such as Mukesh's 'Kisi Ki Muskarahaton ..', Hemant Kumar's 'Aa Ja Sanam Madhur Chandni Mein Hum', and Rabindra Sangeet 'Aalo Amar Aalo'. He evidently found something in my playing to suggest that I start taking individual lessons, at home. Thus began my four-year stint with Indian classical music. Gopalda would visit every Sunday, and teach me for two hours. Through the week, I had to practise for at least an hour a day. I began by learning Raag Yaman Kalyan, the Alaap, Tod & Jhala; the Drut Gat and the Vilambit Gat. That was followed by Raag Bhairav, Kedar, Bihag, Bageshri, Bhairavi, Piloo, Malkaus, Chandrakauns, and finally, the Raag of Kings - Raag Darbari. Gopalda would coax me to practise even more, even at the cost of my play time, and I considered him a hard taskmaster. My father got me a metronome from his lab to keep time. And then, it was suddenly time for my first public performance. On the occasion of Saraswati Puja, Gopalda would get some of his students to perform at a cultural evening at his residence. I played Raag Bihag, in teental, for some twenty minutes. It was the high point of my short-lived musical career. Public performance over, it was time to take the first level examination that would qualify me as some kind of a musician. I appeared for Prayag Sangeet Samiti's Sangeet Prabhakar examination – the equivalent of a High School certificate in classical music – and passed in the first division. By that time I was in the eleventh standard. The seemingly unsurmountable barrier of competitive examinations lay ahead, and we were all swept away in a tide that engulfs students as they approach that stage in life when getting admission to an engineering or medicine course is all they can think of. At least that's how it was, in Varanasi, in the early 1980s; I believe it still is so. I no longer had the time to practise the guitar. One evening, I sadly told Gopalda I was giving up learning the guitar. He was angry at me, but inside, I knew he felt sad. "You had a future in music," he told me. "But I cannot prevent you from trying to make a career elsewhere." I never touched the guitar after that. Recently, Gopalda's elder daughter Sangeeta, who is married to an old classmate of mine, and lives in Boston, appeared on my chat window. She told me, "You may not believe it, but Baba often talks about you."

Knowing exactly just how long it takes to get that note, that beat just right, I find it amazing how music schools that promise foreigners that they would learn to play an instrument in a month, have proliferated in the city. The Outlook magazine, in its December 25 2000 issue, had an article on it headlined 'Karma Kitsch'. There could be no better description. It talked about how Seiji Shimada, from Kobe in Japan, shelled out Rs 3000 to learn hatha yoga and sitar in two weeks flat. His guru, Monilal Hazra of Kedar Ghat justified his promise by saying: "Indians can't master the sitar within a short time; foreigners can because they consume 1 kg of butter and honey every day." The article went on to say: 'Moksha was never any better. Just attend a Monday evening classical concert at the Triveni Music Centre near Pandey Ghat. Dim lights, pictures of Hindu divinities, classical instruments hanging from a damp ceiling and a motley crowd of 14 provide the setting for this eve of musical nirvana. Thirty minutes later, sitarist Monilal Hazra builds up a crescendo over which his companion Nandalal Mishra blurts out: "Music is a meditation. It'll help you achieve inner peace." ' Con artists, all. If you are a Western, or Eastern visitor interested in mastering an instrument, be sure of what you are getting into, and verify the antecedents of the music school or guru you'd be taking lessons from. Here is a short description of the schools that I am aware of.

Kailash Nishad

A very experienced teacher, he has taught several Indian and Western Tabla students who had a deep interest in Indian Classical Music. He holds a Diploma in Music (1989) from Banaras Hindu University and Masters in Tabla(1990) from Allahabad University. He knows English well and so it is easier for foreign students to communicate with him while they learn. As a player, his career highlights include concerts and recordings in Germany, a special invitation performance (1996) for the Indian Consulate General in the United Arab Emirates and the 1998 World Music Festival in Vienna. His recordings available in Audio Cassettes ("Ganga and Friends") and CDs ("Flying East" & "Air is Spirit"). His address in Varanasi is : B 30/ 250 A Nagwa. Phone: 315532.

Triveni Music Centre

This school finds mention in Lonely Planet and Rough Guide. They are located near Dasashwamedh Ghat, and hold concerts by well-known artistes twice every week on Monday and Tuesday. They also sell musical instruments. Their address is : D-24/38, Pandey Ghat, Dashawamedh Road. Phone : 328074.

Sur Sarita

Situated on the Manikarnika, the famous burning ghat of Varanasi, this school has teachers for several instruments including the flute and the santoor. Every evening at 7:30pm, a live music concert is held here. They also manufacture & repair instruments.

Music Melody House

This is a relatively new school next to the Assi Ghat, and has been doing well. They also sell all kinds of instruments, and hold concerts frequently. Here one can sit down next to the Ganga and practice his or her music. Phone : 314747.

Sur Sandhya

Located near Shivala, close to the ashram of Baba Kinaram, the school is headed by an experienced teacher. It's a good place to learn Hindustani classical vocal, as well as the sitar and the flute.

Mumtaz Musical

This school is also at Shivala, in front of the Ratnekar Park. The place is recommended for those who want to learn the Tabla, though other instruments like Sarangi, Sitar, and Flute can also be learnt. A musical concert is held here every evening at 7 pm. Phone : 314749.

Baba School of Music

This school, located at Meer Ghat in the Ganpati Guest House Building, has a fantastic view of the river. As one learns to play the instrument, one gets the feeling of being one with nature, as if they are on an island of peace. The good thing about the school is that they have excellent teachers like Deodhar Mishra, who have cut their own CDs. Manufacturing and repair facility is also available at the school, which holds music concerts thrice a week.

Radhey Shyam Sharma and Brothers

They specialise in the manufacturing and export of high quality musical instruments like sitar, tabla , tanpura and dholak. They are the best if you need to purchase a Veena. Radhey Shyam or Ram Lakhan can be directly contacted on phone at 358427. Their address is D 52/73, Luxmi Kund, Luxa Road.

ও

The Akhadas and Pahalwans of Varanasi

As he or she floats on the Ganga on a boat in the early morning, or takes a walk on the ghats waiting for the sun to rise, a visitor in Varanasi will surely be struck by the sight of many a young or middle-aged man doing push-ups on stone platforms at the ghats, or vigorously swinging a mace. For the resident, it is just another vital ingredient in the city's ancient culture. There is more to the practice of wrestling and body-building in Varanasi than physical fitness. By doing so, a man demonstrates his devotion to Hanuman, the Monkey God. Joseph Alter, the Indian-born American scholar, has possibly written the most in-depth account of life at the akhada in his book, 'The Wrestler's Body'. Much of this section is based on his work.

> What is an akhada? It is a place of recreation for youth. It is a shrine of strength where earth is turned into gold. It is a sign of masculinity and the assembly hall of invigorated youth. Strength is measured against strength and moves and counter moves are born and develop. An akhara should be in an open area where fresh air and sunshine mingle. It should be away from dirt and filth and in a place where the earth is soft. It should be set off by a boundary of some sort and surrounded by thick foliated trees. There should be water nearby.
>
> One should enter the akhara after paying obeisance and offering incense to the Lord. An akhara is where one prays and where offerings are given and distributed. Its earth is saluted and taken up to anoint one's shoulders and head. And then one wrestles and the sound of slapping thighs and pounding chests fills the air. Grunts and groans of exertion echo ominously. One trounces and in turn is trounced. Exercise is done. La-

ziness and procrastination are drowned in sweat. The earth is mixed and finally one salutes the pit and leaves.

Ratan Patodi, in Bharatiya Kushti Kala[1]

The ideal location for an akhara is a cool, clean, quiet area where one can get away from both an atmosphere of domestic obligation and an environment of work. It would be set back from the road under banyan and *neem* trees and demarcated by a low wall. In the center of the akhara stands a large cement structure some twenty feet tall with a flat roof supported by thin posts decorated with blue line paintings of wrestlers exercising and posturing.

Within this structure is a wrestling pit: a raised rectangular platform of soft, fine earth brought in yearly from village fields and raked even and flat. Around the sides of the pit are areas of hard-packed earth. On one side can be found a well and cement trough for bathing. Opposite this, usually, there will be a small temple decorated with paintings of Hanuman, Ram, and Sita, inside of which stands the bright vermilion, cloth-bedecked, flower-garlanded form of Hanuman, the patron deity of every akhara. Inside the akhara premises are a number of small shrines with smaller icons of Hanuman and Shiva, some with many earthen lamps before them. Behind the pit is a shedlike verandah attached to the guru's house where wrestlers change, exercise, and massage one another.

As you enter the akhara, you will see wrestlers or trainees climbing up ropes attached to a neem or pipal tree while others perform *dands* (jackknifing push-ups) and *bethak* (deep knee bends), lift weights, and swing dumb-bells and *gadas* (wooden maces). Although there are no rules that govern the spatial layout of trees relative to earth, air, and water, there is a sense that together they must comprise a picturesque integrated whole: a tableau of mutually dependent elements. The roots of the trees mingle with the water of the well; the air is cooled by the shade of the trees and is scented by their leaves. The earth is bound by the roots of the trees and, like the water, it draws on the ineffable essence of the trees and imparts to them the resources of growth. The water dampens and cools the earth, and the earth keeps the water fresh. The interdependence of natural elements reinforces a notion of the akhara as self-contained, an aesthetic world unto itself.

I spent some time at Akhada Swaminath at Tulsi Ghat to understand the rituals associated with wrestling. Jai and Arif Khan, two young men explained them to me one morning, as they offered me handfuls of soaked gram. Every akhara has at least one shrine dedicated to Lord Hanuman. This shrine is the focus of religious activity in the akhada. The image of Hanuman is cleaned at least twice a week and is anointed with *sindoor* (vermilion paste). His "clothes" are cleaned regularly, offerings are made to him twice a week, he is prayed to every morning when his blessing is invoked, and he is saluted whenever someone enters or leaves the akhada. Most akharas have numerous shrines and temples dedicated to a host of gods, goddesses, godlings, and saints. *Lingams* are often found either in shrines by themselves, at the base of trees, or in conjunction with small images of Hanuman. Many akhadas also have a shrine dedicated to the founding guru. The founders of many akharas are reputed to have been superhuman, saintly men who possessed great spiritual and physical strength by virtue of their strict adherence to a wrestling regimen of diet, exercise, and religious faith. The daily life of a wrestler is a regime of integrated health and fitness drawn out, on, through, and in his body. In this regard the guru is both a taskmaster and a sculptor. Many wrestlers believe that a person must not so much as urinate or drink without first asking his guru's permission. A disciple's role is not to think, but to be moulded and shaped, to allow himself to be cut in the pattern of perfection.

For many wrestlers who labour as dairy farmers, clerks in government offices, cooks and waiters in hotels and sweet shops, dry-goods merchants, policemen, railway personnel, hotel managers, military recruits, and *paan* hawkers, the akhara is a retreat. It is indeed "a world unto itself," a place set apart from the world of work and family, a peaceful place from which to draw strength. After work many men come to the akhara from all over the city of Varanasi simply to defecate, drink some water, bathe, change clothes, and talk with friends. In this social context of camaraderie, the atmosphere and mood of the akhara space is everything, for it charges these simple pleasures with therapeutic significance. In fact, the term '*langotiya yaar*', used to connote one's closest friend, is derived from the loincloth that wrestlers wear – if we can share our loincloths, we can share anything. The mood and aesthetic appeal of the akhara environment is captured in the term *anand* (satisfaction) which is used to summarize the feeling that one comes to the akhara to experience.

Some of the more famous akhadas and pehalwans associated with them are now mentioned. Bansphatak Akhada, located near Mir Ghat, was started nearly 150 years ago by Jaggu Seth. He was reputedly capable of performing 5000 stretches and 8000 situps, and enter the pit immediately. His strength was compared to that of an elephant. Akhada Hanuman Gadi, near Gaighat, is known to have produced champion wrestlers like Mahesh Mishra, Radheyshyam Mishra – all India champion in the welterweight class, and Olympian Janardan Bhargava. Akhada Ramkund produced the famous wrestlers Pandit Swaminath of Sankatmochan, and Olympian Sugreev Lakshar. It also gave refuge to freedom fighters Bhagat

Singh and Chandra Shekhar Azad. Yet another Olympian, Laxmikant Pandey learnt his ropes at the Ramsingh Akhada near Beniabag – which has to date produced some seven thousand wrestlers.

ଓ

On Widows

Varanasi is sometimes called the 'city of ten thousand widows'. The figure, I believe, is an underestimation. The State Women's Commission in West Bengal suggests that the number is sixteen thousand. If one walks along the Ganga, one will see numerous women, alone or in small groups singing and begging for survival. It is a tradition that goes centuries back, when women who did not commit 'Sati' by throwing themselves into their husbands' funeral pyres, would be banished to the city for the remainder of their lives. Here they survive on the doles of the city's residents, and in some cases, on the small sums of money sent by their family members. A small number might take refuge in *ashrams*, but most have to find makeshift shelter. They are the widows who must wait, for death that would reunite them with their husbands. It is a redemption that could take years.

Most of these widows came from Bengal. Bengali writer Narayan Sanyal's famous novel 'Asalitatar Daye' has its central character Anandamohan Ray falling in love with a widow; Tatini. Until social reformers like Ishwar Chandra Vidyasagar advocated and were able to bring a change, young Brahman girls had to be married off before they attained puberty. The social ostracization was such that if parents failed to do so, they married off their daughters even to men in their 60s or 70s. Besides, a man could marry as many girls as he wished, and even received cash from parents for the deed because he 'rescued' these girls, as well as themselves, from becoming social outcasts. The result was inevitable; girls became widows even in their teens, some of them before consummating their marriage.

It is not that the widows belong to impoverished families. A study conducted in 1982 found that 75% of the women came from well-to-do Brahmin families; which no longer wished to spend money to support a mother, but explained away her banishment as a religious, ritual necessity. Deepa Mehta's aborted film 'Water' might have drawn attention to the plight of the widows briefly, but now that the hullabaloo has died out, they have once again been forgotten.

For most widows, every day is a painful routine. It begins with an early morning bath in the Ganga, no matter how cold it is or how swift the currents. Then she goes to the temple for a prayer, and sits outside with her aluminum bowl extended till she manages to collect a few coins. When it is time for the daily *prasad,* she collects it from the temple to fill her stomach. Later, she sits with other widows and sings devotional songs as long as her frail voice will allow her to do so.

There are, however, exceptions; and the stories of Vidya Devi and Krishna Bhamini bear testimony to the courage of widows to chart their own paths of progress. Vidya Devi, a widow from Bihar came to Varanasi in 1920-21. Determined to make the most of her life, she took initiation from Swami Gyananandji, who had started an ashram where widows could be educated. Vidya Devi learnt philosophy and the religious texts, and took on the task of managing the various trusts from him. In 1933, she started the Arya Mahila School. By 1958, it had evolved to a degree college, and there were 1300 students. Krishna Bhamini came to Varanasi as a child widow, from an unconsummated marriage. Charged with a feeling of nationalism and independence, she found the support of other widows in Varanasi who did not look upon widowhood as a burden. She started a school in 1918, which later gained recognition as the Anglo-Bengali Lower Middle Girls School. A prosperous Bengali merchant, Durga Charan Rakshit donated a large sum of money for the upkeep and expansion of the school, and after his death, the school was renamed Durga Charan Girls' School.

ꟹ

Twelve Months, Thirteen Festivals

Hindus believe in worshipping their Gods and Goddesses collectively. The important dates associated with significant events in their lives are celebrated as festivals. In the observance of some festivals, it is essential to pray and perform ceremonies at a temple, or at a community place like a *puja mandap*; others may be performed at home. As the main centre of Hindu religion, Varanasi possibly celebrates more festivals than any other place, giving rise to the popular saying '*Barah Maas, Terah Parva'* (Thirteen festivals in twelve months). The Hindu calendar is a lunar one, and the dates on the Gregorian one keep changing every year.

Makar Sankranti

This festival takes its name from the fact that it is celebrated when the Sun enters the sign of the zodiac called *Makar* (Capricorn). This is considered the most auspicious place for the Sun to be in. Since the calculations for the date are done by the solar calendar, the festival always falls on January 14th. In Varanasi, the festival is called *Khichdi,* after the concoction of rice, pulses and vegetables that is prepared from the new harvest, distributed to the poor and the needy, and consumed at home.

This is also the day when kite-flying fever in the city reaches its peak. For days before Makar Sankranti, all the young men can be seen honing their skills in the open fields in the neighbourhood or from the rooftops of their homes. They prepare their strings, coating them with powdered glass so as to achieve maximum cutting power, and test kites for that perfect balance and aerodynamic shape. On the appointed day, the fields are full of young and old, boys and men launching multi-coloured kites into the air, and competitions between colonies and 'champion' kite-flyers begin. The best sight, of course, is at the river-front, where the breeze is the strongest. Kites dot the sky, as cries of 'Bhak-katey' rend the air, as soon as one kite dives and its sharper string abrades and slices through the string on another. The loser's kite floats gently towards the ground, with hordes of young children scrambling to get it; while he frantically reels in his string lest someone catch hold of that and take even that away from him!

Mauni Amavasya

The festival of Mauni Amavasya takes its name from the prescription that worshippers must not speak a word on this day, in the month of Paush (January-February), when the moon goes into eclipse. The Kashi Khand requires the worship of three images – Trimurti - of Brahma, Vishnu and Mahesh (Shiva), and the offering of the idols to Brahmans as gifts. Devotees begin the day by taking a bath in the Ganga at Prayag Ghat, and then taking the vow of silence. They worship the images of the three Gods at the ghat, and then go to the Vishwanath temple. Returning home, they perform a puja and a yagna (fire ritual), which is followed by donations to a Brahmin. The city sees an influx of pilgrims from neighbouring districts on this day, and the ghats get very crowded.

Basant Panchami

As winter gives way to spring, the people of Varanasi get ready to celebrate nature – *Basant*, spring, is commonly known as *Rituraj*, the King of Seasons. Basant Panchami is observed on the fifth day of the waxing fortnight on the month of *Magh* (January-February). On this day, the Goddess of Learning, Saraswati is worshipped, in every home that there is a student, and at every centre of learning, school, college, pathshala, or university; and the festival is also referred to as Saraswati Puja.

For two days before the puja, idols of Saraswati are on sale in different parts of the city, but especially in the market at Dasashwamedh. As children, this was a festival we would look forward to, because we understood the rites, participated in its observance, and the benefits would directly accrue to us – depending on (as we believed) how devoted and earnest we were. An idol of the Goddess was to be carefully selected, she had to have a benign, caring look. Flowers were bought in large quantities from the Flower Market at Bansphatak the previous evening. Then, the living room would be cleared of all furniture, and the task of decoration would begin. Potted plants were brought in to provide a backdrop of foliage. Coloured paper was cut and strung together to make streamers, which would be hung across the room. Crisscrossing them were long garlands of fragrant jasmine. This whole process took several hours, but tasks were clearly outlined and distributed. Finally, the Goddess would be seated on her wooden pedestal, and my brother and I would get our books and place them beside her. They would stay there, to imbibe all the blessings, all of the following day, which was another bonus that Saraswati Puja brought – no studies for a whole day! Meanwhile, Baba, our father got busy buying sweets and fruits, while Ma occupied herself with getting the Puja essentials together. Just before going off to bed, Baba would make sure that the dhotis we would all wear the next morning were ironed and pleated for that perfect fall.

By the time we woke up on the morning of the Puja, Ma was already awake, bathed and doing the *alpana* (floor painting, with rice paste) around the Goddess's idol. Baba had picked up fresh flowers from our garden. We would quickly bathe, and put on crisp, white *dhotis* and *kurtas*. By seven-thirty, our *purohit* (priest) would arrive. Bishu *da*, as we know him, is no ordinary priest. He is a plastic surgeon at Sir Sunderlal Hospital, but belongs to a family of Sanskrit scholars. Most years, he would change into his regular wear – shirt and trousers, right after doing the Puja, and head straight for the Operation Theatre. We would assemble around the Goddess, and the puja would be performed. After the *anjali* – prayers were said, *prasad* was distributed, fruits, sugar candy, and sweets. My father's students would join us in prayer, they needed the Goddess's blessings as much as we did.

Then, it was time to go to the Banaras Hindu University. Basant Panchami is the university's foundation day. Saraswati is the university's emblem. A procession ran through the main road of the university campus, gaining strength after every hostel, as the beautiful floats designed by the students joined it. The hostels vied to outdo each other every year, but the honours were almost always taken by the Agriculture Faculty (later, Institute), which had the benefit of decorating their float with myriad and plentiful flowers grown by the Horticulture Department. Eventually the floats would wind their way towards the university's foundation stone, set in a field outside the campus walls, where the traditional song – *Kulgeet* – would be sung by students of the Faculty of Performing Arts. Ceremony over, we would return home to a wonderful vegetarian lunch cooked by Ma. For some years, in the evening, the Bengali Association of BHU held a cultural programme, with plays, song and dance staged by the students and faculty.

Shiv Ratri

It was on Krishna Paksha Chaturdashi – the 14th day of the waning moon fortnight, in the month of Phalgun (February-March) that Shiva was married to Parvati. Since Shiva is believed to be permanently residing in Varanasi, his marriage anniversary is celebrated with much pomp and devotion by residents, and visitors to the city alike, in the form of the Shiv Ratri festival. In the entire year, this is the day when the crowds at the Vishwanath temple are at their maximum. Similarly, the new Vishwanath temple in the Banaras Hindu University, and other Shiva shrines such as Kashi Karvat, Manikarneshwar, Brahmeshwar and Dasashwamedheshwar attract a large number of devotees. Devotees wake up early in the morning and head for the Ganga in groups, singing songs in praise of Shiva and Parvati. Some women do not even sleep all night, staying awake in groups, singing devotional songs. They would have kept a fast for all of the previous day, sometimes not even drinking water. They either pick *bel* leaves, *datura* and other flowers and fruit from the trees in their compound, or buy them from flower-sellers on the way. After taking a dip in the river, they fill little copper vessels with *gangajal,* and milk. They arrange all this on a *thaali,* and set a little lamp beside it. They may also add a pinch of *bhaang* as part of their offering. At the temple, they bathe the *linga with* milk, and then with *gangajal. Bel* leaves and flowers are showered, and the fruits offered to Shiva. They light the lamp and circumambulate the shrine, and finally drink the few drops of milk and water that trickle down the *linga,* as *charanamrit* – the nectar that flows past the Lord's feet. It is only after they have given alms to a Brahman that they break their fast, which in some cases stretches as long as thirty-six hours.

Rangbhari Ekadashi

The Rangbhari Ekadashi was a festival originally associated with Lord Vishnu, particularly at the Adi Keshava Temple. It was adopted by the followers of Shiva in the period 1880-1910, during the tenure of Pandit Mahabir Prasad Tripathi as chief priest of the Vishwanath temple, and has hence become one of the important festivals celebrated here. The festival is observed on the eleventh day of the light fortnight in the month of Phalgun. Lord Vishwanath and his consort Parvati are worshipped with *abeer* (coloured powder – hence giving the festival its name 'full of colour'), *bhaang* and sweets. Two silver idols of Shiva and Parvati are installed at the temple, and an umbrella placed above them, from which descends a narrow stream of water, symbolizing the Ganga. The priests cover the idols with *bel* leaves, flowers and garlands, and sing hymns from the scriptures in the honour of Shiva. They sprinkle *abeer* on the images, and then thrown them open to the public. For twenty-four hours, till the next morning, devotees throng in from all over Varanasi and nearby towns and villages to have a *darshan* of the idols.

Holi

Holi is the festival of colour, gaiety and abandon. It is celebrated on the day after the full moon in the month of Phalgun (usually March). The festival has its origins in the villages and forests of Vrindavan, where Krishna and his band of cowherds went about throwing colour on the *gopis,* and serenaded them with song and dance. The songs are sung even today, and the same *pichkaris* – water syringes – are used by revellers to squirt coloured water during Holi celebrations.

For days before Holi, one finds little piles of twigs and rubbish building up in street corners across the city. With spring in the air, it is time for people to do a bit of spring-cleaning in their homes. By the time the day before Holi arrives, that has grown into a huge bonfire. The bonfire, called Holika, dates back to the time of the Asur (Demon) king Hiranyakashyap who ordered his son Prahlad to be burnt because he worshipped Lord Vishnu. He asked his sister Holika to wear the set of non-inflammable clothes she possessed, with Prahlad in her lap. But Holika was a good, sacrificing soul, and she quietly transferred the clothes to Prahlad and got burnt herself. Prahlad was saved, and became Lord Vishnu's greatest devotee. On the night before Holi, at the appointed hour, women circumambulate the Holika and make ritual offerings, after which the bonfire is lit. In today's Varanasi, it is quite a task to keep anything made of wood safe from the hands of marauders desirous of a bigger, fiercer bonfire. If one is not careful, wooden gates, tables or chairs lying outside anyone's home is sure to be carted away and flung into the flames!

On the day of the festival, the celebrations, originally designed for the free intermingling and banter between the sexes, degenerates into a prime excuse for eve-teasing. This is of course, not a recent phenomenon. Sherring, in 1868, observed, 'No woman can venture into the street on these days, without being exposed to insult … It is very difficult for the government to interfere beyond the suppression of licentious pictures, and to some extent, the general giving of abuse.' Groups of young men go about town throwing colour, and abuse. But I remember a far more enjoyable celebration, within the confines of our colony. At about 9 a.m., Professor of Physiology, and long-time Varanasi resident Shyam Behari Shukla would leave home, with his two sons, and buckets of coloured water. The first round of water-play would happen at his immediate neighbours, and then like a Pied Piper, he would lead a team of colony residents around. At each home, the men and boys of the family would be bathed in colour, following which the revellers would be served sweets and salted snacks. The size of the contingent would keep growing, till we would all reach the home of Hiralal, the farmer who once owned the land we all had our homes on. There, under the shade of mango trees, a vast array of sweetmeats would be laid out for all to partake. By that time, the women and girls of the colony would form their own travelling band. But the unwritten code of conduct was strict – while throwing colour on each other was allowed, the boundaries of decent behaviour were to be respected.

By one o'clock in the afternoon, it is usually time to start scrubbing the colour off one's body, and shampoo it out of the hair. In the evening, Banarasi men wear new, spotless white kurta-pyjamas, apply the dry colour – *gulal* - and hug each other in greeting. Then they venture out for a round of intoxication and ribaldry. Either they themselves have prepared the famous *thandai,* with dollops of *bhaang* in it, or their friends have. Copious quantities are drunk, and the tongue loosens to vent fulsome abuse. No one is spared, not even the families of the dearest friends, the policeman on the road, present to keep order, or the most disrespected politicians. Cheaply printed rag magazines, with pornographic cartoons and verse, begin to circulate. Then, a crowd assembles at two points – Assi, and Chowk. These are the settings for the Kavi Sammelans – poet's conferences. Prominent poets from all over Varanasi, and nearby exhibit their mastery over puerile, vulgar yet incisive verse, challenging and abusing each other. This goes on till late at night, after which the men drunkenly stagger home.

Ganga Dussehra

The festival of Ganga Dussehra is observed to celebrate the arrival of the holy Ganga river from Heaven, at the footsteps of King Bhagirath, and through the matted locks of Shiva. It is celebrated on the tenth day of the light fortnight of the month of Jyeshtha (May-June). Devotees first take a bath in the river; some may string a garland of flowers right across the river to denote their love for her – this could be done by swimming, or by taking a boat, while trailing the garland. Then, they worship the shrine of Mother Ganga near the Dasawshwamedh Ghat. Special arrangements are made at this small shrine, and they offer flowers and garlands to the deity. Young girls let flow small images of 'gudda-gudiya' (toy boy & girl) and fruits, in anticipation of a blissful marriage in the future. A special *aarti*, using a lamp with fifty wicks, is offered to the Goddess in the evening, the only time of the year when the lamp is brought out and used by the priests. After praying to the Goddess, the devotees visit Vishwanath temple to have a *darshan* of Lord Shiva, because the two are complementary to one another. If Shiva is the body, then Ganga is the soul, and it is the spiritual assimilation of the two that makes Varanasi *mokshadayini* – the bestower of salvation.

The next morning, a procession comprising leading citizens of the city, including Pandit Kishan Maharaj and Acharya Sitaram Shastri, and groups of devotees collect a mix of water from the five holy rivers, and milk, in small metal containers and head towards Vishwanath Temple for the Mahajalabshishek ceremony. Thousands assemble at Rajendra Prasad Ghat at seven in the morning. Among the devotees are the virginal Brahmakumaris, dressed in white, Naga sadhus, fifty-one Dandi Swamis, Vedic Brahmins, Muria tribals from Chhatisgarh, singing and dancing, beating drums with animal horns; as shehnai players lead the head priest, whose journey is made easier by an umbrella wielding assistant.

Durga Puja

In ancient times, a demon called Mahishasura earned the favour of Lord Shiva after a long meditation. Shiva, pleased with the devotion of the demon, blessed him with a boon that no man or Deity would be able to kill him. Empowered with the boon, Mahishasura started his reign of terror over the world. People were killed mercilessly and even the Gods were driven out from heaven. The Gods went to Shiva for relief and informed him about the atrocities caused by the demon. Shiva, who is normally unaware of the happenings in the material world, became very angry after hearing all this. This anger came out in the form of energy from Shiva's third eye and concentrated to form a woman. All the Gods who were present there contributed their share of energy to this Goddess and thus Durga, the eternal mother, was born. Riding a lion, she attacked

Mahishasura. After a fierce battle, Durga transformed into Devi Chandika, the most ferocious form of the Goddess, and beheaded Mahishasura.

The first Durga Puja in Varanasi was held in the 17th century. Traditionally celebrated by Bengalis, the Durga Puja has over the years evolved into a festival where people from every community participate. There are two kinds of pujas – the *Barwari* (community) Puja and the *Gharwari* (home) Puja. Unlike other pujas, it is not easy to do the Durga Puja at home because of the complex set of rituals and mantras, and only the well-versed Brahmans do so. Community pujas are a different story. They provide people with the occasion to pray, socialize and be entertained, while the organizers of the puja take care of the rituals. Durga Puja is spread over five days, beginning with Shashthi, when the Goddess is established in her *pandal.* The main image of Durga is flanked by those of her sons and daughters – Saraswati, Lakshmi, Kartik and Ganesh. A *pandal* is a decorated tent, set up in any large, open area. Like in Calcutta, organizers of Pujas compete with each other to build the most elaborate and beautiful *pandals.* Some are decorated with *shola* – the soft white material that comes from the stem of a plant that grows in Bengal's ponds. In other *pandals*, craftsmen create patterns with cloth in different colours. Chandeliers are hung from the ceilings of the *pandals*, and bright lights strung outside. The main puja days are Saptami, Maha Ashtami – which is most auspicious, Navami and Vijaya Dashami, when the Goddess is immersed into the river. On the first three days, the food served to the Goddess is then served to all who come to pray in the form of *bhog.* Every *aarti* is a treat to watch, as the drummer who plays the *dhak* keeps up a frenetic beat, and the priest as well as local men and women dance with a smoking lamp.

Being Bengalis ourselves, this was the festival that we looked forward to the most. It was the time of the year when we would get new clothes stitched. Relatives from Calcutta sent clothes too, and we compared notes on how many new outfits we got each year. A month before the puja, Bhakti Maharaj, a kindly priest from the Bharat Sevashram Sangha, would come home to collect our donation. So would Shibu Ghosh, a friend of my father, shop-floor incharge at the Institute of Technology's workshop and chief organizer of the puja at Saradotsab Sangha in Bhelupura. On the morning of Maha Ashtami, my father would make a huge garland of pink *sthalpaddas* (a flower that blooms just in time for the puja, and its Bangla name means Land Lotus) for the Durga at Saradotsab Sangh. This is where we performed our puja, as did most teachers from the Banaras Hindu University and their families. We would have our *bhog* at the Bharat Sevashram Sangh, where hundreds of pilgrims would be seated on the floor, plates made of *sal* leaf placed in front of them, and served steaming hot *khichdi* by the priests of the ashram. It always fascinated me to see them pour *khichdi* with giant ladles out of large stone basins, into the serving buckets. When we had eaten our fill, Bhakti Maharaj would ask us if we were satisfied, and then reach into the folds of his robes and dig out a few sweets, which were the *prasad* of Goddess Durga. In the evening, we would do the rounds of the other *pandals* in the city.

At Ramakrishna Mission on Luxa Road, the *swamis* sing hymns in praise of Sri Ramakrishna, and Durga even today. Durga Puja has been performed here since 1913, when it began upon the initiative of a few devotees from Bankura in West Bengal. The organizers of the puja at Kashi Durgotsab Samiti spent many years finding a permanent spot to hold their festivities, till the Kashi Naresh donated them a piece of land in Shivala in the year 1968. In the 1980s, Eagle Sporting Club in Jangambari always took the top prize in the city for the best decorated *pandal*. The competition for the bigger, grander *puja* has intensified over the years. This year, at Prahlad Ghat, the members of Bal Sporting Club got Krishna Pal, an artist from Kathua, near Burdwan in West Bengal, to create an idol made of two-hundred and fifty thousand cardamom pods; yet another image in Macchhodari was fashioned out of twenty-five kilos of silver. Thankfully, it will not be immersed after the *pujas.* Purists lament the passage of the traditional styles of idol-making, like the *Ek Chala,* where all the images of Durga, Lakshmi, Saraswati, Ganesh and Kartik are built within one semi-circular frame.

Every evening of the *pujas,* after dinner, we would go back to watch a *jatra* organized by the Saradotstab Sangh. The *jatra* is a form of traditional folk theatre from Bengal. The stage is put up in the middle of a large open arena, quite like a boxing ring, and the audience sits around it, on the floor covered with dhurries. The themes for drama are taken from history, or contemporary social issues – they had names like *Shah Jehan, Hitler, Bhalo Manusher Bhaat Neyi* (The Honest Man Always Goes Hungry) and *Pongopaal* (Locusts). The actors and actresses wear costumes that reflect the time when the play is set, king's robes and queen's jewels for those about royalty, swords, maces and guns for those about battle, simple *dhotis* when the setting is in a Bengal village. The performance would go on till two o'clock at night, and we would watch, wide awake. It was the only time in the year when we were allowed to stay awake that late!

On the last day of Vijaya Dashami, everyone assembles at the *pandal* to bid farewell to Durga. Women, after offering *sindoor* to the Goddess, put colour on each other. Then, in a procession, to the beating of the drum and the singing of the song, '*Thakur Jabe Bisharjan... Thakur Ashbi Kotokkhon*' (Goddess, now that you shall be immersed, When will you be back?), the idols are taken to the Ganga and immersed. Hundreds of local residents and visitors hire boats to watch the immersion. After the immersion, families return home to pray to the deities at home. They touch the feet of elders and embrace those of their own age doing *kolakoli* – as the gesture is called. And then it is time to wait for next year's Durga Puja.

Kartik Puja

On the ekadasi (11th day from the no-moon) day of the Hindu month of Kartik, the women of Varanasi participate in a unique ritual on the banks of the Ganga: the celestial marriage of Tulsi with Shaligram Shila. These are the earthly forms of Vishnu and Lakshmi, and the origin of the ritual can be found in the Puranas. The story goes thus. Once the sisters Lakshmi and Saraswati had a terrible fight, and cursed one another. Lakshmi was transformed by Sarawati's curse into a *Tulsi* (ocinum basilicum) plant destined to live on earth forever. At this point, Lord Vishnu intervened to tell Lakshmi, "You will live on earth as a *tulsi* plant, but will return to me when the curse runs its course. On that day, I will be found on the bank of the river Ganga, as a *shaligram shila*, and the people of earth will celebrate our wedding." A *shaligram shila* is an ammonite fossil, more than 400 million years old, and one of the most sacred stones for the Hindus.

On Kartik Purnima, the women gather on the *ghat* in the morning to bathe. They then divide themselves into two parties, one representing the groom's party, the other the bride's. The typical ceremonies of *baraat,* marriage and *kanyadaan* are played out, to the accompaniment of some fifty folk songs. There are verbal duels, each side trading allegations such as Krishna's (Vishnu's incarnation) propensity to flirt with *gopis.* The other notable event on this day is the worship of Bhishma Pitamaha, the great-grand uncle of the Kauravas and the Pandavas from the Mahabharat. An image of him, dying on the bed of arrows shot at him by Arjuna, is made of mud. Devotees pile flowers on him and pray for his soul.

Dev Deepavali

On the full moon night in Kartik, the Gods descend from heaven to bathe in the Ganga. Ordinary human beings share the bathing space, by the thousands. The people of Varanasi welcome them by lighting innumerable *diyas* and bursting crackers. They also guide the spirits of their ancestors to the *ghats* by lighting *akash deeps,* clay lamps hung on top of tall, thin bamboo reeds, all along the length of the *ghats.* Children decorate their respective *ghats* with motifs like the *swastika*, Om, draw images of Ganesh and Lakshmi, and place *diyas* around them. At night, the view from a boat on the river is ethereal. This day also sees the culmination of the Ganga Mahotsav Festival, which is celebrated from the Prabodhani Ekadashi day to Kartik Purnima.

Varanasi's Fairs

If every festival is replete with religious meaning and ritual, a fair – called *mela* in local parlance – is an occasion for entertainment and celebration of culture. Some fairs do have some religious significance associated with them, that only provides the backdrop to the more serious business of having fun. In this section, I shall describe three of the most important *melas*, that are so much a part of the folklore of Varanasi.

Burhwa Mangal

If there is one festival that has attained legendary status, it is the Burhwa Mangal – literally meaning Old Tuesday. The term old is used to refer to the year that has gone by, Mangal refers to Tuesday, when the celebrations began. When Varanasi came under Awadh dominion, Mir Rustam Ali was appointed administrator of the city during the period 1730-1738. He was an *aishpasand* – a lover of luxury, who started a festival through which the royalty and the aristocratic gentry of the city could find an outlet for their cultural enthusiasm. The Raja, and other noblemen, would take out their large boats, called the *bajras,* on the river Ganga. These were decorated with carpets, buntings, flowers and chandeliers and converted into stages where musicians and dancers performed. Most of the performers were courtesans and singers from the royal court. Their rich audience was served sumptuous food, drink and *paan* by attentive waiters, arriving on boats laden with goodies. The commoners who were not privileged to be invited aboard the *bajras* would watch from the ghats, straining to hear the strains of the shehnai or the high-pitched voice of a courtesan. If they wanted to get close, they would get on to a smaller boat, and follow the path taken by the *bajras* over the river.

The Burhwa Mangal was a symbol of the spirit of *mauj-masti* (fun and frolic) that is characteristic of Varanasi. People would say, "There is no other place where such a festival can be held." In every way, it stood for the subtle pleasures of springtime – the outdoors, moderate temperatures and all-night festivities. But by the early 20th century, life became difficult with famine beginning to ravage parts of the countryside. The King lost interest, and by 1923, the Burhwa Mangal was no longer held. Many years later, in the 1980s, some of the notable musicians from Varanasi, namely Pandit Kishan Maharaj, Pandit Ravi Shankar and Ustad Bismillah Khan attempted to revive its former glory. But with the demise of royal patronage, the spirit of the festival was lost, and it remains only as a memory of the grand times that once were on the river Ganga. Writer Vishwanath Mukherjee laments, "If expenses keep rising like this, all festivals in Varanasi will be a casualty like Burhwa Mangal."

Sawan Mela at Durgaji

The rains bring with them another occasion for song and dance. The largest fair in contemporary Varanasi is held throughout the month of Sawan between Durga Kund and Sankat Mochan. Having lived for eleven years in that part of the city, I was able to observe the fair from close quarters. The fair attracts the largest crowds on Tuesday, the auspicious day to worship Durga and Hanuman, and they come from all over the city and its neighbouring small towns and villages. They belong to all the sections of society – the rich and the poor, the able and the disabled, the young and the old. The Tulsi Manas Mandir, with its bright lights, attracts the simple villagers who are awe-struck by the grandeur of the temple as much as by the tableaux of animated scenes from the Ramayan.

The fairgoers come in large groups, taking every conceivable mode of transport. Bullock-carts, horse drawn tongas and buses carry entire joint families, or villages. A bicycle carries a man, his wife and infant on the back seat, and another todler dangles on the rod in front. Auto-rickshaws and 'Vikram' tempos spill over with people who have stepped off trains and buses. In an open space in front of an apartment block just off the main road, the buses park, while the passengers cook, string out their washed clothes (the large Durga Kund is where they bathe and wash), or sleep off in the shade of the bus.

In an open area behind the Durga Temple, a fairground comes up. There are giant-wheels, merry-go-rounds, booths for getting one's photograph taken behind the wheels of a tacky sports car, or next to a Bollywood actress's cutout. All along the road, local entrepreneurs set up stalls selling snacks and sweetmeats – *samosas, jalebis, golgappas, aloo-tikkis, kachoris*. Flower sellers line the entrance to all temples. Bangle and sindoor sellers jostle with vendors of posters, which cover the entire gamut of characters from the mythological to the Bollywood-bred. Others peddle traditional herbs and medicine; some sell cheap pornographic books covered in yellow cellophane and cassettes of bawdy songs. Toys, ribbons and trinkets entice the young; religious objects like images of Gods and Goddesses and garlands of *rudraksh* attract the old. Stalls for shooting balloons, stuck in colourful circles in the form of a target attract macho young men. The balloon sellers and flute sellers wind their way through the crowd, the latter playing from a repertoire of just two or three tunes. Loudspeakers are put up on lamp-posts for the entire stretch of one-and-half kilometres, and coloured lights strung everywhere. The loudspeakers broadcast religious songs, Hindi film music; but that is punctuated by announcements of *'Bhoole-Bichhrey Log'* (People who've been lost). A majority of them are little children. When I mentioned the mela to an old friend of mine, now a software engineer in Boston, she remembered how her mother had panicked upon her disappearance in the mela, when she was ten. She had simply followed a balloon-seller.

Sorahiya Mela

Beginning late in the month of Bhadra (usually September) and carrying on till the month of Ashwin, a sixteen day fair is held at Lakshmi Kund, on Luxa Road near Godowlia to honour the eponymous goddess of wealth. During this period, devotees – mostly women - set up idols of Lakshmi at home, keep a fast and pray that their wealth stays with them. On the last day, which is called Jivitaputrika, they take a bath in the *kund*, offer sixteen kinds of flowers, sixteen kinds of sweets and grain to Mahalakshmi, and then proceed to enjoy the fair. Women buy trinkets and cosmetics from stalls in the fairground, children buy toys and balloons, both feast at the *chaat* stalls, and thereby bring the celebrations to a close.

ʗ

The Ramlilas of Varanasi

Everywhere in the country, the Dussehra festival is celebrated with the staging of the Ramlila, the story of Lord Ram. Their story is based on Tulsidas's Ramcharit Manas. But no Ramlila is endowed with as much pageantry and history as the Ramlila of Ramnagar in Varanasi. The small town of Ramnagar sits across the river from Varanasi. The Ramlila was started by Raja Udit Narayan Singh, who ruled from the year 1765 to 1835. An interesting story surrounds the origin of the Ramlila. Close to Ramnagar, in a small village called Chhota Mirzapur, two brothers Bhonu and Vithal Sahu used to stage a Ramlila. The Raja was a patron, and visitor to the show. One year, when the key scene of 'Ram breaking the bow' was to be enacted, the Raja got late. The actors waited, but when they could hold on no more, they carried on with the scene. The Raja got the news while he was still on his way, and was very disappointed. He returned to his castle, and was clearly miffed that the actors and audience hadn't waited. To add insult to injury, his maharani said, "The *banias* can hold a Ramlila, and you, a king, can't?" She added, laughing, "If you organize a Ramlila here, then even I can watch it." From the next year onwards, the Raja began staging the Ramlila.

During the reign of Raja Udit Narayan Singh, and his successor, Ishwari Narayan Singh, the Ramlila was staged within the premises of the Fort, and in a place called Ayodhya. The current form of the Ramlila was given by Raja Ishwari Narayan Singh, who became king in 1835. He called a meeting of prominent religious leaders and scholars, who wrote out the stages, rituals and locations for the enactment of the epic. They gave shape to the theatrical environment in which to stage the Ramlila – a space of some fifteen square miles, and the time which structures the enactment. Spatially, Ramnagar is laid out in a manner corresponding to the various places mentioned in the epic – Rambagh, Ayodhya, Janakpur, Chitrakoot, Panchvati, and Lanka. The performance shifts from one place to the other over time.

The epic's three great movements, namely Rama's birth to marriage, exile to battle, and triumphant return to his kingdom of Koshala, were divided into five main action groups. For the residents of Ramnagar, the staging of the Ramlila is an intensely emotional affair, and they fiercely protect its form and sanctity. No amplification is allowed in the performance. Even though the audience numbers twenty thousand on an average, a hush falls as soon as the performance begins. Petromax lights are hung on the same kind of bamboo poles from which oil-fired lanterns were hung a hundred years ago. Even the actions of the Raja are under close scrutiny, as I discovered two years after the death of the previous Raja, Vibhuti Naryana Singh. People asked, will the new Raja observe all the rituals? And lamented when he arrived at the scene of enactment in a motor vehicle, instead of the traditional buggy.

In the prelude, which lasts for a day, Lord Vishnu takes on a human form, upon Brahma's implorations, in order to rescue the world from being terrorized by Ravana. The one-hundred and seventy five verses that describe Ram's childhood are recited. On the first day of the performance, which takes place at Rambagh, Ravana acquires the powers that he would later abuse. He asks Brahma for a boon that he would not be killed by anyone other than a human or a monkey. He wins the kingdom of Lanka, and asks his army to disturb the *yagna* that the Brahmans have been performing. His son Meghnad captures Lord Indra, and Brahma grants him the title of Indrajit – the one who conquered Indra. Then, in the night, at a *kund* next to the Durga Temple, Vishnu awaits the birth of Rama, while reclining on his serpent, Sheshnag. Lord Ram is born on the second day of the performance. On the third day, as time leaps forward by a few years, the sage Vishwamitra arrives in Ayodhya to ask King Dasarath for his sons, so that they can save him from the demons. Ram vanquishes the demoness Taraka, and the Gods are elated. Vishwamitra decides to take Ram to Janakpur, where the king is looking for a suitable bridegroom for his beautiful daughter. En route, Ram spots a stone and asks Vishwamitra about it. He is told that the sage Gautama had cursed his wife Ahilya and turned her into a stone, and she had been awaiting the arrival of Ram. Ram frees Ahilya from her curse, and she goes to Heaven after blessing him. Ram and Lakshman arrive at Janakpur, where Vishwamitra introduces the two princes to Raja Janak. The scene of the performance now shifts to Janakpur. The two princes take Vishwamitra's permission to tour Janakpur, and the entire town turns up to admire them. When one lady suggests that King Janak would straightaway get Sita married to Ram, another wonders how such a tender young man would ever be able to break the famed bow. The princes then go to pluck flowers in a garden, where Sita also arrives with her friends. The next day, Janak invites Vishwamitra to bring Ram and Lakshman to his palace. Here, one king after another fails to break the bow of Shiva, leaving Janak disappointed. At that moment, young Ram steps up and with a loud crack, breaks the bow. All break into a cheer, and Sita garlands Ram, accepting him as her husband. Janak then sends an emissary to King Dasarath, informing him about the events.

On the sixth day, Dasarath leaves for Janakpur with Bharat, Shatrughan and the rest of the family as part of the wedding entourage – the *baraat*. Amidst great fanfare, the wedding rituals of Ram and Sita are solemnized. Simultaneously, Lakshman weds Urmila, Bharat Mandavi, and Shatrughan Shutrakirti as per the advice of Vishwamitra. The wedding party returns joyfully to the kingdom of Ayodhya on the following day. They take leave from Vishwamitra, and are welcomed by Kaushalya, the eldest of Dasarath's wives. To celebrate the events, many homes in Ramnagar prepare *pooris* and *kheer* and serve it to all family members on this day. Events take a turn for the worse from the eighth day. Dasarath, who is getting old, decides to anoint Ram, his eldest son, as his successor. At this point, Kaikeyi's (Dasarath's second wife) ears are poisoned by her maid Manthara, as she reminds her that Dasarath had promised to grant her two wishes anytime she desired. Kaikeyi chooses to encash her wishes, asking Dasarath to send Ram into exile, and place her son Bharat on the throne. The king is heartbroken and dumbstruck at this request, but he can do nothing. Ram gracefully agrees to follow his parents' wishes, and seeks their permission to leave. The entire city of Ayodhya goes into mourning.

On the tenth day, Ram leaves Ayodhya, accompanied by Sita and Lakshman. He crosses the Ganga on Kevat's boat after washing his feet, and arrives in Prayag where he asks Bhardwaj Muni for directions to the forest. After paying their respects to Valmiki, they reach Chitrakoot. The residents narrate their tale of woe – Ravana does not allow them to live in peace here – and seek refuge in Ram's company. The next day sees Bharat arrive in Chitrakoot to try and convince Ram to return, after he discovers his mother's actions. The Gods in Heaven seem to be disturbed by the happenings, believing that Ram would be swayed by brotherly affections, but Brihaspati assures them of Ram's steadfastness. The Gods have an ulterior motive – they want Ram to eventually take on the evil Ravana. On this twelfth day of performance, the heartbroken Dasarath dies. In spite of the urging of all, Ram does not return to Ayodhya, and Bharat goes back, carrying his eldest brother's shoes, which he places symbolically on the throne, vowing never to sit on it. This happens on the fourteenth day. The next day finds Ram coping with the travails of living in a forest. As troublemaker Indra despatches his son Jayant in the guise of a crow, to peck at

Sita's feet, Ram shoots an arrow at him and blinds him in one eye. He encounters a pile of bones, which the saints living in the forest tell him, are the remains of those the demons have eaten. Agastya Muni gives Ram a boon that would enable him to kill the demons. The following day, the sixteenth in the performance is a dramatic one. Surpanakha, Ravana's sister is besotted with Ram and Lakshman. She tries to scare Sita away, but Lakshman lops off her nose. To take revenge, Ravana hatches a plan. He lures Ram and Lakshman away and then appears at Sita's doorstep in the guise of a mendicant. Sita is abducted as soon as she steps over the Lakshman Rekha – the protective line that Lakshman had drawn around their home. As he flies to Lanka in his chariot, Ravan fights and mortally injures Jatayu the eagle. On the following day, just before breathing his last, Jatayu is able to tell Ram about Ravana's misdeeds. Ram and Lakshman now set about trying to find Sita. They first go to Pampasar, where they meet the King of Monkeys, Sugreev. The sage Narad also arrives at the spot. Sugreev's able companion Hanuman asks Ram to narrate the chain of events, and then a bond of friendship is formed between the two sides in order to take on a common foe. Over the next day, battle plans are formed, and Hanuman leaps across the sea to Lanka, where Sita is being kept captive. He conveys Ram's message to her, but is caught by Ravan's soldiers. His son Vibhishan sets fire to Hanuman's tail – and that is a fatal mistake. Hanuman sets alight all of Lanka by bounding from one roof to another. On the twentieth day, Ram assembles his army, much of it taken from Sugreev's band of monkeys. Ravana refuses to be intimidated by such a force, inspite of pleas from Mandodari and Vibhishan to make peace. Ram's emissary is booted away by Ravana, and he prepares for war. Magically, a bridge appears across the sea. The next three days are when the battle scenes are enacted. Ravan's favourite son Meghnad, as well as his fearsome brother Kumbhakarna are killed and he goes into mourning. Finally, Ravana himself gets down to the battlefield. Inspite of Ram's attempts, he refuses to die, his heads keep growing back even after Ram cuts them off. Finally Sita is able to figure out from Trijata that only an arrow in his navel would be able to kill Ravan. On the twenty-sixth day, which is Dussehra, Ram finally kills Ravana and the entire audience – which has swelled up to nearly a hundred thousand now - erupts in joy. Ram returns to Ayodhya, the brothers and their families are reunited, and Deepawali celebrated as the entire kingdom lights up lamps to welcome them.

The last two days are the postlude, when the performers are welcomed by the Raja at his fort, fed in front of dignitaries and common folk, and paid for their services. Everyone in the town decorates his home, and the fort is decorated with lights. The costumes and the props – swords, thrones, et al, for the spectacle are all provided by the Raja. One part of the expenses is met from the estate of 'Bhauji Sahiba'. She was the sister-in-law of Raja Ishwari Prasad Singh. She had received a large piece of land as part of her dowry, and pledged the earnings from the land towards the staging of the Ramlila. After her death, her minister Colonel Vindheshwari sold the land and put the money in the bank. The interest from the money is now used to defray some of the Ramlila expenses. The performances are watched by people from all over the region, but it is the *nemis* who watch every episode, and they have been doing so for many years. They dress simply, in white linen clothes, a scarf on their heads. They carry a staff, and their feet are bare. Throughout the performance this group stays together, they watch the Ramlila out of a combination of self-imposed law (*niyam*) and love (*prem*). The audience are not mere spectators, but part of the drama. When Rama goes to the forest, they accompany him on the journey. When he is crowned, they shout 'Bolo Ramchandra Ki Jai', as if it were their own king.

The Ramlila at Ramnagar is undoubtedly the most venerated and grand staging of the epic. Still, all over the city, lesser

Ramlilas are staged in the month preceding Dussehra. Notable among them are the Ramlila at Chetganj, the high point of which is the 'Nakkataiya' – the episode when Lakshman chops off the nose of the ogre Surpanakha – and the procession associated with the event. The Chetganj Ramlila was started by a sadhu by the name of Baba Fatteram. He was a devotee of Rama, and an avid Ramlila-watcher. After several years of travelling to see various Ramlilas, he decided to start one of his own. To raise funds, he thought of a novel scheme: he asked the shopkeepers of the area to keep aside one paisa from their earnings, every day of the year. By the time of the event, a large sum of money would thus be raised. Seeing his devotion, a few wealthy businessmen donated a piece of land to hold the Ramlila.

The Nakkataiya procession consists of a series of floats depicting scenes from the Ramayan, as well as the fantastic. It is, in a way, like a Mardi Gras. Tricksters and magicians, courtesans and cross-dressers, gamblers, singers and actors, they all come together to stage a spectacle of folk drama. Scenes like Gandhi's salt satyagraha at Dandi, Krishna narrating the Gita to Arjun provide a counterpoint to the gaudy ribaldry. The procession begins at the Ramlila ground at Pishachmochan at 11 in the night. The floats and performers are mounted on trucks, bullock-carts, rickshaws and tractor-trollies; some walk along displaying their costumes and showing off feats they are capable of performing. Groups of men sing the *birha* and the *alha* from the back of a truck; in another, women might be singing *bhajans.* Somewhere, children dressed as warriors stage a mock battle; elsewhere courtesans titillate procession-watchers with their sensual dance and beckoning gestures. A swordsman walks along swinging his weapon, occasionally thrusting it towards the crowd who back off in alarm. A fire-eater shoots a flame into the air, drawing gasps of amazement from children. The entire route is brightly lit up, and shopowners lay out their produce for the revellers to buy. Thus does the Nakkataiya procession wind its way through the narrow streets of Varanasi, before reaching Chetganj. Here, Lakshman finally cuts Surpanakha's nose, and brings the festivity to a close.

The Nakkataiya is enacted amidst great festivity at several other locations : Kashipura, Lallapura and Lat Bhairav. The oldest Ramlila, Mauni Baba Ki Ramlila dates back as far as 1554 A.D., before the time Tulsidas's Ramcharit Manas was written. In its early days, the performance was based on the Valmiki Ramayana. Besides being the sponsor of his own Ramlila, the Raja of Varanasi is closely involved with the staging of the Bharat Milap, at Nati Imli. The victorious Lord Ram arrives on his chariot, accompanied by Lakshman, and his brothers Bharat and Shatrughan wait for him on the stage. As soon as he climbs the stage, they fall to Ram's feet, and he lifts and embraces them warmly. Cries of 'Siyawar Ramchandra Ki Jai' rend the ear as the watching crowd lets its emotions flow. The Raja watches the entire episode from the top of his royal elephant, and then leads the victory procession wherein Ram meets his 'subjects'. As per tradition, his chariot is carried on the shoulders of several men belonging to the Yadav community. The waiting crowd, which occupies every inch of space along the narrow path, showers flowers on their regent and the actors of the Ramlila, as the procession winds its way through the city.

Ramnagar Fort

I have been wondering where to write about one of Varanasi's prime attractions – the Fort of the Raja of Banaras, lying across the river from Saamne Ghat. Barring the rainy season, when the pontoon bridge across the Ganga is dismantled, it is fairly easy to reach by taking an auto-rickshaw from Lanka. Its current occupant is Raja Anant Narayan Singh, a Sanskrit scholar who regularly takes in a game of tennis at the club named after his great-grandfather, Prabhu Narayan Singh, in the cantonment. A fairly unimpressive gateway flanked by two cannons welcomes you to the Fort. Inside is another story – a sprawling complex of mansions, temples, tunnels, pavilions, gardens and halls, in various states of disrepair. Too proud to let a hotel chain take over, but without the resources to keep the entire palace in spit-and-polish shape, the royal family continues to live in one well-appointed part of the palace complex.

Built in sandstone procured from neighbouring Chunar, the construction of Ramnagar Fort began during the reign of Raja Balwant Singh, in 1750, and it was completed by his successor Raja Chet Singh. The royal armoury and its collection of vintage cars, a couple of Rolls Royces among them, are now part of a museum. The impressive arms collection includes a WW I vintage Vickers Machine Gun, Austrian Percussion Lock rifles, mathclock guns, duelling pistols from the period 1780-1840, weapons from Burma, African and Japanese swords. There are also howdas of ivory, palanquins of gold and a giant silver crown for the royal elephant – these are brought out during the Ramleela. There's a huge clock, the Dharam Ghari, made by the royal astronomer in 1852, and dusty silks with elaborate brocade work, which leave you wondering about their original splendour. A tunnel infested with bats leads to the temple of Ved Vyas, on the parapet next to the river. From here, one gets a chance to appreciate and wonder at the exquisite stone carvings on the walls and balconies of the royal residence. The balconies allow the royals to have a sweeping view of the Ganga and the city as it rises from her banks.

The palace has welcomed royalty from other parts of the world, including Queen Elizabeth, and King Saud of Saudi Arabia. The latter was so taken in by the vegetarian food served at the Raja's table that he took the cook back with him!

☙

CRAFTSMANSHIP, COMMERCE & CULINARY AFFAIRS

Kartatha so Kyon Kiya, Ab Kyon Pachhtaye
Boye ped Babool ka, Aam kahan se khaye?

Thoughtlessly you do a thing,
then regret the result
If you plant sour Babool,
can you ever get sweet mangoes?

Kabir

ᨓ

Even the simple, mystic Kabir was aware of the pleasures of the mango from Varanasi when he wrote the above *doha*. The son of a weaver, he was also part of the timeless tradition of making the exquisite Banarasi sarees. In Varanasi, creativity finds expression in surprisingly diverse forms. It inspires the finest silks, and the common wooden toy. It can be seen in the diversity of the sweets available in the *mithai* shop, and in the inlay work on brass and copper vessels. Most of this creativity has resulted in profit for the traders of the city. As early as the 2nd century BC, merchants called the city 'Jitwari' – Victorious, because they could reap great profit here. Varanasi has a five hundred year old tradition of making wooden toys. Colourful and sturdy, they imbue the childhood of many a Banarasi childhood with delight. For the traveller, they are a cheap souvenir. Kashmiriganj is the main toy-making area, but most shops are in Vishwanath Gali. More than 300 types of toys are made and sold here. There are figures of animals – cows, bulls, tigers, birds, camels, horses, deer and elephants. There are Russian dolls, one inside another. There are figures of Gods and Goddesses, and tiny utensils for aspiring homemakers. Little wooden containers for keeping *sindoor* are a favourite among women pilgrims. During the festival season, the streets are lined with clay pottery images of Ganesh, Saraswati, Shiva, Ram and Hanuman. There are many shops that sell images in stone. I have a finely carved Buddha, all of an inch high, at my desk. You might find an equally fine image of Nataraj, but six feet tall, at the sculpture shops at Dasashwamedh, or at a shop called Pashan Devta next to the Durga Temple. Sculptors carve out candlesticks and animal figurines, ashtrays and tableware in marble, granite, sandstone and limestone. The *thatheras* and the *kaseras* – metalworkers, ply their trade at Thatheri Bazaar, but many of their wares are on display in Vishwanath Gali. Here you will find shiny pots and vessels in bellmetal, brass and copper stacked on top of each other.

Lord Macaulay, the English scholar, wrote in the 18th century of how the delicate silks from Varanasi's looms adorned the halls of St. James's and of Versailles. In this chapter, I have elaborated on that famous 'export', the silk saree, and on Varanasi's homegrown culinary tradition.

ꟹ

Tana-Bana: The Banarasi Saree

Almost every Hindu bride aspires to be wed wearing a Banarasi saree. Rich and lustrous, it is a garment that can certainly make a woman feel like a queen when she wears it. Silk was originally woven for the deities in temples. Lord Vishnu is called *Tantuvardana* (the Divine Weaver); he is said to have woven the rays of the sun into a garment for himself. It is no surprise that a fair percentage of the city's inhabitants are involved with the design, production and sale of Banarasi sarees. This is also an industry where the Hindu and Muslim communities have a symbiotic, dependent relationship. While the weavers – the *julehas* – are Muslims, mainly from the Ansari community, the traders are Hindus. The origin of the Banarasi saree lies in Mughal times, when the rich silk garments, with threads of gold woven in intricate patterns, became the rage.

The Persian motifs and designs studded with gold and silver remain remnants of Mughal patronage.

The process of making a saree begins with the acquisition of fine silk yarn. In Mughal times, the silk would come from China. Then, Bangalore silk from south India became the raw material as sericulture flourished in that region of India. In recent years, Chinese silk has again become popular because of its low price; most of it entering through Nepal.

Once the yarn has been obtained, it must be dyed in the myriad colours. The colours of the Banarasi saree are subdued in comparison with the rich colours that one finds in Kancheepuram in Tamil Nadu. The coloured thread is rolled on wooden poles, and sold by weight to the weavers. At the loom, the craftsmen weave the basic texture of the saree. In the weaving warp they create a base which is usually 24 or 26 metres long. Within a 45 inch width, some 5600 strands of silk – 120 to an inch - are laid out. Then comes the most important part of selecting the design. Only a few craftsmen are capable of creating the design – they are called the *nakshabandhs*. Popular designs include intricate intertwining floral and foliage motifs, *kalka* (the turban brooch), and *bel* (vine). There are scenes from village and fairs, clouds, dancing peacocks, temples and mosques. The skill and imagination of the *nakshabandh* plays a prominent part in the making of designs. *Nakshabandh* families were brought to Varanasi during the reign of Muhammed Tughlak (1325-1350 A.D.). They were supreme masters of the art of tying designs into the loom. Local artisans and weavers learned this art from these great craftsmen. The *nakshas* (designs) are first worked on paper. This part of the work is called *likhai* (writing). The *nakshabandh* then makes a little pattern of it in a framework of cotton threads, like a graph. This pattern gives guidance to the working of that design into weaving. Once the design is selected, small punch cards are created. Those are guides for the particulars of which coloured thread must pass through which card, and at what stage. Weaver Haqim Ali says that for one small design, a *nakshabandh* requires to create hundreds of perforated cards to implement the concept. Once the perforated cards are prepared, they are knitted with different threads and colours on the loom. According to the design, those are paddled in a systematic manner by the weaver, as he picks up right colours to create the design and weave. The weaver passes the *nar* – a boat-like shuttle made of buffalo horn – through the layers of the warps, and immediately purls along the weft with *zari* or dyed silk yarn by tucking its tubicles along the warp. The arrangement of threads is complex, and operated from a pit below the loom using treadles. The treadles and the warp threads are synchronized – each alternate motion of the foot raising or depressing a different set of warp threads.

Some time ago, there was an interesting story in the Times of India about a unique ingredient in the weaving of the Banarasi saree. Believe it or not, but in Varanasi, the condom plays an important role in weaving Banarasi sarees, particularly on hand looms. As per a rough estimate, the daily consumption of condoms is about six lakh units in the weavers' localities. A weaver working on loom pulls out the condom in half its length and then rubs it on the bobbin. The lubricant on the condom smoothens the bobbin and makes it move faster between threads. No one knows who invented this unique use of condom in saree weaving, but today almost all the weavers have adopted this technique. The convenor of Bunkar Bachao Andolan, Mahfooz Alam, says that there are about 1.5 lakh looms in Varanasi and the average daily consumption is four condoms on each loom. "We use it only for lubricating the bobbin," says Anis of Bajardiha area. From where the weavers procure the huge quantity of condoms is also interesting. Some of them get condoms free of cost, courtesy the family planning department and NGOs dealing with family planning, while majority of them purchase cheaper brands. They generally look for cheaper brands if the free supply is not available. Those registered with the local health centres or having good relations with health department volunteers, get their supplies free.

Till five decades ago, Banarasi sarees would have designs woven with original gold and silver thread, and a weaver could take as long as a year to create one saree. Those sarees could fetch several lakhs of rupees for the weaver. Today, depending on the intricacy of the design, a saree takes between 15 days and one month, in the rare occasion six months to weave.

There are three main types of Banarasi sarees. The most popular are those with an opaque silk base and *zari* (gold or silver coloured thread) brocade. Here, patterns on thick silk fabric are created by using *zari* as the supplementary weft. These saris are also known as *Kimkhab* in old Mughal terminology. The second variety is the Tanchoi brocade. Here silk is used on silk to create designs. The third style is currently very fashionable and resembles the Jamdani style of Dhaka in Bangladesh. This style uses transparent silk as its base, with thicker silk or *zari* as the supplementary weft. The field remains transparent while the designs are opaque.

The main weaving areas that visitors get to see are Madanpura and Reori Talaab, but the real centres lie in the north of the city in the wards of Adampura and Jaitpura, where some five hundred thousand people are involved with the trade. Here lies the Bunkar Colony – Weaver's Colony, a collection of about fifty government-subsidized homes made available to poor weavers. It was in Jaitpura that I met Chand Bhai, one of a family of sixty that has been weaving Banarasi sarees for the last 400 years. He showed me around – weavers busy at work on the looms, complained about cheap Chinese silk that was flooding the market, and about onetime prime minister Morarji

Desai who got craftsmen from Surat to learn the art of making zari, and took away the trade to Gujarat. Once the saree is created, the weavers bring them to Gol Ghar and Kunj Gali, the main wholesale markets. There are several hundred shops here, where every morning weavers from different villages and the city come to deliver 'created' sarees to the market. There are some 10 shops whose annual turnover is believed to be greater than Rs 800 million !

Across the city, it is estimated that over a thousand shops sell Banarasi sarees. It is only in Madanpura that, in the last two decades, some of the saree producers have begun selling part of their production directly to customers. Most shops look alike – white sheets pulled tight over three-inch thick mattresses laid on the floor. White bolsters lean against the walls. Bright flourescent lights and bare bulbs hang from the ceiling. It is an atmosphere of plainness designed to bring out the best in the saree. Business begins only at about 1:00 pm every afternoon, and peaks around 5:00 pm. The shop owner will ask you and your companions to sit down and feel comfortable (I mention the companion because no one ever goes to buy a Banarasi saree alone). He then motions to one of the young men, possibly hanging around the door, and the man bellows to the shop across the lane, "*Ay chhotu, chaar chai laana.*" (Hey kid, get four cups of tea). Then he makes a gentle enquiry, for what occasion is the saree being purchased? Do the buyers have something in mind? Is the girl or woman who will wear the saree fair or dark? How much are they willing to spend? By that time, tea arrives and he asks the customers to drink it while the sarees are being fetched. He beckons another of his men, who ducks into and then quickly returns from inside the shop with a couple of large rectangular white boxes. He flips them open and gently unravels the exquisite creations from the thin white tissue they have been wrapped in. With a magical flick of the wrist, he unfurls the sari causing it to billow out on the white sheet, with its marvellous *pallu* spread open. One by one, he lovingly displays the sarees. If the customer were to ask its price, he says, *"Aap pasand to kariye. Daam sahi laga dengey."* (Go on, choose the one you like. I will be reasonable). He has already assessed what the buyer can afford, and is displaying the best within that price. Then, almost as the enthralled buyers have made up their mind, he throws open an even more exquisite saree. This is a little beyond your budget, he says enticingly, but so beautiful that I could not resist showing it to you. Few can resist the temptation.

For an interesting peep into the history of silk and weaving, the Silk Route Museum, at the Cottage Industries Exposition (CIE) across the road from the Taj Ganges hotel is worth a visit. The building itself is steeped in history. The palace was built by Kashi Naresh, Maharaja Sir Prabhu Narayan Singh Bahadur, and used by him for state banquets. During 1914-1918, the palace served as a war hospital for the First World War troops, and after independence it was converted into an office for Indian Airlines. It has been on lease with the CIE for the last 24 years.

The flight of steps that lead upto the front door itself impart a royal feel to the single-storeyed building, what with visitors being given a red carpet welcome as one climbs up. Inside, the palace has two big halls facing each other. While one used to serve as a dining hall, the other was a dancing hall where the royal family was entertained to an evening of song and dance. The palace sports a carved wooden roof, frescoes painted on the walls, carved Belgian glass ventilators and chandeliers that remind you of a bygone era. A part of the dancing hall has now been converted into The Silk Route museum bringing out the significance of silk. The museum traces the growth of silk, right from the cocoon stage to the actual production of silk. There is a silk worm model, a section enumerating the various types of silk like mulberry, tusaar, eri and mooga, a life-size model of a loom and a village scene depicting silk weaving. There are even old costumes made of the famous *kimkhab* or cloth-of-gold. Further down, there is a section which includes photographs of some famous Indian royalty wearing silk apparel. Next to it is the shopping arena where silk sarees, scarves, ties, shirts, furnishings and cloth material are sold. "If opening a showroom as well as a museum here helps further our business interests, it also helps in preserving the historical monument. We spend a good amount of money on repairs annually," says A R Mir, Chairman-cum-Managing Director, CIE. The rest of the dancing hall is stocked with interior accessory items like silk bedcovers, cushion covers, woollen fashion items, sandal /rosewood figures, paper paintings, cotton table accessories, and brass figures. The dining hall, on the other hand, has been entirely dedicated to carpets, a CIE speciality.

❧

Celebration for the Taste Buds

Varanasi's residents say that because Annapurna, the Goddess of Food, is a permanent resident in the city, no one should ever fear of going hungry. But for the indulgent Banarasi, food is more than something that will merely fill one's stomach. I have a hypothesis: there are several factors that contribute to the development, availability and consumption of the best of Banarasi cuisine. The first is the practice of fasting. If one keeps a fast on so many occasions, it is only to be expected that the period of denial be ended with something that is a feast for the taste buds. The second is the frequent celebration of festivals. Every occasion calls for its own unique preparations that must be consumed at home and distributed to friends, neighbours and relatives. Finally, the male orientation towards bodybuilding ensures a supply chain of nourishing food, from milk, *ghee* and *rabri* to preparations made out of gram and pulses.

I have earlier described the scene at the wholesale market for milk products, Khoya Gali. From here, the makers of sweets buy the raw material to craft some of the most succulent, juicy sweets made anywhere in India. The sweet-making tradition in Varanasi is based on *khoya* as a key ingredient, but is strongly influenced by the Bengali tradition that uses *paneer*. It is believed that during the freedom struggle, sweets from Varanasi were used to stoke up a nationalist feeling among Indians. The tricolour *barfi*, originating from the famous Shri Ram Bhandar in Thatheri Bazaar, is one such example. The unique thing about the sweet is that no artificial colours are used : the green comes from pistachio, the orange from saffron, the *khoya* base provides the white layer. The *halwais* at the shop, Raghunath Prasad and Hanuman Prasad, created other sweets by the names of Gandhi Gaurav, Jawahar Laddoo, Madan Mohan and Vallabh Sandesh, after Gandhiji, Jawaharlal Nehru, Madan Mohan Malaviya and Vallabhbhai Patel respectively. Today, the shop has two more branches, but the original probably has the best tasting sweets. My personal favourite is the Malai Samosa, a small pyramidal sweet with a thin outer layer of *khoya,* stuffed with a pistachio-nut paste.

While Shri Ram Bhandar has tradition going for it, the most popular sweet shop in the city probably is Ksheer Sagar at Sonarpura. This is a shop which fuses the Banarasi and Bengali traditions with stunning effect. It has taken the soft, juicy rosogolla, already legendary, and added a dash of saffron to it to create the fantastic orange rosogolla. My favourite *kheerkadam* has a juicy centre and a coating of white, powdered *khoya* which simply melts in the mouth. The *barfis,* on the other hand, must be bitten into and chewed upon so that the delicate flavours in them can be released into the mouth. Jalajog

Sweets, at Godowlia, is another Bengali shop owned by the Lahas. Their *rasogollas* and *chumchums* are syrupy sweet, while the *sandesh* made from palm jaggery is soft and delectable. One of the shop attendants, Jamini, always added a few extra sweets to our order whenever my parents bought sweets. Madhur Jalpan, an old shop in a lane just after the Kanhaiya Chitra Mandir, on the way to Chowk, is famous for its *kheermohan*; Shree Rajbandhu in Kachauri Gali for its *pedas* and *namkeens* made in pure ghee; Kamdhenu Sweets, a relatively new shop at Gurubag, for its *sandesh*. Madhu Bahar, a shop at Assi, has a wide array of sweets, but it is the *rabri* they make that makes a trip here worth making. Rich, with a texture that tantalizes the mouth before you eat it, this milk preparation is the finest in the city. You will find most sweet shops in Varanasi selling *rabri* in the evening. It is an indulgence that few miss out on. While most sweet shops sell *gulabjamuns,* those from the suburb of Pandeypur have a reputation of their own. It is said that one should never try to eat them with a spoon, or break a piece off using one's fingers. The way to eat the *gulabjamun* is to hold it gingerly between the forefinger and the thumb, and plop the whole thing into one's mouth. Other newer shops that have continued the *mithai*-making tradition in Varanasi are Vaishali Sweets in Lanka, where the one-armed owner expertly packs the creations of his *halwai,* and Raj Sweets in Kabir Nagar, close to our home in Durga Kund. Finally, giving in to the pressures of modernization, Varanasi also has its first air-conditioned sweet shop called Annakoot Sweets opposite Natraj cinema, near Rathyatra, who serve *mithai* warmed up in a microwave oven.

The typical breakfast in Varanasi consists of *kachori-subzi,* and *jalebis.* Every corner shop prepares these in the morning, and barring the large shops, their stock is exhausted before 10 am. Jalebi-making is nothing short of an art. The *halwai* is a man with the classic evidence of partaking of his own creation in large quantities - a rotund middle. He sits cross-legged wearing a singlet and a *lungi*, in front of a large flat pan, in which bubbles hot oil. He pours the batter into a small container with a hole at the bottom. Then, with a flourish, he begins to pour the batter in a thin stream on the boiling oil, his hand moving in small circles to create the spiral pattern of the *jalebi*. Just when the *jalebi* is firm enough, he breaks it into smaller pieces, and turns it over. Next, he lifts it with tongs and dunks it into a vessel full of syrup. The syrup soaks into the hot, fried crust, which changes colour to become golden-brown. The *jalebi* is ready to be served and savoured.

When it is evening, and certainly when the Banarasi family is out shopping, *chaat* figures on their eating-out agenda. The most famous place is of course, Kashi Chaat Bhandar at Godowlia. Their *aloo-tikkis, golgappas, chholey, dahi-vadas* and *raj kachoris* are sublimely spicy. A couple of *chaatwallahs* in Lanka do roaring business, thanks to BHU students starved for spice in their hostel meals. Every evening, however, especially at festival time, hundreds of *chaatwallahs* set out in residential colonies and marketplaces, with their offerings on a handcart, clanging their ladles against huge iron plates that are set on top of kerosene stoves. The plate has spicy potato puree around it, and when someone orders the *chaat*, they simply turn up the flame, add a dab of oil, draw in the required amount of potato, sprinkle spices, and hey voila, the *chaat* is ready. The same vendor has an earthen jar containing *dahi-badas*, and a large pot of *jaljeera* water for *golgappas*. When eating from these carts, one simply forgets about hygiene and gives in to temptation.

If there is anything that contributes to the Banarasi's sense of *masti* – fun, it is the consumption of *thandai*. A popular saying goes thus:

Bhang Gang Dou Bahin Hain, Rahti Shiv ke Sang
Bhajan karan ko Bhang hai, Bhav Taran ko Gang
Bhaang and Ganga are sisters, they stay with Shiva
Just as prayers accompany Ganga, Bhang is a must with song.

A cooling drink made with milk, dry fruits – almonds and pistachio, cardamom, *thandai* becomes intoxicating when *bhaang* (cannabis paste) is added to it. Its consumption is seen as a form of devotion to Shiva. The most popular place in the city to have *thandai* is Godowlia, where shops like Mishrambu, Thandai Corner, Raju Thandai Ghar, Thandai Bahar, Shiva Thandai, Banarasi Thandai Ghar and Thandai Lok do roaring business in the evening.

As a Banarasi, I may be accused of bias, but it is true that the *Langda Aam* of Varanasi is legendary. An appreciation of this variety of mango involves full involvement of the senses. First, sight. It is green in colour, even when ripe. Upon peeling one sees the uniform golden orange pulp, ready to be eaten. The skin of the *langda* is so thin, that locals call it *aasmani* - you can see the sky through it after you've eaten the mango. Then, smell. It smells sweet, so sweet that if you stand next to a pile of ripe *langdas,* you will be compelled to pick one and start peeling it. Then, touch. A good *langda* is firm on the outside, even when fully ripe. The skin is smooth. When you cut it, the juicy flesh encourages you to sink your teeth. It has a small kernel, allowing you to savour as much fruit as possible. And finally, taste. Sweet, but not cloying. A *langda* has no fibre, only a soft but firm pulp. One wishes that one could associate a sound to the glorious fruit, but the only sound I can think of is the slurp from the mouth of the one who eats the fruit. Every summer, the *langdas* ripen in June. When we lived in the university quarters, our *langda* tree would bear five hundred fruits in peak years, and two to three hundred in the lean ones. We, like most Banarasis, would cool the fruit in pails full of water, and eat at least three or four mangoes every day. Poet Bedhab Banarasi has the last word:

Kashi Kabahun Na Chhodiye, Vishwanath ko Dhaam
Marne par mukti miley, Jeete langda Aam
Never leave Kashi, Vishwanath's holy place ...
When you die, you'll get salvation.
When you're alive, you'll get Langda Mango.

No description of Varanasi can ever be complete without a reference to Paan. Poems and songs have been written about it, the Kamasutra prescribes it as an integral part of courtship and seduction. The simple indulgence and addiction towards the betel leaf, coated with lime and *kattha,* sprinkled with tobacco and areca nut, is characteristic of every long-time resident of the city. While the city's roads and any conceivable, unoccupied corner are stained with splotches of red *paan* juice, spit out with accuracy and hygienic unmindfulness, the lips of every *paan* enthusiast are permanently stained in red. This 8000 year-old chewing habit is best described by them, in these words: " It lightens up the countenance, relieves hunger, stimulates the organs of digestion, disinfects the breath and strengthens the teeth." I do not know about the first four claims, but can say with a fair measure of confidence that the last one is patently untrue. In the city, one is never out of sight from a *paan* shop. Everyone has their personal favourite, but Keshav Paanwala at Lanka, Kuber Tambul Bhandar at Godowlia and Bhelupura, Baiju Bhaiya's shop in Mahamoorganj, Kishan Lal at Sigra and Babunandan and Ram Narain in Thatheri Bazaar are well known. Guests are welcomed with *paan,* friendships and business deals cemented by its sharing. The wealthy have taken its consumption to the level of elaborate ritual, where the ingredients are taken out of carved silver *paandaans,* and the spit captured in brass or silver spittoons. There has been occasion when one *paan* shop in Godowlia achieved great popularity. It was said that once you had *paan* there, you kept coming back. Eventually, it took the Narcotics Squad to find out that the smart *panwallah* spiked his *kattha* mix with opium juice, and sent him to jail. In popular culture, the song *Khaike paan Banaras waala* (Don, 1978) became a rage thanks to Amitah Bachchan's capers where he turned the simple act of eating a *Banarasi paan* into a chartbursting song.

ഗ

EPILOGUE

I spent the first twenty years of my life in Varanasi. I go back, at least once a year, when I walk down the shady university roads, watch the sun rise over the Ganga, and the *aarti* in the evening. I pig on *kachoris* in the morning, and *rabri* in the evenings, knowing that the amount of walking I do in the city would help me burn all the calories away! It has been fifteen years since I left, but there has been little change -–it has got more crowded, lots of flashy shops have come up, but the essential character of the city remains intact. I guess, if things haven't changed in several centuries, they wouldn't within my short lifetime.

I have always wondered why Varanasi can't be a clean, orderly, yet ancient place – say like Bhaktapur in Nepal – which is smaller but so picture-pretty. Why can't Unesco declare it a cultural heritage site, and support preservation and restoration efforts? And why on earth should Uttar Pradesh Chief Minister Mayawati go around spending millions constructing marble monuments and parks instead of making sure that the city (and the state) has adequate power supply, good roads and drainage? Somewhere, I think, our politicians and administrators have lost their way completely. Private citizens can do much, as they are already doing in Varanasi, but without the active intervention of a sagacious government, only limited progress can be made. We have, in Varanasi, a microcosm of much of the culture and heritage that India has to offer. I would only like to end with the plea that, let us not allow it to completely degenerate into an urban mess. Let the City of Shiva, the City of Light, show the way.

☙

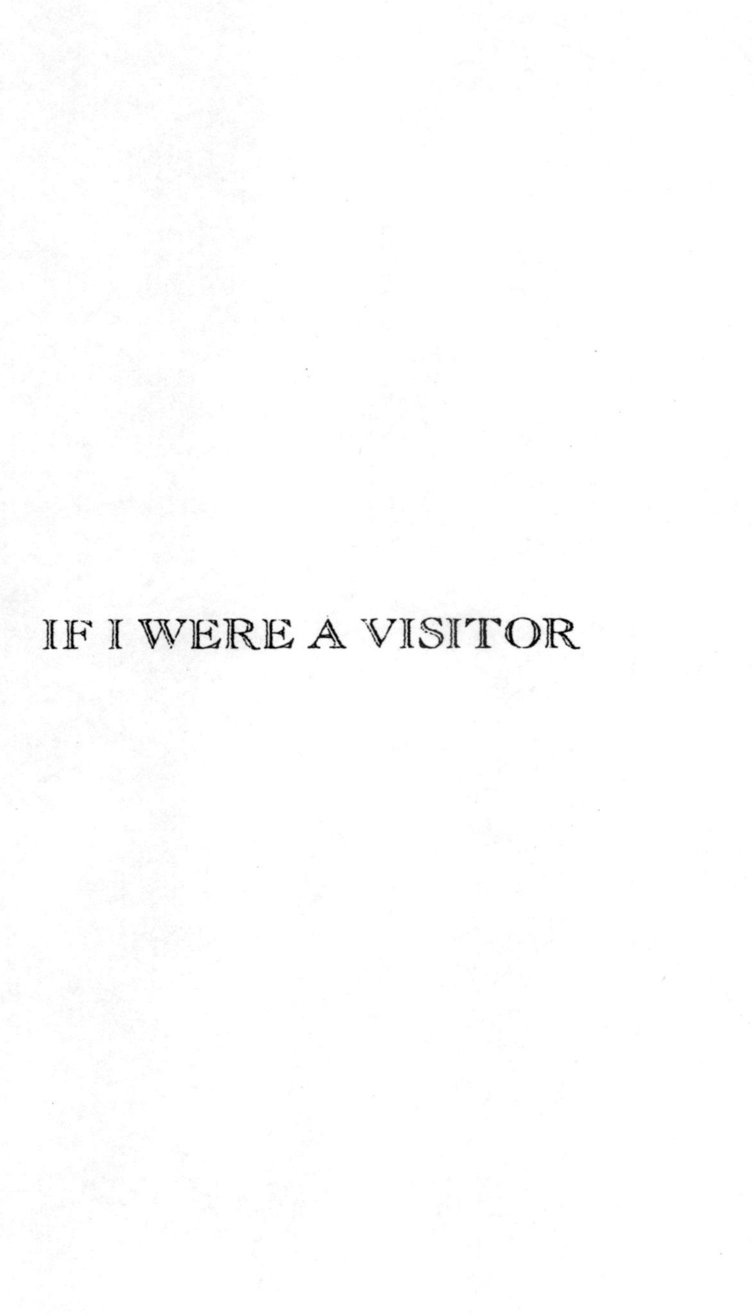

IF I WERE A VISITOR

Should I, shouldn't I? Having debated the question in my mind, I finally concluded that it would only be fair for me to provide all those travel essentials that would enable the visitor to plan his or her trip to the city. By Indian standards, Varanasi is a tourist-friendly place. There are myriad options to choose from in every department, so to speak: accomodation, food, transport. While some tourist guides and shopowners might overcharge for their services and merchandise, it is all, I think, part of the need to bridge the developing and developed world divide. Ultimately, my advice is – be prepared, haggle at every step, and learn from friendly locals and other travellers. In this chapter, I have attempted to list as many facilities and options, as much information as possible, that the visitor to Varanasi might need.

GEOGRAPHIC LOCATION; CONNECTIONS

Varanasi lies in the middle of the Indo-Gangetic plain, at a mean sea level of 77m, where the latitude 25.18° E intersects longitude 83.1° E. It is situated on the western bank of the Ganga, and along the only stretch of the river that flows from south to north.

The city is well connected by air, road and rail. The airport is situated 26 kms from the city centre, at Babatpur. There are connections by air to New Delhi, Agra, Lucknow, Khajuraho, Kathmandu, Mumbai and Bangalore. The main railway station is Varanasi Cantt, though there are smaller stations, Varanasi City and Kashi. Mughal Sarai Junction, 16 kms away, is an important junction from where one can catch trains that bypass Varanasi but reach major cities in the country like Kolkata, New Delhi and Mumbai. There are two main bus stands, one next to cantonment railway station, the other at Golgadda. Uttar Pradesh Roadways operates bus services to Allahabad, Gorakhpur and Lucknow; there are private bus services to a host of nearby towns.

Phone Numbers (Varanasi Area Code : 0542) & Addresses

Varanasi Cantt. Railway Station : General Enquiry – 348031, 348131, 348231; Reservation Enquiry – 135, 131

Roadways Enquiry : Bus station, Cantonment – 2343476; Bus station, Golgadda – 2330740

Airport Enquiry : 2343742

Important Distances, by Road

New Delhi	765 km
Kolkata	681 km
Allahabad	125 km
Agra	565 km
Lucknow	286 km
Gorakhpur	212 km
Bodh Gaya	243 km
Patna	246 km
Sunauli (Nepal border)	308 km

Airlines Offices : Indian Airlines, 52 Yadunath Marg, Cantonment, Phone – 2343746, 2345959, Airport Phone – 2622090, 2622494; Jet Airways, 1st Floor, Krishnayatan Building, The Mall, Cantonment, Phone – 2511444, 2511555, Airport Phone – 2622795, 2622796; Air Sahara, Mint House Motel, Nadesar, Phone – 2343094, 2511489, Airport Phone – 2622334, 2622547

Foreigners' Registration Office, Srinagar Colony, Siddhgiri Bagh, Phone - 2351968.

Government of India Tourist Office, 15B The Mall, Cantonment, Phone – 2343744

Government of Uttar Pradesh Tourist Office, Parade Kothi, Cantonment, Phone – 2343486, 2342368

Tourist Information Service, Varanasi Cantt. Railway Station, Phone - 2346390

Head Post Office, Vishweshwarganj, Phone – 2332050, 2331899; Head Post Office Mahmoorganj, Phone – 2330050; Head Post Office Cantt, Phone – 2345988; Head Post Office, Banaras Hindu University, Phone – 2368325.

CLIMATE

There are four distinct seasons in Varanasi: winter, from November to February, a brief spring in March, the hot season from April to June, and the rainy season from July to September. The festive month of October is a transitional one. Temperatures range from a cool 4-5 degrees Celsius minimum in December/January to a baking 44 degrees maximum in May and June. In summer, hot winds called the *loo* blow through the plains of north India, and Varanasi is no exception to the heat that they bring. The normal rainfall in a year is 1000 mm, and the average number of wet days in a year are 48, mostly between June and September. Winters can sometimes get foggy, delaying flights. All said and done, the best time to visit the city is from October, when the city is truly in a festive mood, to March.

GETTING AROUND

As I have mentioned before, the city's roads are congested. Metered taxis are unavailable. Local city buses do ply, but are crowded and uncomfortable. The best option is to hire autorickshaws, or to simply hop on to one that plies from point A to point B – one may simply flag a passing auto-rickshaw down, if there are available seats. Auto-rickshaws typically carry five passengers and those sitting in front must perch themselves precariously beside the driver. It is also possible to hire an auto-rickshaw all for yourself, but negotiate the rates in advance. A good way to find out the best fare is to ask a local before hiring your transportation. For a leisurely ride, cycle rickshaws are a good bet, if one doesn't have any qualms about human-drawn carriages. Again, rates must be negotiated beforehand. For the luxury-seeking, hotels and travel agencies will provide chauffeured cars, with or without air-con; they usually have a rate by the day, subject to the condition of a maximum distance covered. If you do propose to stay in the city for a while, just buy a bicycle. I find it to be most convenient, if I do not plan to ride really long distances. Some shops in Lanka, just outside the Banaras Hindu University, even allow you to rent a bicycle. Finally, nothing beats walking, when you are exploring the ghats and the lanes; and a boat ride down the river. The normal charge from Assi Ghat to Manikarnika is Rs 150, but that goes up in peak seasons. If you want to do the Panchkoshi Yatra circuit, hiring an auto-rickshaw is a good idea. It would take a full day, if you started at 8:00 am. My recommendation for a good auto-rickshaw driver to take you around would be Mahendra Kumar Bharti at the Durga Kund auto-rickshaw stand. You can also leave a message for him at 313535, the phone number of his next-door neighbour!

WHERE TO STAY

Visitors in Varanasi have a wide range of options, from the luxurious to the very, very basic. Your choice of digs could be dictated by how comfortably you'd like to stay, what you can afford, whether you seek the peace and comfort of a hotel in the outskirts or would like to be in the thick of the action, and how much you are willing to compromise on service. In sum, there's something for everyone in Varanasi. If you are visitng for the first time, it is advisable to book a room in advance, both to avoid disappointment in the peak tourist season, and the touts who hang around the railway station, airport and bus station.

At the top end are the five-star hotels, mostly clustered in the Cantonment area. They offer all modern conveniences, including swimming pools, business centres, travel desk, 24-hour coffee shops, health clubs, tennis courts, shopping arcades, bar, speciality restaurants, central airconditioning, and most importantly, back-up electricity supply – essential because the entire state of Uttar Pradesh suffers severe power shortage. Here's a list of hotels, in three broad categories.

TOP-END

Taj Ganges, Nadesar Palace Ground; Ph. 2345100-17
Clarks Tower, The Mall, Cantonment; Ph. 2348509
Clarks Varanasi, The Mall, Cantonment; Ph. 2348501-10
Hotel Hindustan International, Maldahiya; Ph. 2351484-90
Varanasi Ashok, The Mall, Cantonment; Ph. 2346020-30
Radisson Hotel, Cantonment
Best Western Kashika, The Mall, Cantonment; Ph. 2348091
Palace on Ganges, Assi Ghat; Ph. 2315050, 2314304

MID-RANGE

Alka Hotel, Mirghat; Ph. 2328445, 2328474
Diamond Hotel, Bhelupura; Ph. 2276696-9
Hotel Ajay, Lahurabir; Ph. 2344763
Hotel Baradari, Maidagin; Ph. 2330040
Hotel Budhha, Lahurabir; Ph. 2343686, 2344378
Hotel de Paris, 15 The Mall, Cantonment; Ph. 2346601-08
Hotel Ganges View, Assi Ghat; Ph. 2313218
Hotel Garden View, Sigra; Ph. 2360851, 2361093
Hotel India, 59 Patel Nagar, Cantonment; Ph. 2343309, 2342912
Hotel Jai Ganges, Maldahiya; Ph. 2345951-54
Hotel M.M. Continental, The Mall, Cantonment; Ph. 2345272-73
Hotel Malti, Vidyapeeth Road; Ph. 2356844, 2351395
Hotel New International, Station Road, Lahurabir; Ph. 2350805
Hotel Padmini International, Mahamoorganj; Ph. 2220972, 2222274
Hotel Pallavi International, Hathua Market, Lahurabir; Ph. 2356939-42
Hotel Pradeep, Jagatganj, Lahurabir; Ph. 2204963, 2204594
Hotel Pushpanjali, Lahurabir; Ph. 2343776
Hotel River View, Brahma Ghat; Ph. 2334565
Hotel Sidhharth, Sigra; Ph. 2358161, 2351852
Hotel Sun-Shiv, Aurangabad; Ph. 2350468
Hotel Surya, Varuna Bridge Road, Cantonment; Ph. 2348330, 2343014
Hotel Temple on the Ganges; Assi Ghat, Ph. 2312340
Hotel Vaibhav, Patel Nagar, Cantonment; Ph. 2346588
Hotel Venkatesh, Maldahiya; Ph. 2345777
Tourist Bungalow, Parade Kothi, opp Rly. Station; Ph. 2343413,

BUDGET

Ambasasador Hotel, Lanka; Ph. 2312711
Hotel Ashok, Sigra; Ph. 2350058
Hotel Empire, Godowlia; Ph. 2392129
Hotel Faran, Nai Sarak; Ph. 2351653, 2350683, 2358968
Hotel J K International, Luxa Road; Ph. 2392141
Hotel Lara India, Dasashwamedh Road, Ph. 2320323
Hotel Manasarovar, Parade Kothi, Ph. 2343546
Hotel Nar-Indra, Parade Kothi; Ph. 2343586
Mint House Motel, Nadesar, Ph. 2343819
Shahi River View Hotel, Assi Ghat; Ph. 2366730
Shalimar Hotel, Varuna Pul; Ph. 2346227

Small guest houses / lodges find favour with foreigners who intend stay to for longer periods. The most famous among backpackers is Yogi Lodge, D8/29 Kalika Gali, off Vishwanath Gali, Phone: 2392558, and has spawned a host of imitators like Old Yogi Lodge, and New Yogi Lodge. Others are mentioned below.

Amrit Guest House, Bhojubir; 2313264
Ganga Guest House, Pandey Ghat; Ph. 2321137
Om Vishwanath Lodge, Sonarpura; Ph. 2311832
Puja Guest House, Lalita Ghat; Ph. 2326102
Rahul Guest House, Gangotri Vihar, Nagwa; Ph. 2366614
Sandhya Guest House, near Shivala Ghat; Ph. 2313292
Scindhia Guest House, Scindhia Ghat;
Shanti Guest House, Garwasi Tola, near Manikarnika Ghat; Ph. 2322568
Trimurti Guest House, near Vishwanath Temple; Ph. 2393554
Vishnu Guest House, Pandey Ghat.

Besides these, several local residents offer paying guest accomodation. A list of the same can be obtained from the Uttar Pradesh Tourism office at Parade Kothi, near the cantonment railway station.

DHARMASHALAS

Meant for Hindu pilgrims, dharmashalas do not require advance reservation – one only has to try his or her luck. They offer both rooms and dormitories, and the accomodation is pretty basic.

Annapurna Telwala Dharamshala, Chhoti Gaibi; Ph. 2350025
Bagla Dharamshala, Hauz Katora; Ph. 2329219
Baranwal Seva Sadan, Badi Piyari; Ph. 2355801
Beriwala Atithi Bhavan, Ramapura; Ph. 2357117
Biharilal Jain Dharamshala, Maidagin; Ph. 2334980
Bireshwar Pandey Dharamshala, Ramapura; Ph. 2320862
Buddha Burmese Dharamshala, S17/330 Cantt;
Dudhwala Dharamshala, Bulanala; Ph. 2354670
Harsundari Dharamshala, Godowlia;
Jaipuria Atithi Bhavan, Godowlia; Ph. 2352709, 2352674
Kamala Dharamshala, Dasashwamedh; Ph. 2321499
Karnataka Guest House, Hanuman Ghat; Ph. 2313422
Kashi Mumuksha Bhawan, Assi; Ph. 2311187
Kesharvani Dharamshala, K43/53 Vishweshwarganj;
Khunkhunji Dharamshala, Bulanala; Ph. 2354704
Lakkhiram Dharamshala, CK13/40 Sukhlal Phatak;
Maharana Ranvir Dharamshala, Terhineem; Ph. 2327461
Maheshwari Dharamshala, Saptasagar; Ph. 2354134
Parsvanath Digamber Jain Dharamshala, Bhelupura; Ph. 2312892
Purushottam Dharamshala, Ramapura; Ph. 2328014
Sri Atithi Bhavan, Mukimganj; Ph. 2331595
Sri Kishan Beriwal Atithi Bhavan, Luxa Road; Ph. 2321550

Sri Krishna Dharamshala, Englisia Line, near Cantt; Ph. 2346164
Sri Marwari Yuvak Sangh, Luxa Road; Ph. 2358612
Radha Krishna Dharamshala, Gyanvapi; Ph. 2321726
Sri Marwari Sewa Sangh Dharamshala, Bhadaini; Ph. 2310226
Sardar Vallabhbhai Dharamshala, Andhra Pul; Ph. 2346221
Sindhi Dharamshala, Misir Pokhra, Godowlia; Ph. 2358441
Tulsiram Dharamshala, D40/2 Lakshmanpura

The only Muslim guest-house that I know of is Muslim Musafirkhana, CK 50/229, Dalmandi; Ph. 2342458. The other cheap places to stay are: Railway Retiring Rooms at Cantt. Railway Station, Ph. 131/135 – you must have a valid train ticket; YMCA, Ph. 355895; International Guest House, Ph. 2362558, 2364491; and the Circuit House – if you have clout in the government, Ph. 2511223.

RESTAURANTS

A large number of eateries in the city serve up a delectable fare, but nothing beats homemade food. So as a visitor, one must certainly try to befriend a local, and get an invite at least for one meal ! For other times, here's a partial list of restaurants across the city. None of the restaurants, barring those in 5-Star hotels are allowed to serve alcohol. A meal for two can cost as little as Rs. 100, and remember that most places do not accept credit cards. It would be advisable to drink only bottled water evrywhere you go.

3F Restaurant, Upendra Nagar, Durga Kund
Achar Chatni, Best Western Kashika, Cantonment
Adit, Varanasi Ashok, Cantonment
Aiyar Café, Raman Katra, Dasahwamedh
Aman Restaurant, Ravindrapuri
Amarpali Restaurant, Sonarpura
Amrapali Restaurant, Clarks Varanasi, Cantonment

Anamika Coffee & Kulfi House, Shastri Nagar, Sigra
Ashiana Restaurant, Varuna Pul
Baba Restaurant, Hathi Phatak, Dasashwamedh Ghat
Baker's King, Subzi Mandi, Orderly Bazaar
Bread of Life Bakery, Shivala
Cakes & Bakes Bakery, Jagatganj
Canton's, Hotel Surya, Varuna Pul
Chahat Restaurant, opp. Natraj Cinema, Sigra
Coffee House, Bhelupura
Darpan, Hotel Pallavi International, Hathua Market, Lahurabir
El Parador, Maldahiya
Garden Restaurant, Godowlia
Gokul Sweets & Restaurant, Bhelupura
Gopal Sweet House, Lahurabir
Haifa, near Assi Ghat
Isha, Hotel Malti, Sigra
Kashika, Tourist Bungalow, Parade Kothi, Cantonment
Kerala Café, Bhelupura
Kesari Restaurant, Dasashwamedh Road
Labela Chinese Restaurant, Lanka
Madhur Jalpan, Hauz Katora, near Godowlia
Mandap, Hotel Taj Ganges, Nadesar
Marwari Bhojnalaya, Bulanala
Mela, Hotel MM Continental, Cantonment
Mughal, Hotel Baradari, Maidagin
Neelam, Diamond Hotel, Bhelupura
Novelty Restaurant, Bhelupura
Palki, Hotel Vaibhav, Patel Nagar
Palm Springs, Hotel India, Patel Nagar
Pizzeria Vatika, Assi Ghat
Poonam, Hotel Pradeep, Jagatganj
Pragati Café, Ganesh Katra, Chowk
Rajshri Restaurant, Baradeo
Shahi Restaurant, Gurubagh
Shanti Guest House Rooftop Restaurant, near Manikarnika Ghat

Sindhi Restaurant, Bhelupura
Sona Rupa, Vishweshwarganj
The Host Restaurant & Café, Lanka
The Palms, Hotel Hindustan International, Maldahiya
Win-fa, Lahurabir
Ye Café at Home, Lanka

At the end of that list I can only say, *bon appetit!*

SHOPPING

So, you have arrived in Varanasi, settled down, hopefully comfortably at a hotel or guest house, explored the city, and would now like to do a bit of shopping – and thereby contribute to the local economy. The main shopping areas are Dasashwamedh, Chowk, Godowlia, Thatheri Bazaar, Lahurabir, Nichibagh and Lanka. Varanasi recently had its first mall at Rathyatra, but it remains just a novelty among locals. Most of the souvenir shops are concentrated in the Vishwanath Gali - though the big hotels have a reasonable, albeit pricey, collection.

For silk, simply head to Chowk and Thatheri Bazaar (Akashdeep Sarees, Chitrakala Sarees, Sri Vishwanath Co., Champaklal Sarees, Kanhaiyalal, Banaras Saree Niketan, G.N Brothers); Madanpura and Pandey Haveli (Ali Ahmad Ilyas Ahmed, Dilnashi Sarees, G.G. In Style, Sartaj Sarees Group); or Kunj Gali (Garib ki Dukan, Anil Brothers, Ashok Brothers, Jalan Sari House, Ramratan Amarnath, Atmaram Harishankar). These are where the weavers bring their masterpieces everyday. Chand Bhai can be found at H.A. Malai & Co – Mughal Textiles, J 29/44 Husain Pura, Naibasti, Jaitpura; Ph. 2331043.

While you do get silk in Vishwanath Gali, the narrow winding lane is crammed with other novelties. These include lacquered wooden toys (Aggawal Toy Emporium, J R Ivory Arts & Curio, Banaras Toy Museum); brassware and *puja* items like lamps, candlestands, *sindoor* holders, bells, conches; cheap cotton clothes – gaily printed T-Shirts and pajamas, scarves, kurtas, and handbags; tobbaco sellers; and colourful glass bangles. For the local perfume, or *attar*, Chowk is a good place to shop, with Ayodhya Prasad Lakshmi Chand, Kashi Vishwanath & Co. and Kashinath & Co. offering a range of smells.

As a write, I think it would be patently unfair if I did not list bookstores in the city. So here goes: Bhargav Book Depot, Chowk; Book World, Hathua Market; Chaukhamba Sanskrit Bhavan, Chowk; Chaukhamba Classica, Chowk; City Book Shop, Godowlia; Gautam Pustak Mandir, Bulanala; Globe Book Centre, Lanka; Harmony, Assi Ghat; Indica Books, Godowlia; International Publicity, Maldahiya; Nagri Book Stall, Orderly Bazaar; Motilal Banarasidass, Chowk; National Book Agency, Bulanala; Pilgrims Book House, Durga Kund; Sharda Sanskrit Sansthan, Jagatganj; Universal Book Company, Godowlia.

TRAVEL AGENCIES

Abhiyan Tours & Travels, Mint House, Nadesar; Ph. 2345535, 2346727
Air People, Varuna Bridge; Ph. 2340562
Akash Ganga, Gulab Bagh, Sigra; Ph. 2320527
Anand Travels, Sindhi Dharmashala, Luxa Road; Ph. 2322855
Asia Travel & Tours, Maldahiya; Ph. 2351484, 2357873
Brand Link Travels, Rajabazar, Nadesar; Ph. 2345366
Durga Shakti Travels, Trilochan Bazar; Ph. 2334595
India Travel Services, Thatheri Bazar; Ph. 2320628, 2329426
ITDC Transport Unit, Hotel Varanasi Ashok; Ph. 2346032
Kushinagar Travels & Tours, Sigra; Ph. 2224026, 2331612
M.N. Travels, Harishchandra Ghat Road, Sonarpura; Ph. 2355650

Oasis International Tours & Travels, Patel Nagar; Ph. 2345595
Overseas Travel, Dasashwamedh; Ph. 2321465, 2393840
Radiant Services, Misir Pokhra, Godowlia; Ph. 2351218
Raj Travels, Maidagin; Ph. 2391595-6
Saraswati (India) Travel Services, Cantt.; Ph. 2346652, 2348734
Sita World Travels, The Mall; Ph. 2344692, 2342447
Shri Shubh Travels, Ananta Gate, Nadesar; Ph. 2344844, 2344944
Sunny Travels, Hotel Jai Ganges, Maldahiya; Ph. 2344435
Surabhi Travel & Tours, Cooperative Building, Nadesar; Ph. 2348632
Tour Aids, Hotel India, Nadesar; Ph. 2346881, 2345627
Travel Bureau, The Mall; Ph. 2346621, 2345530
Travel Corporation of India, Sri Das Foundation, The Mall; Ph. 2345281, 2346209, 2346210
Travel Point, Hotel Malti, Sigra; Ph. 2223864, 2220944
Travel Zone, Patel Nagar; Ph. 2348184-5
Varuna Travels, Sonarpura; Ph. 2393370-71
Vijayshri Travels, Rani Kuan, Chowk; Ph. 2326035, 2321930
Unique Travel, Jiyapura, Chetganj; Ph. 2356565, 2356401
World View Travel & Tours, Mint House, The Mall; Ph. 2346357, 2345530
Yatrik Tours & Travels, Bank Colony, Mahamoorganj; Ph. 2361454, 2360969

IMPORTANT HOSPITALS

Sir Sundarlal Hospital, Banaras Hindu University; Ph. 2368436, 2368169
Heritage Hospital, Lanka; Ph. 2367977, 2366726, 2366728
Shivprasad Gupt Hospital, Kabirchaura; Ph. 2333719-20
Marwari Hospital, Godowlia; Ph. 2394611, 2321456
Railway Hospital, Cantonment; Ph. 2342538
Ramkrishna Mission Hospital, Luxa; Ph. 2312727, 2320776
Jan Kalyan Hospital, Mahamoorganj; Ph. 2360063
Mata Anandmayee Hospital, Shivala; Ph. 2310186

GLOSSARY

Aangan	Courtyard
Aarti	Fire ritual
Acharya	Learned teacher
Ahir	Milkman caste
Akash	Sky
Akhara	Wrestling arena, also school
Amrit	Nectar of immortality
Apsara	Dancing girl, in Heaven
Ashram	Monastery
Attar	Perfume
Bahi Khata	Ledger
Baraat	Bridegroom's party & procession
Bhaang	Cannabis Indica, is chewed
Bhajan	Devotional song
Bhakti	Devotion
Brahmacharya	Abstinence
Chaiwallah	Tea seller
Charas	Marijuana
Chaupal	Village square
Chhena	Cottage cheese
Chowk	Central square in a city
Daan	Offering, donation
Damaru	Shiva's rattledrum
Darshan	Holy view
Dharmashala	Pilgrims' hostel
Dhoti	Traditional, wraparound garment for men
Dhuni	Sacred fire
Diya	Oil lamp
Dwarpal	Doorman
Gada	Mace
Gali	Lane
Gangajal	Ganges water

Ganja	Cannabis, is smoked
Gayaki	Singing style
Ghat	Riverbank
Ghee	Clarified butter
Gopi	Female cowherd
Guru	Teacher
Halwai	One who makes sweets, confectioner
Havan	Ritual purification by fire
Imli	Tamarind
Janapada	Kingdom
Jugalbandi	Musical partnership
Juleha	Weaver
Kachauri	Fried bread, stuffed with pulses
Kanyadaan	Ritual of giving away the bride
Katha	Story
Khatik	Vegetable seller
Khayal	Imagination; a style of singing
Khichdi	Mishmash made with rice and pulses
Kotwal	Guard
Kund	Water tank
Lagan	Perseverance
Langda	A kind of mango, which Varanasi is famous for
Lathi	Staff, made of bamboo
Lila / Leela	Performance
Linga	Shiva's phallus
Lungi	Wraparound skirt, worn by men
Maalish	Massage
Malmala	Muslin
Mandap	Covered arena for public worship
Mandi	Grain market
Mandir	Temple
Mantra	Invocation
Masjid	Mosque
Math	Seat of any religious sect

Mazaar	Muslim memorial, shrine
Mithai	Sweetmeat
Mohalla	Part of a city; Locality
Muhurta	Auspicious moment
Mundan	Head shaving ceremony
Nag	Cobra
Naksha	Design; map
Nala	Drain, not to be confused with mythological character
Namaaz	Prayers, done five times a day
Namkeen	Salted savouries
Nankhatai	A kind of biscuit
Naresh	King
Paan	Betel leaf
Pahalwan	Wrestler; Bodybuilder
Panch	Five
Panda	Enabling priest
Pandit	Priest; Learned Person
Pathshala	School
Peepul	Ficus
Pranam	To pay obeisance
Prasad	Food of the Gods
Puja	Prayer
Pujari	Worshipper
Pustakalaya	Library
Rickshaw	Tricycle
Riyaaz	Practice singing or playing
Sadhana	Ardent devotion
Sadhu	Holy man
Samadhi	Tomb
Sangam	Confluence
Satti	Vegetable market, usually wholesale
Shakti	Power
Shastra	Sacred text; knowledge
Shikhara	Peak

Shishya	Disciple
Sindoor	Vermillion
Supari	Arecanut
Sur	Tune
Swayambhu	Self-manifest
Taal	Beat (in music)
Taazia	Float brought out in a Muharram procession
Takhat	Wooden bench; Seat
Taleem	Provide education
Teeka / Tika	Red mark on the forehead
Thana	Police station
Thathera	Metalworker
Tikki	Patty
Tirtha	Pilgrimage
Tonga	Horse drawn carriage
Tulsi	Basil
Veshti	Cotton vest, worn in South India
Vrat	Keep fast
Yantra	Instrument
Yatra	Journey
Zarda	Chewing tobacco

BIBLIOGRAPHY

Altekar, A.S. 1947. Benares and Sarnath - Past & Present. Varanasi: Banaras Hindu University Press.

Barman, Arijit. December 25 2000. Karma Kitsch. New Delhi, Outlook Magazine

Beal, Samuel (ed). 1969. Buddhist Records of the Western World. Delhi: Oriental Books Reprint Corporation.

Bhatt, G.P. (ed). 1997. Kashi Khanda. New Delhi: Motilal Banarasidass.

Chandramouli, K. 1995. Kashi – The City Luminous. New Delhi: Rupa & Co.

Dar, S. L. and Somaskandan. 1969. History of Banaras Hindu University. Varanasi: BHU Press

Das, G.N. 1991. Couplets from Kabir. New Delhi: Motilal Banarasidass

Devi, Savita. 1998 *'Maa ... Siddheshwari'*. New Delhi: Roli Books

Dikshit, Rajeev. July 31 2000. Safe Sarees, not Safe Sex. New Delhi: The Times of India

Doshi, Esha Basanti. 1965, District Gazetteer of Varanasi. Lucknow: Government of Uttar Pradesh

Eck, Diana L. 1982, Banaras, City of Light. New York: Alfred Knopf

Hertel, Bradley R. and Cynthia Ann Humes (ed). 1993, Living Banaras – Hindu Religion in Cultural Context. Albany: State University of New York Press

Kinsley, David. 1998, Tantric Visions of the Divine Feminine. New Delhi: Motilal Banarasidass.

Knappert, Jan. 1995, Hindu Mythology. London: Diamond Books

Lannoy, Richard. 2002, Benares, A World Within a World. Varanasi: Indica Books

Mitra, Swati (ed). 2002, Varanasi City Guide. New Delhi: Eicher Goodearth Limited

Patodi, Ratan. 1973. *Bharatiya Kushti Kala* (The Art of Indian Wrestling). Indore: Bharatiya Kushti Prakashan

Prinsep, James. 1996 reprint. Benares Illustrated in a Series of Drawings. Varanasi: Vishwavidyalaya Prakashan.

Rau, Santha Rama. February 1986, Banaras: India's City of Light, in National Geographic Magazine. Washington D.C.: National Geographic Society.

Shankar, Dr. Hari. 1996, Kashi Ke Ghat. Varanasi: Vishwavidyalaya Prakashan

Sharma, R.C and Bimla Poddar. 2002, Vaisnava Contribution to Kasi, Seminar Proceedings. Varanasi: Jnana Pravaha.

Sherring, Reverend M.A. 2001, Benares, The Sacred City of the Hindus in Ancient & Modern Times. New

Delhi: Rupa & Co. (First published in 1868)

Singh, Bhagwati Sharan. 1988, Varanasi. New Delhi: National Book Trust

Singh, Rana P.B. 1989, Where Cultural Symbols Meet – Literary Images of Varanasi. Varanasi: Tara Book Agency

________ (ed). 1993, Banaras: Cosmic Order, Sacred City, Hindu Traditions. Varanasi: Tara Book Agency

Sukul, Kuber Nath. 1974, Varanasi Down the Ages. Varanasi: Bhargava Bhushan Press

Vidyarthi, L.P., Makhan Jha and B.N. Saraswati. 1979, TheSacred Complex of Kashi. New Delhi: Concept Publishing.

INDEX